RENFREWSI

RENFREWSHIRE

A Scottish County's Hidden Past

DEREK ALEXANDER AND GORDON MCCRAE

BIRLINN

First published in 2012 by
Birlinn Limited
West Newington House
10 Newington Road
Edinburgh
EH9 1QS

www.birlinn.co.uk

ISBN: 978 1 84158 799 8

British Library Cataloguing-in-Publication Data
A catalogue record for this book is available from the British Library

The Publisher gratefully acknowledges the
support of the Gordon McCrae Trust towards
the publication of this book

Typeset by Brinnoven, Livingston
Printed and bound by GraphyCems, Spain

Contents

	Acknowledgements	vii
	List of Colour Plates	xi
	List of Illustrations	xiii
	Foreword	xix
	Introduction	1
1	A History of Renfrewshire Archaeological Studies	5
2	Palaeolithic Renfrewshire	15
3	Mesolithic Renfrewshire	19
4	Neolithic Renfrewshire	23
5	Bronze Age Renfrewshire	35
6	Iron Age Renfrewshire	53
7	Roman Renfrewshire	71
8	Early Historic Renfrewshire	81
9	Early Medieval Renfrewshire	95
10	Later Medieval Renfrewshire	117
11	Early Modern Renfrewshire: An Introduction	147
12	Post-Medieval Renfrewshire	151
13	Agriculture to Industry	171
14	Renfrewshire in the Industrial Revolution: (1) Water Power and Canals	207
15	Renfrewshire in the Industrial Revolution: (2) Steam and Railways	223
16	Early Modern Renfrewshire (1850–)	241
	Conclusion: The Future of Renfrewshire's Past	261
	Appendix: List of major archaeological investigations	265
	Select Bibliography and Further Reading	267
	Index	277

Acknowledgements

The authors would like to acknowledge their debt to the many fieldworkers and researchers whose contributions to Renfrewshire history and archaeology have made this book possible. Most of their names are listed in the bibliography and throughout the text, but special mention should be made of Frank Newall, Sylvia Clark, Eileen Malden, Stuart Nisbet, Alan Steel, the staff of Paisley Museum and Library, and the members of Renfrewshire Local History Forum especially Bruce Henry, Stephen Clancy, John and Ann MacDonald. We are particularly grateful to John MacDonald for supplying information on the Second World War sites and Bruce for the Barrhouse results. Thanks are also due to the many people who have previously worked in the county and who have provided the results of their work both for the text and as illustrations. Among these are Lawrence Keppie for Barochan Hill and Brian Kerr for Cathcart Castle. Others have provided access to old slide collections. Most notably, George Newall gave access to many of his late father Frank's slides and Eileen Stables to her husband Danny's.

In addition, numerous archaeological organisations are also to be thanked for information on recently excavated developer-funded sites. CFA Archaeology Ltd for Titwood and Elderslie; GUARD for information on Rais Tower, Neilston Church and Paisley Abbey; and Addyman Archaeology for Kilbarchan Old cemetery. In particular, AOC Archaeology Group, including former staff such as Murray Cook, and current staff Ciara Clarke, were very generous in supplying reports and illustrations for the large number of sites worked on in the west: M77, Floakside, West Acres, Braehead and Mar Hall Hotel. Indeed my own employers, the National Trust for Scotland, also allowed inclusion of material on Greenbank, Holmwood and the Weaver's Cottage.

For illustrations, we are grateful also to Jim Devine at the Hunterian Museum, Katinka Stentoft of Glasgow Museums and Amanda Robb of East Renfrewshire Libraries. The staff of the Royal Commission on the Ancient and Historic Monuments of Scotland were also extremely helpful; Alex Hale provided information on their recent survey work in East Renfrewshire and Ian Parker drew up the plan of Duncarnock so it could be included in the book. Other organisations such as Historic Scotland, the National Museums, the National Archives of Scotland and the British Geological Survey were also supportive.

This work started back in 1997 and despite a productive start it slowed down. Its format has had to change over the years but it is hoped it forms an introduction to the subject. It is by no means complete and at best forms the authors' personal favourites.

I acknowledge here a huge debt to my fellow author, Gordon McCrae, whose sudden death in 2005 robbed Renfrewshire's history and archaeology of a true champion. Gordon's deep understanding of the local area and his boundless energy and enthusiasm spurred me on to find out more, and it is fitting indeed that the book is dedicated to his memory. Fortunately, Gordon had completed large chunks of text which form the second half of the book. I am extremely grateful to the McCrae Trust, based in the University of the West of Scotland (Gordon's workplace), and its committee members, including Isobel McCrae, for providing considerable financial support to see the book published at last. Andrew Simmons and Birlinn Press were both helpful and patient. Finally, thanks are due in particular to Stuart Nisbet for providing so much help and information, to Alan Steel for helping with the index, and to my partner Ingrid Shearer who slaved over the illustrations and without whose sharp eye for detail the work would not have looked as good.

Derek Alexander
March 2012

This book is dedicated to the memory of

Gordon McCrae

1947–2005

List of Colour Plates

———◆———

1 Jet beads and spacer plates from South Mound necklace, Houston

2 Craigmarloch vitrified wall showing inner and outer stone wall faces with mass of vitrified wall core in between

3 Duncarnock hill fort with rampart visible from the north-west across Glanderston dam

4 Samian bowl from the Antonine period Roman fort at Whitemoss near Bishopton

5 Lurg Moor Roman fortlet from the north-west

6 Arthurlie Cross in Barrhead

7 Denniston motte, Milton Bridge, on ridge above Gryffe Water near Kilmacolm

8 West front of Paisley Abbey with its original twelfth-century door and later lancet windows

9 Silver coins from the hoard found in Bell Street, Renfrew

10 Finely carved tomb recess of Sir Robert Sempill, First Lord Semple, in the Collegiate Church, Castle Semple

11 Coffins found during rebuilding of graveyard wall at Kilbarchan Old Parish Church

12 Plan of Eaglesham village by John Ainslie in 1789 including Moat Hill in centre of village green

13 Busby waterfall and mill foundations

14 Crofthead Mill and Neilston village

15 One of the octagonal gun positions at East Yonderton anti-aircraft battery, Houston

16 Erskine House and grounds, 1774 by Charles Ross

List of Illustrations

1 Gordon McCrae on fieldwork at Johnstone Castle
2 Map showing major topographic features in Renfrewshire
3 Plan of Cuff Hill cairn by excavator Robert Love in 1874
4 Plan and elevation sketch of Knockmade homestead 1890
5 Stone artefacts including a Neolithic stone axe found in Neilston
6 Capelrig cross-base during excavation by Kelvingrove Museum staff in 1926
7 Map showing major archaeological excavations undertaken in Renfrewshire
8 Horn and upper part of skull of a wild ox or aurochs found in Cowden Glen, Neilston
9 Map of major Mesolithic and Neolithic sites in Renfrewshire
10 Selection of Mesolithic flint tools (1), Neolithic flint tools and axes (2, 6 and 7), and Bronze Age arrowheads (3–5), stone battleaxes (10–12) and flat bronze axes (8 and 9)
11 One of the plain bowl Neolithic pots found in pits under the Roman layers at Whitemoss, Bishopton
12 Large cup-and-ring marked boulder found in Bluebell Woods, Langside
13 One of the four cup-and-ring marks on the bedrock outcrop in Craigston Wood, Johnstone
14 Map of major Bronze Age settlements and burial cairns in Renfrewshire
15 Bronze Age hoard of two decorated axes and a dagger from Gavel Moss near Lochwinnoch
16 Lugtonridge beaten bronze shield now in London
17 Plan of excavation trenches on South Mound, Houston in 1974 and south of the road in 1976
18 Chart from South Mound skeletal remains found in 1976

19 One end of a spacer plate jet bead necklace found at the South Mound

20 Plan of Picketlaw hut circle excavation showing heavily robbed outer wall, inner ring and central hearthstones

21 Plan of Knapps palisaded homestead

22 Plans of possible Bronze Age homesteads

23 Plan of West Acres Bronze Age house and two smaller structures found on the route of the M77

24 Reconstruction drawing by Alan Braby of West Acres house

25 Map of major Iron Age and Roman sites in Renfrewshire

26 Plans of small Iron Age forts

27 Plans of Duncarnock and Dunwan forts

28 RCAHMS survey plan of Duncarnock fort

29 Renfrewshire's largest hill fort, Walls Hill, Howwood

30 Crop-mark of three ditches around the summit of Corslie Hill, Houston. The square feature in the centre is the base of Barochan cross

31 Crop-mark enclosure at Shiels and the earthwork enclosure in North Wood, Pollok Park

32 Ditched and palisaded enclosures at Braehead and Mar Hall, Erskine

33 Mar Hall entrance to ditched and palisaded enclosure with Erskine Bridge in background

34 The small but perfectly formed Langbank comb can now be seen in the National Museum of Scotland

35 One of the Meikle Cloak cave rotary querns (left) with modern replica at the NTS Weaver's Cottage, Kilbarchan

36 Barochan Roman patera and one of two bronze handles found at the same time in 1886

37 Diggers take a rest beside the excavated west gate of Barochan Roman fort. Note the upright markers in the trench indicating postholes.

38 Renfrewshire's Roman forts at Barochan and Whitemoss and the Lurg Moor fortlet

39 Map of Early Historic sites in Renfrewshire

40 Titwood palisaded enclosure dating to eighth–tenth century AD

41 Two Norse silver armlets found in Port Glasgow

42 Barochan Cross: the finest of Renfrewshire's crosses

43 Surviving cross-shafts in Renfrewshire

44 Two of the three early historic sculptured stones at Inchinnan: the possible shrine lid in the foreground with the recumbent cross slab behind

45 Reconstructed outline of the cross found at Newton Woods, Elderslie, and the Dumb Proctor cross at Lochwinnoch

46 Feudal sites in Renfrewshire

47 Renfrewshire mottes

48 Sherd of twelfth–thirteenth century white gritty pottery and a fifteenth–sixteenth century 'jetton' found at Denniston motte, Milton Bridge, near Kilmacolm

49 The earthen ring-work of Robert Croc around the later stone tower of Crookston Castle

50 Plan of the enclosure castle at Duchal, near Kilmacolm

51 Reconstruction sketch of Duchal Castle on its promontory between two rivers

52 Plan showing original extent of Elderslie moated site, location of buildings and excavation trenches

53 Map of medieval castles, churches and other sites in Renfrewshire

54 Reconstruction drawing of Crookston Castle fifteenth century tower – cut away to show storage cellar, great hall, and chambers above

55 East elevation of Cathcart Castle with inset of moulded plaster heraldic shield found during the excavations

56 Stanely Castle sitting in middle of the reservoir built in 1838 and with the stump of the Stanely Cross in the foreground

57 Plan of Old Bar Castle, Erskine, showing castle buildings in south-east and outer courtyard beyond

58 Fine ashlar stonework of well found at Old Bar Castle

59 Nineteenth-century drawing of The Peel remains at Castle Semple Loch showing stairs to first floor and inner rebates of gun loops in basement. Inset shows bronze cannon found in loch.

60 Four-seater sedilia in the south choir wall, Paisley Abbey, thought on stylistic grounds to be late fourteenth century

61 Possible layout of the medieval buildings of Paisley Abbey and its Precinct showing the line of the now famous drain

62 Castle Semple Collegiate Church built in 1504 by John, first Lord Semple

63 Fifteenth-century burial tomb of Sir John Ross of Hawkhead and his wife in Renfrew Old Parish Church

64 Effigy of Sir Patrick Houston (d.1450) within Houston Parish Church

65 Map of post-medieval sites in Renfrewshire

66 The Argyll Stone (also known as St Conval's Chair) at Inchinnan close

to the spot where The Duke of Argyll was captured after his failed rebellion in 1685

67 The fifteenth-century tower of Newark Castle on the far left with the late sixteenth-century ornate wing added by Patrick Maxwell in the foreground

68 Plan of Newark castle showing two main phases and excavation trenches that located the outer barmkin wall that linked to the doocot tower

69 Houston Mercat Cross topped by a later sundial

70 Map of early industry in rural Renfrewshire

71 Greenbank House built by Robert Allason in 1760s with inset of clay tobacco pipes found in field to west

72 Old Kilbarchan Church with medieval grave-slab built into wall in foreground

73 Kilbarchan graveyard plan of excavation of coffins. Inset shows teeth with notches possibly caused by biting thread.

74 Map showing eighteenth-century industrial and transport related sites

75 MacDowall's Georgian mansion house at Castle Semple was one of the earliest of its type built in Scotland

76 Extract of Greenbank House estate plan showing lint mill beside the White Cart

77 Remains of the eighteenth-century Margaret's Mill just upstream from Duchal Castle with date of 1760 on re-used lintel

78 Plan of the excavated farmsteads of Floakside and Barrhouse

79 Extensive remains of limestone quarries, coal pits and over 28 clamp kilns at Corseford

80 The Weaver's Cottage in Kilbarchan is typical of early eighteenth-century houses combining both workshop and house

81 Map of industrial water-powered sites in Renfrewshire including mills, lades and dams

82 Interior of the brick-built Busby mill tunnel

83 Broadlie Mill, on the Levern Water, with Neilston village and parish church on the hill behind

84 Mills on the Black Cart in the new planned town of Johnstone

85 Elevations of typical Renfrewshire mills

86 Map of nineteenth-century sites including houses, farms and transport features

87 View of the chimneys and spires of Paisley from south-east with the canal aqueduct crossing the White Cart

88 Timber ponds at Port Glasgow

89 Map of nineteenth-century mills, industrial sites and railways

90 Plan and section of cutting through Greenock Reservoir No. 1

91 Coal workings exposed during the digging of foundations for the Fever Hospital site at Cowglen, Thornliebank in 1937. The unexcavated pillars would have supported the roof of this shallow mine.

92 Engraving of Caldwell House (centre) and tower (left) with a working draw-kiln for lime production in the foreground

93 Different types of Renfrewshire lime draw-kilns

94 This replica of the 1811 steamboat *Comet* can be seen at Port Glasgow

95 Map of late nineteenth- and twentieth-century industrial sites and houses in Renfrewshire

96 The Balgray dam, part of the Gorbals Reservoir complex built at Barrhead

97 Anchor Mills, Paisley, showing the different building phases

98 Industrial archaeology – the Inchinnan swing bridge built in 1923

99 Cathcart paper mill with Sunnyside villa and Holmwood House above

100 Map of twentieth-century sites including, dams, reservoirs and Second World War sites

101 The huge Thornliebank printworks run by the Crum family from 1789 until it closed in 1929

102 A concrete shelter and ammunition store of the East Yonderton anti-aircraft battery with another gun emplacement behind

103 Extract of 1780 Castle Semple Estate map showing abandoned farm/village sites at Fleemingston, Hersington and Chapelton.

Foreword

Stuart Nisbet

———◆———

This book was conceived by the authors more than 20 years ago. An early version surfaced as *Renfrewshire's Historic Monuments – a Heritage under Threat*, published by Gordon McCrae in 1990. This article explored the neglect of archaeology and history in the region under a number of headings. These ranged from the lack of co-ordinated understanding of Renfrewshire's physical heritage, to what could be done to increase awareness of the neglect. These concepts evolved, with the help of Derek Alexander, into this book, under the vernacular title of the 'Great Work'.

It could perhaps be claimed that Gordon was an archaeologist in disguise (Fig. 1). This does not mean that his sizeable musical and theatrical talents, nor his bunnet and wellies, were a masquerade for his principal hobby. Nor was his profession as an academic librarian a cunning subterfuge, although it was undoubtedly a great help with source material. Gordon's disguise was that he avoided being compartmentalised into an archaeologist or historian. He favoured more diverse methods, combining fieldwork with historical sources and numerous other disciplines, ranging from geography to industrial archaeology. His over-riding principle was that, if a question or threat arose about a historical site, the first thing to do was to visit it. Over the years, this led to a deep and very practical knowledge of the Renfrewshire landscape. It also introduced many others to his practical approach, through numerous field trips.

One of Gordon's biggest challenges was the erroneous but surprisingly prevalent view that 'not much had ever happened' in Renfrewshire. Gordon believed that this was simply because little had been published, or to put it more crudely, that nobody had actually looked in the first place. Sorting this oversight became his main pastime. Part of the process was the co-founding

Figure 1   Gordon McCrae on fieldwork
at Johnstone Castle (Bruce Henry).

of Renfrewshire Local History Forum in 1988. This is an amateur society where like-minded enthusiasts research, survey or publish on a diverse variety of archaeological and historical interests. Gordon's multidisciplinary approach did not mean that the results were amateurish. In fact, both authors have degrees in archaeology. Despite this, Gordon was more likely to offer you a boiled sweet than baffle you with academic jargon. As part of this user-friendly communication process, he also put a great deal of work into developing a practical vocational course on Renfrewshire's History and Archaeology at Paisley University (now the University of the West of Scotland).

Gordon's knowledge of the landscape and history of Renfrewshire was unsurpassed. However, he had one weakness, namely, that he encouraged and inspired others to write much more than he published himself. Fortunately, this long-standing problem has been resolved by the publication of this practical guide by Gordon and Derek, which fills a yawning gap in the history and archaeology of the old county of Renfrew. The authors would be the first to admit that the contents represent only the tip of the iceberg of interesting sites in Renfrewshire, and it will have fulfilled Gordon's ambition if it continues to inspire others to investigate new sites in the future.

Introduction

There have been several surveys of Renfrewshire's history and architecture, but we believe this is the first to attempt to list the surviving buildings, archaeological sites and monuments in roughly chronological order and historical context. It is a job that needs to be done. Renfrewshire is one of Scotland's smallest and most densely populated counties and comprises the modern council areas of Renfrewshire, East Renfrewshire and Inverclyde. Men and women have lived here for more than 8,000 years, and throughout that time they have cleared, planted, flooded, drained, built, rebuilt and engaged in all sorts of agricultural, industrial, religious and military activities. During the last century and our own times, they have continued to do these things at an ever-increasing rate with the result that many of the relics of former days have been obliterated by 'developments', decay and vandalism. The remaining castles, mills, hill forts, cairns, hut circles and carved stones are chance survivors and represent a way of finding out about the distant past. The purpose of this book is to increase awareness of these monuments and, with due regard to personal safety and private property, encourage people to visit them and develop an understanding of the archaeology of the county.

One of the main problems for the beginner is the jargon – what historians and archaeologists call things and how they divide up time. Students of the past divide the last 6,000–8,000 years into several periods based on their interpretation of the surviving remains. These take the form of field monuments such as hill forts, enclosures, castles, farms, houses, burial sites and smaller finds – or artefacts – like flints, pottery and coins.

We have included monuments just outside the boundaries of the former Renfrewshire because they demonstrate periods of the county's history for which there are currently no recorded monuments. We have described the periods for which there are no monuments because they represent a challenge to future local archaeologists and historians (there must be unrecorded

Mesolithic, Bronze Age, Proto-historic, medieval and industrial monuments because there are large areas where systematic fieldwork has never taken place). Some of the regrettably large number of Renfrewshire monuments that have been destroyed have also been included.

Renfrewshire provides a wide variety of landscapes (Fig. 2). Situated immediately to the south of the Firth of Clyde, its north and north-western boundaries are formed by the banks of the River Clyde and the shore of the Firth of Clyde; the river running for a distance of 7.5km before becoming the Firth which forms c.31km of the county boundary. The banks of the river between Renfrew and Erskine are becoming more heavily built up, and it is difficult to appreciate how this area must have looked when farmland and forest spread along the water's edge. This upper stretch of the Clyde is, for the most part, inaccessible due to the built-up area and some farmland. As such, it is often difficult to tell how close the river is, and the best way to view this stretch of the river, in the absence of a road along the edge, is from the Erskine Bridge, from a plane coming into land at Glasgow Airport, or when sailing down the Clyde on the *Waverley* paddle steamer. After Erskine Bridge, the Clyde opens out into the Firth proper to become visibly more tidal, characterised by extensive mud flats along the foreshore and backed by the raised beach-line. Further westwards still, the towns of Port Glasgow, Greenock and Gourock, with their harbours, revetted sea fronts, and shipyards have greatly altered the shoreline. Beyond Gourock the nature of the shoreline changes; it is more exposed to the effects of the open sea and consists of ribs of seaweed-strewn bedrock.

Much of the eastern boundary of Renfrewshire follows the line of the White Cart from its head streams in the moors to the south-east of Eaglesham downstream into the suburbs of south Glasgow where the boundary cuts across westwards from Muirend to Barrhead before turning northwards past Crookston to the Clyde beside the old power station site at Braehead. The c.50km-long south-western boundary of the county cuts across a broad range of level-topped volcanic hills and moors, which form the watershed between Renfrewshire and Ayrshire. The high ground is broken by the Loch Libo and Lochwinnoch 'gaps', which are the principal routes from the lowlands of the Cart basin to the south-west.

It is advisable for any one visiting the sites listed in this book to use Ordnance Survey maps. The best set of maps are the 1:25,000 Ordnance Survey Explorer Series, which provide the necessary topographic detail for locating a number of the more isolated sites on the high ground.

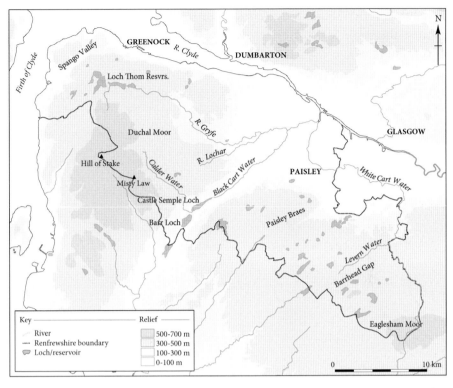

Figure 2   Map showing major topographic
features in Renfrewshire (Ingrid Shearer).

Many of the sites are on private property, and inclusion in the book does not imply right of access. Permission to visit them should therefore be sought from the nearest farm, house or estate office to ensure right of access. Some of the buildings are in a very dangerous state. Please treat these, and the mines and quarries mentioned in the text, with the greatest of respect. We have found that waterproofs and a good pair of boots are as essential as maps and a compass. Some of the sites are in the Guardianship of the State under Historic Scotland, others are in the care of The National Trust for Scotland or are made open on a regular basis by private owners. An essential resource for anyone wanting to find out more about any archaeological site in Renfrewshire or indeed Scotland is the Royal Commission's database CANMORE, which can be accessed through their excellent website (http://www.rcahms.gov.uk).

1

A History of Renfrewshire Archaeological Studies

———◆———

The current understanding of the archaeological remains within Renfrewshire is built upon a variety of sources. Prior to the 1950s very little systematic archaeological fieldwork had been undertaken, although information on a limited number of sites and discoveries can be gleaned from early sources such as old maps and documentary records, some dating back to the eighteenth century.

THE EIGHTEENTH CENTURY

Some of the first references to archaeological sites in Renfrewshire can be found in *The History of the Shire of Renfrew* written by George Crawfurd in 1710 and updated by William Semple in 1782. This parish by parish account of the county mainly focuses on family histories but a number of archaeological sites are mentioned briefly, including the 'vestiges of an Old British Camp' in the lands of Rosshall (now only visible as a crop-mark). What appears to have been an extensive spread of cup-and-ring rock carvings at Hairlaw Craigs near Barrhead are described as 'seventy-two small holes of an oval form about an inch deep in the stone', spread out over 30 yards. This description was accompanied by the unusual interpretation that 'tradition hath handed down, that a battle was fought there, and these holes were where the feet of their tents stood', although they admitted to not knowing what truth there was in the story. Such early references form a record of sites some of which have since been destroyed or are less well preserved. Of the 72 cup-marks at Hairlaw, for example, it has been reported that only five are now visible.

Another excellent source of information on archaeological remains are the parish descriptions compiled by the local ministers in the late eighteenth century and published in the *Statistical Account of Scotland* (1791–99). These descriptions often include a section on antiquities and other curiosities within the parishes. The entries are very variable in detail, and some parishes have no recorded sites. However, others provide detailed accounts of sites, many of which were destroyed by agricultural improvements or the finds subsequently lost. An excellent example is the description of the discovery of cists close to the South Mound at Houston as reported by the Rev John Monteath, which is worth quoting at length:

> . . . when the country people in this parish were digging for stones to enclose their farms, they met with several chests or coffins of flag stones, set on their edges, sides and ends, and covered with the same sort of stones above, in which were many human bones of a large size, and several skulls in some of them.

This report was checked and confirmed during the excavations on the South Mound in the 1970s. However, a number of other sites from which artefacts were recovered were not as fortunate. The reference to the urns containing human bones found close to the Knock Hill near Renfrew still remains the best source of information on a site which was completely destroyed during the construction of a housing scheme in the 1950s.

Unfortunately the early map coverage of the county, such as Blaeu's map of 1654, tends not to be detailed enough to show archaeological sites. It is really only with the work of the Ordnance Survey from the second half of the nineteenth century onwards that archaeological sites are indicated on maps.

THE NINETEENTH CENTURY

The Ordnance Survey maps provide a record of a number of sites that have subsequently been destroyed or altered. For example, the first-edition Ordnance Survey map marks the fort at South Branchal, between Bridge of Weir and Kilmacolm, which is now covered by a conifer plantation, planted probably in the 1950s or 1960s. In addition, it illustrates an enclosure on Byres Hill in Barshaw Park, Paisley, which was subsequently destroyed by the construction of a golf course.

The OS maps are also essential for understanding the contemporary nineteenth-century landscape. Many of the farmsteads created during the agricultural improvements of the late eighteenth century or early nineteenth century are shown on the maps, sometimes as ruins already abandoned by the mid nineteenth century. The first edition OS maps and subsequent editions are invaluable for tracing the development of many of the industrial sites such as mills and quarries.

By far the most intriguing reference to an archaeological site discovered in the county in the nineteenth century, but now destroyed, is the description of the Overlee weems. These were a series of stone-built houses discovered at Overlee, Cathcart, in 1808 and first reported by Revd Dr Smith of Cathcart in the *New Statistical Account* of the parish and retold in later accounts. It is reported that there were over 42 houses, 36 in an arc on the lower ground with 6 higher up. The stone houses were partially subterranean 4–5ft high and 8–12ft square. The interior of each was paved, with a central hole for a hearth. The date of these features remains unknown, although the reported use of coal and the presence of a dozen hand-mills for grinding grain may suggest a first millennium AD or later date for their occupation. Unfortunately the site of these enigmatic structures was quarried away and is now covered by a combination of a railway line, houses and playing fields. Whether any parts of the structures survive remains unknown.

Although Cuff Hill cairn was excavated following its partial destruction for road-stone in 1874, it is actually just outside the county boundary, in Ayrshire (Fig. 3). Probably the first excavation in Renfrewshire proper was on the feudal earthwork motte at Milton Bridge near Kilmacolm by the local minister and historian Revd James Murray in 1894 when he cut a trench right through the mound down to subsoil.

Unfortunately, Renfrewshire did not attract the attention of a scholarly antiquarian like John Smith of Dalry, whose work in Ayrshire is well known. Only two volumes of William Hector's *Archaeological & Historical Collections Relating to the County of Renfrew* were published in the 1890s, focusing on the remains in the parish of Lochwinnoch. Why other volumes on other parishes were never produced is unclear, but the existing volumes provide descriptions and illustrations of both Barr Castle and the Peel in Castle Semple Loch. The drawing of Knockmade in these volumes is one of the earliest plans of an earthwork site in the county (Fig. 4). It is a pity that David Christison, who surveyed many of the hill forts in Ayrshire, also in the 1890s, did not extend the range of his fieldwork into the neighbouring county. Perhaps

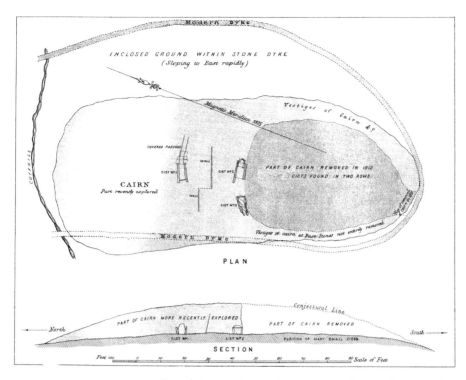

Figure 3   Plan of Cuff Hill cairn by excavator Robert Love in 1874
(reproduced with permission of the Society of Antiquaries of Scotland).

the major exception to Renfrewshire being included in a national survey
is in the work of MacGibbon and Ross, as numerous castle sites featured in
their magnificent five volumes on *The Castellated and Domestic Architecture of
Scotland* and in their three volumes on *The Ecclesiastical Architecture of Scotland*.
Although a number of the crannogs along the mud-flats of the Clyde were
investigated in the late nineteenth century, including one at Dumbuck, the
site at Langbank West in Renfrewshire was not excavated until the opening
years of the twentieth century.

TWENTIETH CENTURY

Although a number of local history books, such as Murray's work on
Kilmacolm (1907) and Pride's volume (Fig. 5) on Neilston (1910), were
published in the first half of the twentieth century, there appears to have been
a lack of archaeological study in Renfrewshire, in contrast to many other

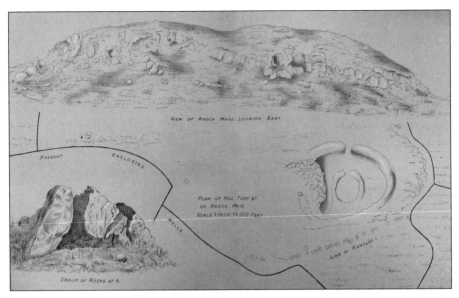

Figure 4   Plan and elevation sketch of Knockmade
homestead 1890 (William Hector).

counties. One notable exception to this was the small excavation undertaken by A.D. Lacaille and the staff from Kelvingrove Museum when they removed the Capelrig Cross from its position in Barcapel field, Crookfur, Newton Mearns, in 1926 (Fig. 6). It is surprising that the presence of some major sites, like the hill forts of Craigmarloch and Duncarnock, were not recorded until the Marginal Land Survey undertaken by Richard Feachem of the Royal Commission on the Ancient and Historic Monuments of Scotland in the 1950s.

The rise of popular archaeology in the 1950s and 1960s saw the start of the single most important source of data to be gathered for Renfrewshire archaeology; namely, the contribution of the amateur archaeologists. The data was collected by local archaeologists who walked different parts of the county in their spare time and recorded any archaeological sites or artefacts. The artefacts were often deposited in Paisley Museum, and reports were published in *Discovery and Excavation in Scotland* (DES), produced annually by the Council for Scottish Archaeology. A quick glance through these volumes indicates that there were a number of dedicated amateurs working in Renfrewshire, including W.F. Lonie, W.O. Black and T.C. Welsh. The survey work tended to focus around the areas where each individual lived,

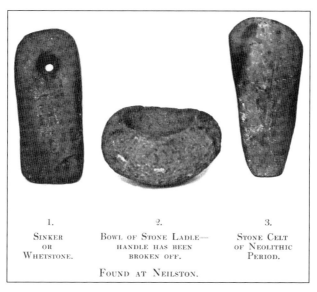

1.
SINKER
OR
WHETSTONE.

2.
BOWL OF STONE LADLE—
HANDLE HAS BEEN
BROKEN OFF.

3.
STONE CELT
OF NEOLITHIC
PERIOD.

FOUND AT NEILSTON.

Figure 5   Stone artefacts including a Neolithic
stone axe found in Neilston (Pride 1910).

and thus the survey coverage is varied. For example T.C. Welsh, who was a
keen historian and prolific fieldworker, concentrated around Eaglesham and
Eastwood. One of the most productive fieldworkers was Frank Newall, who
between 1955 and 1978 contributed (either singly or jointly) over 170 entries
to *Discovery and Excavation in Scotland* for Renfrewshire and has intermittently
contributed another 15 entries since then. It was on the results of his field-
walking that Newall published an article that focused on the early open
settlement in the Renfrewshire uplands (1961–62) in which he identified a
number of different types of unfortified prehistoric settlements.

If archaeology in Renfrewshire can be considered to have had a heyday,
then the concentrated spell of fieldwork during the second half of the 1950s
and into the 1960s surely must be it. Frank Newall undertook the first
modern excavation within the county on the Roman fort at Whitemoss, near
Bishopton, and followed this with an investigation of the large Iron Age
fort at Walls Hill in 1956, the results from which were published by Paisley
Museum (1960). The prehistoric and medieval homestead site at Knapps, near
Kilmacolm, was similarly excavated by Newall in 1961–62 and published
again by Paisley Museum (1965). Of the eight excavations undertaken in the
1950s and 1960s half of them (Walls Hill, East Green, Whitemoss and Knapps)
were undertaken by Newall. The excavations on Knockmade, in 1959–60

Figure 6   Capelrig cross-base during excavation by Kelvingrove
Museum staff in 1926 (Culture and Sport Glasgow (Museums)).

and 1967, and Craigmarloch, 1963–65, also fit into what Newall termed a
series of 'type site' excavations. The radiocarbon dates from Craigmarloch
were among the first in Scotland and as such were much discussed at the time.
Unfortunately, the results of these last two sites were not published until
almost 20 years later, in 1996.

In the 1970s, Frank Newall produced a series of papers in the *Western
Naturalist*, the journal of The Renfrewshire Natural History Society,
published by Paisley Museum. In these papers, he produced period reviews
of the evidence for the Stone Ages (1974), the Bronze Age (1976), the Iron
Age (1978) and the Romans (1975). These reviews were complemented by
reports on a number of fieldwork projects; the artefactual remains of the
Late Neolithic activity from around Gryffe Reservoir (1972) and the rescue

excavation in advance of the destruction of a Bronze Age cairn at East Green, near Kilmacolm (1973). This extensive list of publications forms the backbone of published archaeological research to date in the county.

Newall's work around Gryffe Reservoir was prompted by large-scale planting of conifer plantations and marks the start of rescue excavations in advance of commercial developments from the 1970s onwards. The 1970s also saw the formation of the Renfrewshire Archaeology Society, which undertook a number of excavations, most notably at the South Mound, Houston, in 1974, directed by Daniel Stables, which led to further work to the south of the mound by Alex Morrison of Glasgow University in 1976. These excavations were carried out in advance of proposed tree planting and road construction, while Jack Scott undertook excavation in advance of factory construction at Shiels, Govan, in 1973–74.

The 1970s also saw the first sustained interest in medieval castle sites. Levan, Mearns, Old Barr, Crookston and Cathcart castles were all investigated but once again the first report, the Castle Levan article, took over 20 years to reach publication and, apart from Crookston, the others remain unpublished. Such backlogs of unpublished work were systemic in archaeology prior to the 1990s due to the nature of funding at the time, which often focused on the fieldwork to the detriment of post-excavation analyses and writing up. The lack of final reports for so many sites and the limited distribution of much of Newall's published work has undoubtedly stifled research in the area and has delayed preparation of syntheses, such as this one. This problem was partly addressed in 1996 with the publication of *Prehistoric Renfrewshire*, pulled together and edited by one of the authors (DA), in which reports appeared on Craigmarloch, Knockmade and Shiels, among others. Progress is currently being made on some of the other outstanding reports.

Unfortunately, the Archaeology Society appears to have petered out in the early 1980s until its rebirth as the Renfrewshire Local History Forum (RLHF) – Archaeology Section in 1988 under the guiding influence of one of the authors (GM), Bob Turner, Alan Steel and Irene Hughson. This group holds a series of lectures and provides a forum for discussion of archaeological matters in Renfrewshire (http://rlhf.info). It was in the early 1990s that probably the most exciting archaeological discovery was made: the Paisley Abbey drain, and the Forum were involved in the publication of the results. The RLHF also produces a journal, while the Archaeology Section has undertaken a number of surveys, including Moyne Moor, Neilston, and has continued the research into 'type sites' with the excavation of an unenclosed hut circle at Picketlaw and the post-medieval farmstead at Barrhouse, both just outside Neilston.

Small pieces of research work have been carried out on a number of the sites looked after either by Historic Scotland, as at Newark Castle, or the National Trust for Scotland, with work at Greenbank House, Holmwood House and the Weaver's Cottage, Kilbarchan. Local authorities have also commissioned some research, for example, Renfrewshire Council sponsored work on the site of Renfrew Castle and on the traditional birthplace of Sir William Wallace in Elderslie. Most significant was the work on the Paisley Abbey drain co-ordinated by John Malden, then of Paisley Museum.

Since the turn of the millennium, developer-funded archaeology has really made an impact in Renfrewshire with many sites investigated by professional archaeology field units. At Braehead, for example, a large multi-ditched enclosure was dug in advance of IKEA in 2001. Traces of later prehistoric roundhouses and a nineteenth-century farmstead at Floakside, south of Newton Mearns, were excavated during the upgrading of the A77 to motorway. A palisaded enclosure was discovered at Titwood on the line of the Southern Orbital (Eaglesham bypass) and close by a Bronze Age ring-groove house was excavated at West Acres in 2003. The last five years have also witnessed the first archaeological work within two churchyards at Kilbarchan and Neilston. As recently as 2007, another massive multi-ditched enclosure was investigated at Mar House Hotel golf course (formerly the grounds of Erskine House) in the shadow of Erskine Bridge.

Survey work has continued to identify new sites across the study area and those that have been destroyed. In 1971, Sylvia Clark published a list of industrial archaeological sites in Paisley, and when she updated this in 1998, it was apparent that most of the sites had been demolished. Outside Paisley, the study of early industrial remains of Renfrewshire from bleach-fields, to cotton mills, limestone quarries and kilns has been championed by Stuart Nisbet. He has perfected the art of matching good documentary research with the field remains and is without doubt the most prolific contributor to the Forum Journal with over 12 articles to his name. He has almost single-handedly placed Renfrewshire's rural industrial past in its rightful place as one of the earliest and most innovative counties within Scotland.

Perhaps the most sustained survey work in recent years has been that undertaken around Eaglesham by Robin and Susan Hunter where numerous farms have been recorded in detail. The recent work by the Royal Commission on the Ancient and Historic Monuments of Scotland reviewing their database

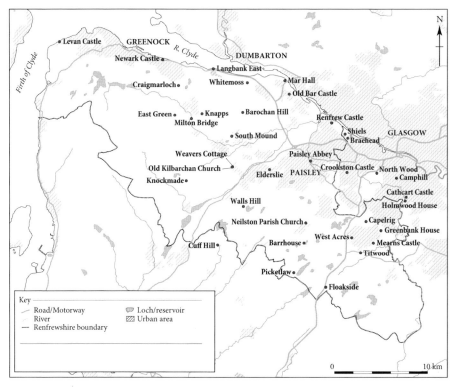

Figure 7 Map showing major archaeological excavations
undertaken in Renfrewshire (Ingrid Shearer).

records for East Renfrewshire involved the first measured surveys of a few
sites including Duncarnock hill fort. In 1996, it was stated that although there
were no known burnt mound sites in Renfrewshire, it was only a matter of
time before one was found. The recent RCAHMS survey has now found
three sites (Alex Hale, pers. comm.).

It is clear from the above review of previous work in the county that,
despite the regular omission from national syntheses, Renfrewshire has a
great wealth of archaeological remains (Fig. 7). This book attempts to draw
together much of the information for the first time in an effort to highlight
the depth of history and archaeology and to encourage future research and
protection for this wonderful cultural heritage.

2

Palaeolithic Renfrewshire

BEFORE *c*.7500 BC

———◆◆◆———

This introductory section is not so much about 'setting the scene' as it is about the actual formation of it. For the purposes of this book, we need only mention those geological periods and features that were exploited at various stages in the history of human settlement of the county.

The form of Renfrewshire is a result of geological processes that occurred over a huge timescale. It is far more difficult to conceptualise the geological processes that led to the formation of this landscape than to imagine the relatively recent (certainly in geological terms) activities of humans. Standing on the Gleniffer Braes, looking out northwards, over the densely built-up areas around Paisley, it is indeed difficult to picture the enormous mass of a glacier, perhaps up to 1,000 metres high, extending out southwards from Loch Lomond. However, this is perhaps an easier concept to grasp than the fact that around 70 million years ago Scotland formed part of a larger land mass, which included Greenland and North America.

The underlying rocks of Renfrewshire were formed in the Devonian and Carboniferous periods, around 400 to 300 million years ago. Sedimentary rocks such as red sandstone and limestone, which were laid down by rivers, or as sand dunes, are among the earliest rocks in the area. Ancient volcanoes produced hard igneous rocks, such as basaltic lavas, which burst through these older sedimentary layers, and the remains of these volcanic plugs and intrusions form the hills to the west and south of the county. Above the volcanic rocks more sediments were laid down as soil or peat, which fossilised over time to become seams of coal, a much exploited resource in later periods. These sediments form the low-lying areas around Paisley and Renfrew.

It is probable that prior to the glaciation the land mass of western Scotland was first shaped by rivers that flowed eastwards before they flowed to the west. Around a million years ago after a gradual decrease in temperatures, all of Britain, apart from the tops of the highest mountains, would have been covered in ice as far as the south of England. Renfrewshire would have been sealed underneath a mass of ice coming southwards from Loch Lomond before spreading east and west. Fluctuations in the temperatures during the Ice Age led to periods of ice either accumulating or melting, when glaciers either expanded or contracted. Between 11,000 and 10,000 years ago was the last cold period when the ice would have extended as far south as the southern end of Loch Lomond.

As the glaciers moved, either advancing or retreating, they scoured the landscape, removing the softer rocks and leaving the hard rocks exposed as hills, such as Misty Law, or Duncarnock, many of which later proved ideal defensive sites in the Iron Age. The glaciers also widened some of the existing river valleys, such as the Calder Valley in Muirshiel Park, with its characteristic U-shaped profile. In addition, the glaciers lifted and carried much of the scoured material, rock and sediments, only to deposit them elsewhere, often forming elongated rounded hills known as drumlins, of which the hills around Inchinnan and Oakshaw, Paisley, are good examples. Large rocks were also transported by the ice, and a particularly fine example of such a glacial erratic can be seen at Clochoderick, near Lochwinnoch, the name of which suggests it was a major landscape feature in the Early Historic or Medieval period.

The fluctuations in the ice cover affected the sea level. At the end of the last Ice Age, more than 10,000 years ago, northern Europe underwent major climatic and geomorphological changes. When the climate warmed, the frozen ice sheets and glaciers melted, causing an initial rise in sea level, followed by an uplifting of the land, which had been compressed by the weight of the ice. A complex state of flux between uplifting land and rising sea resulted in the creation of raised beaches in some areas of Scotland, while in others the coastline was submerged.

With this warming of the climate, the retreating ice and the formation of thin soils, new land became open to colonisation, firstly by tundra vegetation, followed by the spread of birch woodland, and eventually the establishment of elm, hazel, oak and pine forest. As the vegetation changed, so did the types of animals. By 8000 BC, red deer, bear, aurochs (wild ox), wild boar and beaver were all present in the mixed deciduous woodlands of Scotland.

HORN AND UPPER PART OF SKULL OF *BOS PRIMIGENIUS*,
FOUND IN INTERGLACIAL BEDS IN COWDEN GLEN,
NEILSTON.

Figure 8   Horn and upper part of skull of a
wild ox or aurochs found in Cowden
Glen, Neilston (Pride 1910).

Remains of so-called Irish elk (giant deer), wild ox (Fig. 8) and horse were
recovered from layers of clay and peat during the construction of the railway
line through the Barrhead Gap at Crofthead in the nineteenth century. Not
all of the country was covered in forest; there would have been areas of scrub
and marsh, as well as coastal and upland tracts all supporting different flora
and fauna. Following the spread of vegetation northwards were small groups
of humans, hunting and gathering for food and living in temporary shelters.

The earliest human occupation in Britain has been dated to around 500,000
years ago from evidence in the south of England. Any evidence for such
early (Palaeolithic) settlement further north has been removed by later glacial
erosion. Although recent excavation evidence may suggest a date as early as
9000 BC, after *c.*7000 BC there is conclusive evidence for the earliest human

groups in Scotland. These groups of people may have had at least three points of origin. Many may have come from England to the south, while others may have come from Ireland, to the west. In addition, it is also possible that as the sea level rose and flooded the North Sea basin, which would have been an extensive plain during the early postglacial period, some groups may have been gradually pushed from the north-east towards Scotland. The complexity of the situation is apparent in the archaeological record, where no single site could be said to display uniform traits of any single place of origin.

3

Mesolithic Renfrewshire

7000–4000 BC

In Scotland, the earliest human occupation has been dated to *c*.7000 BC on Rhum, with other early sites established along the western seaboard before 6000 BC on Jura, Ulva, Arran, Oban and Islay. However, this picture may be biased by the areas where Mesolithic material has survived, been located and studied. Many experts feel that it is likely that the known early sites are not in fact the earliest sites, and that still earlier remains wait to be found. Recent excavation work at a height of around 2,000 feet up Ben Lawers in Perthshire has uncovered evidence of Mesolithic activity.

The evidence in Scotland and the rest of Western Europe suggests that Mesolithic people lived in small semi-nomadic groups, perhaps formed by extended family units, occasionally coming together in larger groups. They exploited different resources for food and raw materials, probably within relatively set areas, and only moved further afield to obtain specific items. They hunted animals, fished and gathered wild plants and shellfish. Hard stone (flint, chert, quartz and volcanic glass) was chipped into small fragments and used for tools, sometimes hafted together in groups to form arrows and other composite tools. Bone, wood and antler were also used as tools, either as shafts or as implements in their own right. Shelters may have consisted of light, tent-like structures, constructed from a wooden framework covered in animal skins. There is evidence to suggest that, in some cases, shallow hollows were excavated to provide shelter and, indeed, the remains of a circular timber hut dating to the Mesolithic has recently been excavated in East Lothian.

Previously, some scholars thought that these small groups would have moved frequently to exploit seasonally available resources, such as ripening fruit or salmon runs in rivers, but current thinking prefers a less subsistence-dominated lifestyle, often allowing, at least in theory, more prolonged stays at favoured locations. Settlements or campsites are often found beside water, in areas where more than one economic resource could be exploited, for example, beside lochs, the sea or river estuaries, with access to both terrestrial and riverine or marine resources.

The archaeological evidence for these small groups is often difficult to find and interpret, especially the scanty remains left by flimsy structures. The majority of Mesolithic sites have been identified by scatters of flint or chert tools recovered from ploughed fields or sand dune areas. There are also the visible remains of shell middens, which form upstanding mounds, as at Cnoc Sligeach, on Oronsay, or as spreads of white shells visible against the dark soil of ploughed fields, as at Inveravon, in West Lothian.

The lack of hunter-gatherer material has been identified as one of the problem areas of Renfrewshire archaeology, and some researchers have set about finding evidence for such activity. On the basis of the distribution of Mesolithic sites throughout Scotland, it is possible to build up a picture of the environmental niches where more than one type of resource could be accessed, and this information can be applied to the topography of Renfrewshire.

Where would we look for traces of the first settlers who came to the area around 8,000 years ago? If, as seems likely, the interior of the county was wooded, the most probable campsites would be on the shoreline or on the river valleys. Where, then, was the Mesolithic coastline of Renfrewshire? The answer lies in recent studies of the peat mosses at Paisley, Linwood and Barochan. These suggest that the base of these peat bogs accumulated as the ice melted after the Loch Lomond re-advance (after 8000 BC). Rising sea level (8000–6000 BC) scoured away the peat below the 8m contour. The margin was re-colonised by peat towards the end of the Bronze Age or later. Geological maps (the Ordnance Survey Drift editions) indicate that the main drainage patterns of West Renfrewshire are basically unchanged since Post-Glacial times. A combination of these peat studies and the drift maps offers a reasonably clear picture of the coastline that the Mesolithic communities exploited and suggests that sites might be found at various levels in alluvial river valleys and on coastal deposits above the 8m contour line.

Unfortunately, many of the likeliest locations of Mesolithic activity in Renfrewshire cannot be surveyed. From Wemyss Bay to Langbank, for example, the raised beach is built over, afforested or under crops. Between Langbank and Inchinnan extensive green-belt development offers some opportunity for

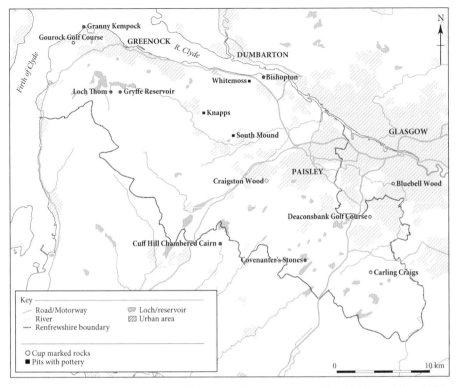

Figure 9   Map of major Mesolithic and Neolithic
sites in Renfrewshire (Ingrid Shearer).

survey in the short term. The most likely locations are ploughed fields on or
above the 8m contour around Inchinnan, Georgetown, Linwood, north of
Paisley, and along the Gryffe, Black Cart and Lochar rivers.

Each potential site has to be approached carefully, starting with a
reconstruction of the Mesolithic topography, soil, beach profile and tide.
But the effort is worth making. Unfortunately, there are no remains of
shell middens in Renfrewshire, but the location of other Mesolithic sites
throughout Scotland, and their preference for environmental niches where
more than one type of resource could be accessed, could suggest where sites
are likely to be found.

Linwood Moss appears to have been a brackish lake before becoming a peat
bog and would have provided an ideal location for hunting and gathering a
wide variety of species.

Recent field-walking of ploughed fields behind the raised beach at Bishopton
(Fig. 9) produced a number of small pieces of flint, which represent the first

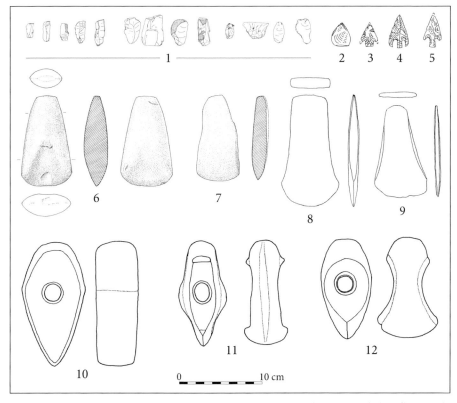

Figure 10   Selection of Mesolithic flint tools (1), Neolithic flint tools and axes (2, 6 and 7), and Bronze Age arrowheads (3–5), stone battleaxes (10–12) and flat bronze axes (8 & 9) (Derek Alexander).

pieces of evidence for the earliest human activity in Renfrewshire and could date back 6,000–8,000 years ago, prior to the adoption of agriculture. These pieces of flint are thought likely to be of Mesolithic date because of their length (Fig. 10, no. 1). Other pieces of what have also been considered to be Mesolithic flints were recovered while excavating the Bronze Age burial cairn, the South Mound, at Houston. Isolated finds of Mesolithic flint have also been made in the hills around Loch Thom, behind Greenock, and suggest that the occupation of inland and upland areas during this period needs to be investigated further.

4

Neolithic Renfrewshire

*c.*4000–*c.*2500 BC

◆◆◆

The Neolithic was thought to have been characterised by a number of significant changes from the Mesolithic, including the construction of semi-permanent settlements, and the production of food through the use of both domesticated plants and animals. These farmers were also believed to have constructed communal tombs. Many tombs may have been used to house the remains of a community's ancestors, to define the limits of their territory and thus legitimise their rights to that territory through the veneration of their ancestors. Technological innovations are also apparent in their material remains; Neolithic communities made pottery and used polished stone tools, such as axes. These changes used to be seen as a Neolithic 'package' adopted wholesale by the Mesolithic hunter-gatherer communities. Current thinking, however, suggests that this process of change was by slow acculturation of the indigenous Mesolithic hunter-gatherer groups who acquired these new techniques and ideas through exchange networks and kinship ties with farming groups in other areas of Britain and ultimately on the Continent. As during the Mesolithic, there must have been contacts between Southern Scotland, Northern England and Ireland. It appears likely that hunter-gatherer groups in some parts of the country did not initially adopt all this Neolithic package at once but chose different parts at different times, and in some cases pottery may have been adopted prior to the use of either farming techniques, or more permanent settlements.

The actual evidence for Neolithic settlement structures is very sparse in Scotland, as in the rest of Britain. It is dominated by the village groups in the

23

Orkneys, as at Skara Brae, Links of Noltland and the excavated settlement at Barnshouse. In addition to these settlements, there is the important island site of Loch Olabhat, North Uist. On the mainland, however, settlement evidence is rare. A couple of exceptions are the large timber halls at Balbridie in Aberdeenshire and the recently excavated examples at Claish, near Callander and Crathes, on Deeside. It is likely that, as in the Mesolithic, the majority of domestic structures would have been of light wooden construction leaving few detectable archaeological remains. Certainly, there are no known or excavated Neolithic settlement sites in Renfrewshire. Fortunately, this lack of settlement evidence in Scotland is contrasted by the abundance of burial and ritual sites.

During the Neolithic, treatment of the deceased members of communities formed a major part of everyday life and is reflected by the number and diversity of funerary sites. Evidence from a number of sites throughout Britain suggests that bodies of the dead may have been placed on raised platforms set within purpose-built enclosures until the flesh was removed by the elements and scavengers. The presence of such structures on which the dead were exposed has been argued for at Balfarg Riding School in Glenrothes, Fife. Once this process of de-fleshing or excarnation was complete, some of the bones, usually the long bones or skulls, were removed and placed within stone tombs or under earthen mounds. The placing of the bones probably formed part of a complex ritual ceremony involving the community as a whole, possibly including feasting and special offerings. These rituals may have been cyclical/seasonal, and access appears to have been required to the bones within the tombs in order that they could be taken out and reused or new bones added. Access to the bones was often provided by means of a passage to the chamber within the tombs.

Neolithic tomb sites have been identified in a number of different forms of megalithic chambered cairns and earthen long barrows throughout Scotland. The different types are characterised, for example, by their different plans of entrance passages and chambers, and form reasonably geographically distinct groups.

Renfrewshire lies on the eastern limits of the distribution of one of these types, the Clyde Cairns. Although there are no known chambered cairns within Renfrewshire itself, there is one at Cuff Hill, near Lugton, Ayrshire, immediately to the south-west of the current study area. This cairn is an example of the small Bargrennan group of chambered cairns, which display a combination of structural features of both early Clyde Cairns and passage-graves. This monument is located on the eastern flank of Cuff Hill *c*.1km south-west of the Renfrewshire/Ayrshire boundary. The cairn is situated in a walled plantation of trees on a small plateau halfway up the south-east facing slope of Cuff Hill. It consists of a partially robbed-out mound of stones, approximately 45m long by 15m across, roughly aligned north-west to south-east (Fig. 3). Three stone-lined cists or burial chambers are set into the cairn at right angles to the main alignment. The amount of labour and organisation involved in the construction of such a cairn certainly suggests a more sophisticated society than that of the hunters and gatherers of Mesolithic times. The present condition of the monument is the result of destruction and excavation in the nineteenth century. On Ainslie's map of the 1790s there is no trace of the cairn or the road, which currently runs along the valley. The site appears to have come to notice in 1813 when according to Robert Love, 'mercenary and brutish labourers' began removing the stones to construct the road. They also smashed through two rows of cists, some 2.1m by 0.9m by 0.9m, and some 0.6m by 0.6m. This account comes from a letter written by Andrew Aitken, a lime burner from Overton. He witnessed the destruction and appealed to Dr Robert Patrick of Hessilhead, the landowner, who stopped the destruction, built a wall round the site and planted trees on it. Contemporary accounts say that many people visited the area to view the remains. They were again disturbed in the winter of 1863–4 by the construction of a fox's earth. In the course of this work a 'limestone cist, with three capstones' and uprights of whinstone, was discovered. The uprights constituted a passage apparently 0.6m by 0.6m. Human bones and a humus-like deposit were also reported. Eventually, in the spring of 1874, Ralston Patrick of Trahearne and Robert Love excavated the cairn for the Society of Antiquaries in Edinburgh. The excavation lasted two days and involved 12 men and 'most of the remaining undisturbed part was turned over'. They found nothing except an internal, discontinuous, flat-stone walling, which seemed to them to be retaining the eastern part of the cairn.

Given the destruction of the last century, it is difficult to reconstruct the history of the cairn. It is possible that the walling discovered by Love's excavation is evidence that the cairn was extended from a simple Clyde cairn. It is also conceivable that the small cists described in Andrew Aitken's letter were later, Bronze Age, cists set into the Neolithic cairn. If this is the case, it is likely that Cuff Hill had a long history as a ritual site at any time between 4000 BC and *c*.2000 BC.

The surface appearance of the cairn is a long oval mound, wider at one end. Although not numerous, similar mounds have been identified by field workers at Auchenfoyle Farm near Kilmacolm and Knockbartnock Farm near Lochwinnoch, although their identification as manmade mounds still requires to be tested by excavation.

It has been suggested that the apparent lack of chambered cairns in Ayrshire and Renfrewshire is a result of their destruction due to improved farming methods and the clearance of land for agriculture, and that, originally, the concentration of monuments may have been similar to the dense spread of monuments located in the southern half of the Isle of Arran, in the Firth of Clyde. However, this argument has been questioned because, although there are records of the destruction of Bronze Age cairns in Ayrshire, there are no records of chambered cairns, which would certainly have been more difficult to remove. It remains possible that few chambered cairns were built in the area, and perhaps the communities who lived in Renfrewshire travelled to ritual centres elsewhere, as on Arran, at particular times of year. Certainly, pieces of pitchstone, a dark volcanic glass found on Arran, was used for making chipped stone tools which have been found on sites in Renfrewshire.

Lithic scatters (spreads of chipped stone such as pitchstone, chert, quartz and flint) and polished stone axes can be used to identify the location of other Neolithic sites. A leaf-shaped arrowhead found at Gryffe Reservoir is characteristic of the Neolithic (Fig. 10, no. 2). The presence of arrowheads reflects the use of the bow for hunting. A yew longbow was discovered in 1990 on a remote peat bog at Rotten Bottom in the Tweedsmuir Hills, Dumfries and Galloway Region, and has been dated to c.4040–3640 BC, thus making it one of the earliest examples from Britain and Ireland. Polished stone axes are also recovered as isolated finds throughout Scotland. Sometimes the stone from which these axes were crafted can be attributed to particular geological sources, like Killin in Perthshire, while others were made of local glacial cobbles. A number of such axes have been found across Renfrewshire. The petrology or geological rock type of a few Renfrewshire axes has been identified and these appear to have come from a source at Tievebulliagh, in Northern Ireland. Two stone axes were found in a ploughed field close to Harelaw Dam (Fig. 10, nos 6 & 7) along with a cannel-coal disc bead. A flake has broken off the blade of the larger of the two axes, probably during use, while the smaller example exhibits wear around its narrower end where it was probably mounted in a wooden handle. Axes would have been used for clearing areas of forests for farmland, and the pollen record indicates that small-scale clearances during this period were relatively common. Axes would also have been used for carpentry during the construction of settlements. They therefore were a very important tool and, given the effort needed to make them and the distance over which some were apparently exchanged, it is clear that they were regarded as status symbols as well as utilitarian tools.

Sherds of Neolithic pottery can also be found, in association with flints and polished stone axes, on ploughed fields. The production of pottery reflects a major technological change in the control of fire. The process of transforming the raw material, clay, into a finished product, a pot, may have held great symbolic importance, and thus the pots themselves appear to have been important in more than just a functional role. The first pots were round-bottomed, plain bowls and were reasonably uniform in style across not only Scotland, but the rest of Britain. However, by 3500 BC different regional styles had evolved with different shapes and forms of decoration, especially on the upper part of the vessels. A form of pottery called Grooved Ware has been found on a number of Late Neolithic sites from ceremonial sites such as the henge complex at Balfarg, Glenrothes in Fife, spreads of pits, as at Wellbrae in Lanarkshire, to the complex settlement site at Skara Brae in Orkney. Grooved Ware appears to represent a pan-British pottery style. A single sherd of Grooved Ware was recovered from forestry plough-furrows around Gryffe Reservoir, south of Greenock.

Pits cut into the subsoil containing sherds of possibly deliberately broken pots appear to represent the remains of an important form of ritual. A number of such pit sites have been discovered in Renfrewshire – usually while excavating other later sites. Sherds of plain round-based Neolithic bowls were recovered from three adjacent pits under the centre of the Bronze Age burial cairn, the South Mound at Houston, when it was excavated in 1974. The largest pit was cut into the bedrock below the cairn. The most complete pot, of coarse fabric with slightly out-turned rim, was c.14cm in diameter and stood c.10 cm high. One of the other bowls was of a finer fabric, burnished on the exterior and with a pronounced lip just above the base. From the same location, pieces of charcoal and burnt hazelnut shells were also recovered. Hazelnut shells are a very common find on Neolithic sites and indicate that hunting and gathering probably still played and important role in the provision of food. These pots are now stored in Paisley Museum.

During the excavation of the Roman fort at Whitemoss, Bishopton a number of pits were also located from which sherds of a number of round-based plain Neolithic bowls similar to those from the South Mound were recovered (Fig. 11). The pots had out-turned (rolled-over) rims, and one had

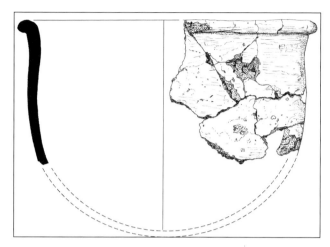

Figure 11   One of the plain bowl Neolithic pots found
in pits under the Roman layers at Whitemoss, Bishopton
(SC 1146760 © courtesy of RCAHMS (Jack Scott
Collection). Licensor http://www.rcahms.gov.uk).

what has been described as a 'lug handle', a common feature on Neolithic
plain bowl pottery, while another had a noticeable shoulder. The similarity
between the description of these pots and those from the South Mound is
remarkable, and once again burnt hazelnut shells were also recovered. A
radiocarbon date of 3943–3520 BC was obtained from charcoal samples from
one of the pits. It is possible that a series of stake-holes found beneath the
Roman headquarters building may also be of Neolithic date. More recently,
another two radiocarbon samples from a pit containing wood and hazelnut
charcoal from Titwood, Mearns, but without any associated artefacts,
produced Neolithic dates of 3640–3370 BC and 3660–3510 BC.

Towards the end of the Neolithic, there is evidence from the rest of the
country for the construction of extensive ceremonial complexes such as
henges and stone circles. What appeared to be the remains of a henge, a
ceremonial enclosure with internal ditch and external bank, was located by
aerial photography on the flat land beside the Clyde at Shiels farm, Govan,
but excavation in 1974 showed it to be a much later Iron Age enclosure. More
recently, the remains of the Covenanters' Stones on Moyne Moor have been
surveyed, and these six large stones may represent the collapsed remains of a
Late Neolithic/Early Bronze Age stone circle. The stones lie within a fenced-
off area on the north side of a recently constructed track which leads around

the southern flank of Lochend Hill on Moyne Moor, near Neilston. The stones are situated *c.*200m west of the remains of the Bronze Age cairn on Lochend Hill. There are seven stones lying flat in two parallel rows running south-west to north-east. There are three stones in the northern row and four in the southern. The stones are all thin slabs and vary in length from around 1.0m to 2.2m. Local tradition links the stones with the Covenanting movement in the seventeenth century, and there may be some truth in this, but the site could easily represent the remains of a much earlier ritual site: a Late Neolithic/Early Bronze Age stone circle. To the north of the stones, there are two 7.5m-long, turf-covered mounds, aligned south-west to north-east, and both have arrangements of stones at their south-west ends. Could these mounds represent small elongated cairns similar to those found on Biggar Common in Clydesdale? Certainly, the ritual associations of the area are not in doubt, what with the presence of the nearby cairn and the stones themselves. The recovery of sherds of Late Neolithic/Early Bronze Age Beaker pottery from the upcast of a drainage ditch 100 metres to the south-west of the stones strengthens this interpretation. These ritual sites may have been used for ceremonial purposes at specific times of year, perhaps for celebrating particular rites of passage, points of change in the life cycle, such as birth, marriage and death. Ceremonies may have involved feasting and the use and deposition of specific artefact types. Fragments of broken pottery and burnt bone are often found within pits or ditches on such sites.

Single standing stones may also have marked significant locations in the landscape. The exact date of the standing stone known locally as 'Granny Kempock' in Gourock is unknown. It might date back to prehistory or it could be more recent. It was certainly standing in the seventeenth century when it is recorded that a Mary Lamont, who was burnt as a witch, confessed to plotting to throw the stone into the sea. It stands on top of a cliff looking out over Kempock Point and is surrounded by iron railings. The stone, which stands 1.8m high and is 0.6m in diameter, is a mica-schist. It is called 'Granny' Kempock as it looks like the cloaked and hooded figure of an old woman. There are a number of local customs associated with the stone. Local married couples passed round the stone to gain luck, and sailors and fishermen would seek successful omens there before setting out. There are another two standing stones on the Paisley Braes.

Much of the ritual and beliefs of early societies can only be guessed at, and, along with the ceremonial sites, rock carvings are among the most enigmatic. Scottish rock carvings consist of designs, usually shallow scoops or cups often

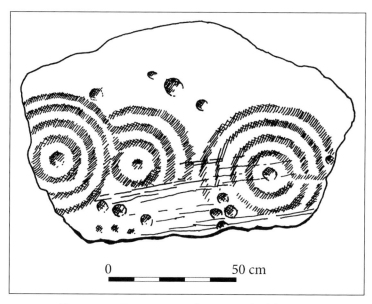

Figure 12   Large cup-and-ring marked boulder found in
Bluebell Woods, Langside (redrawn by Derek Alexander).

surrounded by rings pecked into stone. Cup-and-ring marked rock art can be found across Atlantic Europe from Portugal to Orkney. The abstract symbols of circles and cups were pecked out of the rock some time between 3000 and 1500 BC during the Late Neolithic and into the Early Bronze Age. Professor Richard Bradley is an expert in rock art and thinks these specialised symbols probably had different meanings depending on where and in what context they were used, as does the cross symbol in Christianity. Some appear on ceremonial monuments, others in open landscapes (like the recent discoveries on National Trust for Scotland ground at Ben Lawers on Loch Tay), while some are included in individual burial cists.

Renfrewshire has a limited number of identified areas of rock art, mostly in the form of cup-and-ring marks. Although the rock carvings in the county appear to be evenly spread, they tend to be located at the junction between farming land and upland areas, perhaps lending some weight to the interpretation that these stones marked boundaries between the altered/ domesticated farming landscape and the wild/natural woodland, scrub and moors; a distinction between what was perceived to be tame and wild. A particularly fine example of a cup-and-ring marked rock was found in Bluebell

Figure 13   One of the four cup-and-ring marks on the bedrock
outcrop in Craigston Wood, Johnstone (Derek Alexander).

Woods, Langside at the start of the twentieth century and used to be on display
in Kelvingrove Museum (Fig. 12). It displays three cup-marks surrounded by
three to four concentric rings. The largest set has a gulley running out from
the central cup through the rings. There are a further 14 single cup-marks
on the stone. The site of the wood, which overlooked the White Cart, is now
covered in houses. One of the few *in situ* rock carvings in Renfrewshire can
be found in Craigston Wood, Johnstone (Fig. 13). There were reputedly five
cup-and-ring marks at this site, and at least four are evident. They are located
at the south-western end of a small stone quarry, about 15m off the road in
Craigston Wood. Much of the surrounding ground is covered in similar small
quarries. The cup-and-ring marks are carved into a sloping face of bedrock,
which has been cleared of turf and has been partly defaced with spray paint
and leaves and moss have made it the rock extremely slippy. The cups are
about 5cm in diameter and the rings are 16–21cm in diameter. Three of the
four have gutters running down from the central cup. This site is a Scheduled
Ancient Monument.

Another less well-preserved set of cup-and-ring marks can be found on
Deaconsbank Golf Course beside the doocot, close to the railway line. The

best time to visit might be in winter when there are fewer golfers and the sunlight is low. Low sunlight is essential, as the cup-and-ring marking on this bedrock outcrop is extremely faint. There are very residual traces of two rings at the western end of the outcrop, but the rest of the mark has been quarried away. The surface of the outcrop is pitted by large circular quarry scoops, which were probably for millstones. The turf has recently been removed from the surface, and another very faint but complete cup-and-ring mark that has at least three rings is visible at the east. There are other examples on Gourock Golf course.

About 19 single cups are cut into several of the glacial rocks known as the Carling Craigs, near Eaglesham. These average 50mm diameter and 12mm deep. There are no associated features such as rings, and any other marks are clearly natural. Although many well-known commentators accept these to be manmade cup-marks, others have raised doubts as to their artificial nature in view of other, water-worn, markings on the rocks.

Rock carvings are notoriously difficult to date but, from their presence in burial cairns in other areas of Scotland, they clearly continued in use or, at least, were often reused in the Bronze Age.

The end of the Neolithic and start of the Bronze Age is marked by the appearance of a new form of pottery, called Beaker pottery, which is fine and highly decorated with comb-tooth or twisted-cord impressions. Chambered tombs of the Neolithic appear to have gone out of use in the late third millennium BC; many of the passageways and chambers were blocked up, and sherds of Beaker pottery have been recovered from some of these deposits. The communal tomb appears to be replaced with burial of individuals within stone-lined graves or cists, sometimes individually or in groups, below round cairns, sunk into earlier monuments, or in flat cemeteries. These graves are usually accompanied by burial goods, including Beaker pottery, or jet necklaces. All these grave goods are seen as prestige items that reflect the status of the deceased and of the mourners. This period sees the rise in power of the individual and possibly the creation of hierarchies based upon the control of prestige items and resources. By controlling access to such items, the social elites constantly reaffirmed their position in the social hierarchy.

Beaker pottery was found by Frank Newall during his survey work around Loch Thom and Gryffe Reservoir where he systematically walked forestry plough-furrows collecting artefacts. This fieldwork revealed 14 concentrations of artefact scatters, many located on small knolls. Beaker and Grooved Ware sherds were identified at a number of these locations, along with quantities of flint and chert implements. A number of barbed and tanged arrowheads (sometimes found in Beaker funerary assemblages) have been recovered: a buff chert one from Lurg Moor, a white flint one from Lochwinnoch, and one of dark green Arran pitchstone from Scroggy Bank. Such arrowheads are characteristic of the Early Bronze Age and are often found in cists accompanied by Beaker pots. In addition, Newall proposed that some of the simpler hut circles within the Gryffe Reservoir area may be of Beaker, or Early Bronze Age date. This theory still needs to be tested through excavation.

5

Bronze Age Renfrewshire

*c.*2500–600 BC

———◆———

Technological change, most noticeably resulting from the adoption of metals, marks the start of the Bronze Age (Fig. 14). This change contrasts with the evidence for continuity in many other aspects of the archaeological evidence. There is no clear break between the Late Neolithic and the Early Bronze Age; one merges into the other. This continuity of tradition is evident from the presence of many Early Bronze Age artefacts and burials on Late Neolithic sites. Bronze artefacts seem to have fitted into an existing pattern of prestige items such as decorated pottery, jet necklaces and stone axes, all used to display the social status of their owner, although few bronze artefacts have been recovered from graves. The rise in status of the individual within society is marked by the placing of such status symbols in cist graves and may represent evidence for a hierarchical society.

The Bronze Age was initially defined by a typological division of bronze tools and weapons into Early, Middle and Late phases. The technological changes from simple to complex were used to construct artefact typologies with relative chronological significance. Many artefacts of bronze are recovered individually or in groups (hoards) from bogs and other wet sites. It is possible that the deposition of bronzes in hoards and their deliberate destruction is part of a ritual comparable to the earlier Neolithic pottery deposits. Unfortunately, due to the often isolated nature of their deposition, it is difficult to relate these artefacts to a wider settlement pattern. A number of explanations have been proposed for the deposition of hoards; some were accidentally lost, others were the stock or scrap of a metalworker, while others were considered to be votive deposits or offerings to deities.

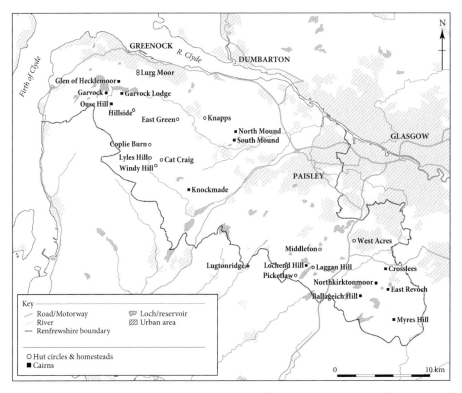

Figure 14   Map of major Bronze Age settlements and burial cairns in Renfrewshire (Ingrid Shearer).

The first metalworkers used soft metals such as copper, gold and, more rarely, lead. Copper flat axes, similar in shape to the stone axes, were among the earliest forms made in single piece moulds during the Early Bronze Age. Bronze, a mixture of copper and tin, was later used to produce other weapons and tools. During the Middle Bronze Age more complex two-part moulds were used to produce tools such as flanged axes, palstaves, looped spearheads, dirks, rapiers, chisels, punches, hammers and small bronze razors. Two flanged axes, one decorated with chevrons, and a ribbed dagger were found at Gavel Moss near Lochwinnoch (Fig. 15). On typological grounds, these are thought to date to 1500–1600 BC. These artefacts are one of the few prehistoric finds from Renfrewshire that are repeatedly incorporated into national syntheses and can be seen on display in the recently refurbished Archaeology Gallery in Kelvingrove Art Galleries and Museum in Glasgow.

Another flat axe was found in the Levern Water near Pollokshaws, while a decorated socketed axe was found at Cardonald near Paisley (Fig. 10, nos

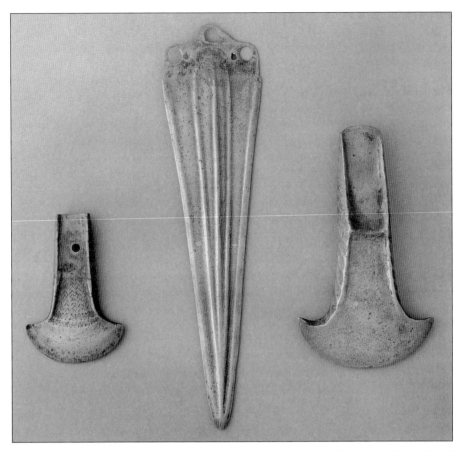

Figure 15 Bronze Age hoard of two decorated axes and a dagger from Gavel
Moss near Lochwinnoch (Culture and Sport Glasgow (Museums)).

8 & 9). A small hoard of three bronze artefacts was recovered from close
to a possible settlement site at Middleton farm near Newton Mearns. This
included a socketed axe, a tanged chisel and the broken remains of an
unidentified bronze object over 10cm long. In addition to axes, spearheads
were a common artefact of the Middle and Late Bronze Age. A socketed,
looped spearhead with a central rib and flanged sides was found in Linwood
Moss, Kilbarchan; another double-looped socketed spearhead was found in
Bennan Loch, Eaglesham; and finally, a tanged flat spearhead was found
at Langstilly near Lochwinnoch. Daggers were characteristic of the Early
Bronze Age; these became longer rapier forms in the Middle Bronze Age
and finally developed into leaf-shaped slashing swords in the Late Bronze
Age. Late Bronze Age metalwork is characterised by an increase in weapon

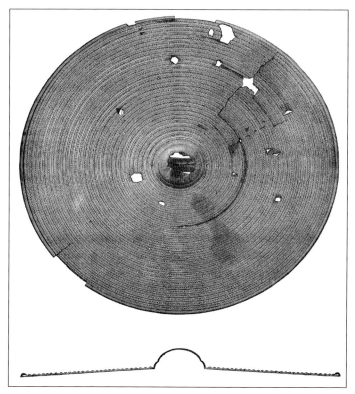

Figure 16   Lugtonridge beaten bronze shield
now in London (John Smith 1890).

manufacture and the production of sheet bronze cauldrons and ceremonial
shields. Lead was added to the copper and tin to allow it flow better in more
complex moulds and also to be beaten out into flat sheets. Two swords have
been recovered from the River Clyde at Bowling, close to Renfrew, along
with a chape for the bottom of a scabbard. Six bronze shields were found
arranged in a circle in a peatbog at Lugtonridge, just over the border in
Ayrshire. Only one of these shields now survives and is on display in the
Society of Antiquaries in London (Fig. 16).

Bronze tools did not completely replace stone tools; for example, stone axes
continue in use in the Early Bronze Age. Some examples have drilled holes in
order to receive a wooden shaft, and these have been termed battleaxes or axe-
hammers, depending on their size. It is possible that some of these stone tools
were made in imitation of metal examples. Although associations with other
datable artefacts are few, battleaxes appear to date from approximately 2000–

1600 BC. A number of these battleaxes have been found in Renfrewshire. An early type was found at Barochan near Houston (Fig. 10, no. 10), while two intermediate-developed types were found at Lawfield, at Kilmacolm and Wheatlands farm, near Kilbarchan (Fig. 10, nos 11 & 12). All of these were recovered as isolated finds and none are from reliable contexts such as settlements or graves. With the progression of the Bronze Age, new types of pottery, such as food vessels, which appear to be a combination of Late Neolithic pottery types and Beaker decorative motifs, and larger urns, become the norm. The former are commonly found in cist burials with crouched inhumations, whereas the latter are found with cremations. Plainer large cinerary urns, sometimes collared or cordoned, were used to hold the cremated remains. Cinerary urns have been found at Knock farm, near Renfrew, and two groups each of four cremations, of which four were covered in well-decorated urns, were found at Paper Mill farm, Newlands, Cathcart. There are a number of references to the discovery of other possible urns, as at Craigmarloch, Kilmacolm.

A large number of simple round cairns have been recorded throughout Renfrewshire. In East Renfrewshire there is one on the summit of Lochend Hill, near Neilston, c.200m east of the Covenanters' Stone. Overlooking both the Harelaw Dam and the Long Loch, the remains consist of a partially robbed, turf-covered, flat-topped cairn c.9.5m in diameter and 0.8m high. There is another excellent example at North Kirktonmoor, above Eaglesham. Two cairns located close to East Revoch farm, Eaglesham, were mostly removed in 1836. The site of the southern cairn, which lies c.250m west of the farm, consists of a disturbed area of ground c.27m in diameter, and several urns containing burnt bones were found when it was removed. More survives of the northern cairn, which is situated c.400m north-west of the farm. The turf-covered mound of stones measures c.30m in diameter and 1m high. Seven cists filled with burnt bones were located within this mound. Construction work in 1825 removed the majority of a cairn which formerly stood on the north-east side of the Eaglesham to Mearns road at Crosslees farm. It is reported that a large empty cist containing burnt bone fragments was found at this time. The large capstone for this cist was built into the wall at the roadside. Other examples can be found at Myres Hill and Ballageich Hill, Eaglesham, both over 20m in diameter.

Over in Inverclyde, there are many cairns on the ground around Loch Thom. The remains of a turf-covered stone cairn are located close to the summit of Garvock hill overlooking Loch Thom. The cairn is c.9–10m in

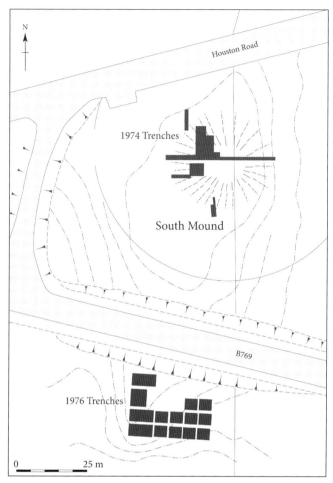

Figure 17   Plan of excavation trenches on South Mound,
Houston in 1974 and south of the road in 1976
(redrawn Derek Alexander).

diameter and stands up to 0.9m high. A stone-filled hollow in the centre
suggests that it has been robbed. On Ouse Hill, a cairn overlooks Loch Thom
and Gryffe Reservoir from the south. Situated on a north-facing slope c.500m
south-west of Dowries Farm Hill are the remains of a cairn 12.5m long by
10.5m wide, and up to 1.5m high.

As with the cairns at East Revoch and Crosslees, the one at Knockmade
near Lochwinnoch was discovered in the nineteenth century. The local
farmer removed a large mound of earth and stone 9m long by 6m from the
field c.100m north-west of the prehistoric homestead on Knockmade Hill.

Under the mound, he discovered a large capstone, which had fragmented into three bits, and when this was lifted pieces of burnt wood and ashes were recovered.

However, without excavation, it is impossible to determine when many of these cairns were constructed and what their functions were. They can vary from Neolithic or Early Bronze Age burial monuments to post-medieval clearance cairns.

During land improvement in the eighteenth century a number of cists were recovered from a field to the south of the South Mound near Houston. Excavation of the South Mound was carried out in 1974 by Danny Stables of the Renfrewshire Archaeology Society, while the area to the south of the mound was excavated in 1976 by Alex Morrison of Glasgow University (Fig. 17). The South Mound was found to be a low cairn over 30m in diameter and 0.6m high, built on top of a natural rise. A number of early features were located below the mound but the main find was a large, rubble-built cist, with a bedrock floor, covered with a large capstone. The cist was 1.2m long, 0.6m wide and 0.6m deep, while the capstone was 1.5m long, 0.9m wide and 0.3m thick. When the capstone was removed, the cist was found to contain a pile of cremated human bone, a small flint knife and an almost complete decorated food vessel. Excavation in the area to the south of the mound uncovered the remains of the cist cemetery partially robbed out in the eighteenth century. In a rock cut pit the cremated remains of a child and an adult male were found, accompanied by an adult female inhumation (Fig. 18). Artefacts included fragments of a food vessel, similar to that found in the cist below the mound, a large number of jet beads, from more than one spacer-plate necklace (Plate 1), and fragments of a bronze awl (Fig. 19). The bronze awl may have been mounted in a wooden handle and is probably the earliest metal implement found in Renfrewshire. On the other side of Houston village, there is a possible cairn similar to the excavated example, but its remains are very indistinct. It is surrounded by a circular dry-stone dyke and is known as the North Mound,

Gravel extraction in 1964 from a small ridge along the southern bank of the River Gryffe on the eastern outskirts of Bridge of Weir located a short cist. The cist, which measured 1.2m by 0.6m, was formed of four side slabs covered by a large capstone. It was found to contain the contracted skeleton of a 19-year-old girl but lacked any grave goods. Without the presence of datable artefacts, this cist can only tentatively be compared to other Bronze Age short cists. Another form of possible Bronze Age ritual site consisting of

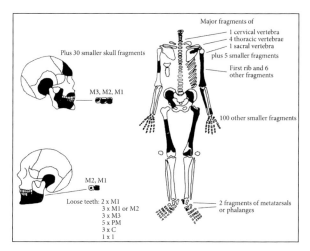

Figure 18   Chart from South Mound skeletal remains found in 1976 (Alex Morrison; reproduced with the permission of Glasgow Archaeology Society).

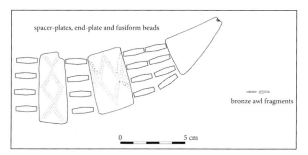

Figure 19   One end of a spacer plate jet bead necklace found at the South Mound (redrawn by Derek Alexander).

a small annular ditched site, termed a ring-ditch, was discovered by aerial photography where it was revealed as a crop-mark in a field at Longhaugh Lodge, near Bishopton. Excavations of ring ditches in other parts of the country have revealed them to be of various dates from the Neolithic to the Iron Age, but the majority are thought to be of Bronze Age date.

One type of monument which has been increasingly identified in upland areas throughout southern Scotland, most notably by the work of the Royal Commission on the Ancient and Historic Monuments of Scotland in Nithsdale and Annandale and by Tam Ward in Clydesdale, is the burnt mound. These enigmatic mounds of burnt stone are often found close to water sources and have been interpreted as either cooking sites or as prehistoric saunas. The lack of artefactual remains may support the latter interpretation. For many years, no burnt mounds had been discovered in Renfrewshire, but recent survey work by Alex Hale and RCAHMS surveyors has located two new examples at East Revoch and South Kirktonmoor, both near Eaglesham. The former site lies 0.5 km north-north-east of East Revoch farm in a boggy area beside a stream. It is an oval grass-covered mound 10m by 7.5m and 1m high. A spade-dug test-pit in the top of the mound found burnt angular stone fragments and black soil. Furthermore, excavation by AOC Archaeology Group in advance of a quarry at Floak for the M77 found the truncated remains of a hearth and a flattened burnt mound, which sealed three pits. One of the pits was lined with wood and may have been the cooking trough.

As with the Neolithic period, the settlement evidence for the Early Bronze Age in Scotland is sparse. The majority of unenclosed hut circles in Renfrewshire are probably of mid to later Bronze Age date or even Iron Age. The remains of a hut circle at Picketlaw, near Neilston, were recently excavated. It had been identified in the 1950s when the local farmer tried removing some of the stones in order to improve pasture. The site is located c.40m west of a small stream, which issues from an area of blanket peat c.2m deep. This bog forms the south-western end of Moyne Moor. Following a survey of the site, it was excavated over three seasons by the Renfrewshire Local History Forum – Archaeology Section under the direction of Derek Alexander and Bruce Henry. Excavation revealed the partially preserved remains of a curvilinear stone wall c.12m in diameter (Fig. 20). This wall was 1.2–1.3m wide and consisted of large stones forming an inner and outer kerb retaining a core of smaller stones. The wall was only one course high, and an entrance 0.5m wide was apparent in the south-eastern side. An area of paving was located inside the entrance and led up to a stone-filled ditch concentric to the outer wall. This ditch enclosed an area c.3.5m in diameter and may have originally held timber posts for supporting the roof. In the centre of the house was an area (1.2m by 1.0m) paved with large flat stones, which was interpreted as a central hearth. Certainly, the soil within the centre of the hut was a lot darker than that outside and contained numerous charcoal flecks. Artefacts recovered from the site include quartz pebbles, some of which had been flaked much like flint, and a number of pieces of plain coarse pottery, probably from upright bucket-shaped vessels with flat rims typical of the Bronze Age. The majority of the pottery was found outside the house, perhaps suggesting that just as much activity happened in the open as under the dark

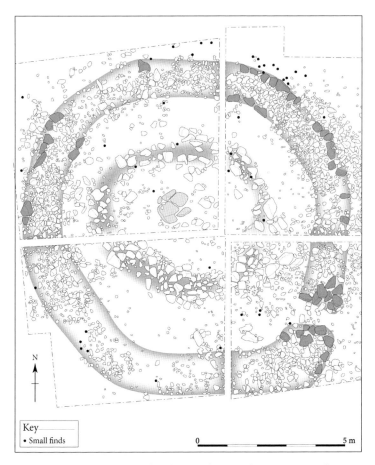

Figure 20   Plan of Picketlaw hut circle excavation showing
heavily robbed outer wall, inner ring and central hearthstones
(Ingrid Shearer).

roof. Radiocarbon dates of charcoal from around the hearth indicated that
the site was occupied in the Middle Bronze Age between 1400 and 1000 BC.

Not far from Picketlaw, there is another hut circle located at the foot of
a natural scarp just below the top of the ridge on the south-eastern flank of
Laggan Hill looking over the small stream towards William's Hill. Here the
hut circle is smaller, only c.6.6m in diameter, and is defined by earth and stone
banks up to 2.5m wide. Its western side is cut back into the hill slope, and the
entrance may have faced to the east.

Frank Newall excavated what appeared to be a small ring cairn at East
Green Farm, near Kilmacolm, prior to its destruction for building purposes.

This consisted of an outer kerb *c.*12.8m in diameter with an entrance in the south-west, enclosing a central chamber 7.2m long by 3.8m wide. The space between the inner and outer kerb was filled with cobbles on the north-western side. No conclusive burial deposits were found associated with the cairn, and it overlay an organic-rich black layer, which sealed a number of pits, two of which contained sherds of prehistoric pottery. Those from pit 6 were of a very coarse, ill-fired vessel while those from pit 1 were finer. Both fabrics were interpreted as sherds from Bronze Age cinerary urns. The excavator tentatively suggested *c.*1500–1000 BC as an approximate date for the site. However, with the lack of burial deposits it is perhaps tempting to interpret this site as a hut circle similar to Picketlaw.

As with the cairns, most of the upstanding examples have been found in the upland areas of Renfrewshire. A couple of good examples are visible in Muirshiel County Park at Windy Hill and Lyles Hill. Located at the foot of the north-western slope of Windy Hill, the first hut circle consists of a ring of stones *c.*11m in diameter, which can be traced sticking up through the heather and rushes. The walls consist of a bank of earth and stones *c.*1.5m wide. The inner slope of the bank at the south-west, upslope side, is the best preserved. Around 4m in from the downslope, north-eastern side, there is a slight terrace which runs across the interior and could represent a stepped floor surface. Large stones are visible around the circuit of the wall, and there is a notable concentration on the eastern side, adjacent to a rush-filled stream channel. The Lyles Hill example is sheltered from the worst of the wind, between the two summits of Lyles Hill looking northwards to Craig of Todholes. This large hut circle measures *c.*12m in diameter over walls 2–3m wide. The bank forming the wall of the hut circle is well preserved on all but the eastern side and stands up to 0.4m high. A modern field drain has been cut down close to the eastern side, while a small outcrop of bedrock on the western side may have been quarried for building stone.

Further north, two clear hut circles are located to the north and south of a small conifer plantation on the south side of the Green Water, *c.*1km south-west of Hillside Farm. The northern hut circle (NS 2929 6967) is located on the north-west side of a small tributary stream, which runs into the Green Water. It is *c.*12.3m in diameter over a large boulder wall up to 1.5m wide. There is a 1.5m-wide entrance gap in the eastern side and another possible gap in the west. The remains of a smaller possible structure *c.*5m in diameter are attached to the south-west side. The southern hut circle (NS 2925 6945) is similarly constructed of large boulders and is *c.*12.3m in diameter over walls

1.8m wide. Within the centre of this hut circle there is a dense spread of stone, whether this represents a later structure or some form of internal division as seen at Picketlaw remains unknown. A further spread of stones lies to the north and north-west.

Another couple of fine examples of hut circles lie on the edge of Lurg Moor, above the steep slope overlooking the eastern end of Greenock. The first site is located to the east of the Lady Burn and appears as a circular platform with earthen banks visible to the south and north. The eastern side has been badly damaged by the foundations for a double wooden pole power line and its associated restraining wires, while the south-western side has also been damaged by similar wire stays for another wooden pole power line to the south-west. The circle is *c*.12–13m in diameter with banks *c*.0.2m high in the interior and up to 0.5m high on the exterior. Stone is visible in the south-west on the exterior where the bank has been disturbed. A low curvilinear field bank runs up the gentle slope westwards on the opposite side of the burn and may represent the remains of a field system associated with the hut circle. The second hut circle is located *c*.300m south of the previous example and is altogether better preserved. It is situated at the foot of a low rocky scarp, which may have provided a degree of protection from the westerly prevailing winds. To the east, there is a small expanse of boggy ground from which the Lady Burn issues northwards. The wall of the hut circle is clearly defined, especially on the interior, by large boulders protruding through the turf. Measuring *c*.9m in diameter over walls *c*.0.8m wide, the internal area is *c*.7.5m in diameter. The entrance is on the downslope side facing eastwards. Vegetation cover within the interior is markedly different with turf covering the southern half, heather and rushes covering the northern half. This clear-cut division between the vegetation cover may simply reflect drainage, but perhaps it could also represent differences in the underlying deposits resulting from the original function of each side of the house.

It is possible that the construction of such open settlements, incorporating widely spaced hut circles, accompanied an increase in the division of the landscape for agricultural purposes. Small field-banks enclose areas adjacent to the hut circles at Gotter Burn West and may have been a small agricultural plot or enclosure for livestock.

This increased division of the land may be partly a result of a deterioration in the climate towards the end of the Bronze Age, *c*.1000 BC when it became wetter and damper. This led to an increase in the growth of peat in the uplands and the abandonment of more marginal land. Bronze Age field-banks have been sealed below peat at Moss of Achnacree, Argyll. In Renfrewshire, it is also possible that settlements are preserved below areas of peat in the uplands. Another effect of this climatic deterioration may have been crop failure and increased pressure on agricultural land, perhaps resulting in the appearance of small defended settlements.

A number of Late Bronze Age homesteads (one or two huts surrounded by a low bank or fence) have been identified in Renfrewshire. The small multi-phased site at Knapps, near Kilmacolm, may have been defended by a wooden palisade or fence during this phase (Fig. 21), although some of the pottery found was of Neolithic date. This homestead was one of the first in Southern Scotland to be completely excavated. Now overgrown with thick vegetation it sits at the bottom of the steep slope to the south of Kilmacolm Golf Course looking down the valley to Knapps Loch. The site was excavated

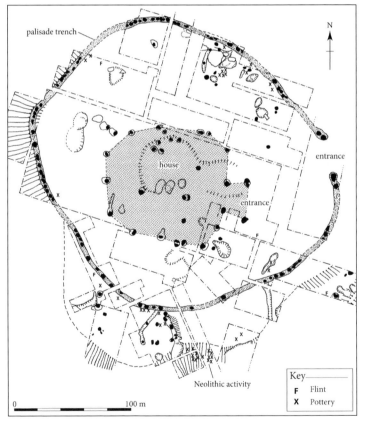

Figure 21   Plan of Knapps palisaded homestead
(redrawn by Derek Alexander).

by Frank Newall in 1964, revealing that it was multi-phased. The earliest occupation may belong to the Neolithic while the latest use of the site was in the fourteenth and fifteenth centuries (see below). The middle phase of occupation may have belonged to the Late Bronze Age or Early Iron Age although without radiocarbon dates this is unsure. During this phase the site was surrounded by a wooden fence set within a narrow slot, enclosing a sub-circular area c.27m long by 23m wide. There was an entrance gap c.2.5m wide in the north-east. Within the fence was a sub-circular arrangement of post-holes, which appeared to define a house 9–10m in diameter with a possible porched entrance facing eastwards. Artefacts recovered from the site which may date to this phase of its occupation include sherds of coarse pottery and fragments of shale bracelets.

In some cases, hut circles and small enclosures are found together. For example, the site which lies c.50m west of the natural rock outcrop called Cat Craig, up in Muirshiel Country Park, includes a homestead (Fig. 22) and at least two hut circles, although other huts have been reported in the vicinity. The homestead consists of a central stone-built hut c.7m in diameter within boulder walls 2–3m wide. The exact outline of the house is difficult to determine because of the numerous large boulders scattered across the site but a clear line forming an inner wall face can be seen on the north side. This central hut may have a smaller structure immediately to the south-west, and both are surrounded by the remains of an earth and stone bank, which if projected round would enclose an area c.28m in diameter. The north-western, upslope, section of this bank is the best preserved. To the south of the homestead, just above the burn, are the remains of two poorly preserved hut circles. The upslope example is more of an oval than a circle and measures c.10.5m long by 9.5m wide. The wall circuit is visible best on the south-west to north-east side. The lower hut circle is smaller and measures c.8m in diameter over walls c.1m wide. The curve of the bank and protruding stones are most apparent on the western side, the rest being covered in thick heather.

Another small homestead site was identified at Middleton Farm (Fig. 22), between Newton Mearns and Neilston and surveyed by Bruce Henry in 1992. This site is about 30m in diameter and has a scooped-out house platform 10m in diameter in the north-east. The discovery of a small hoard of Middle Bronze Age artefacts from close to this site, including a socketed axe and a tanged chisel, suggest occupation in the middle of the second millennium BC.

A similar homestead site was excavated at Knockmade Hill, near Lochwinnoch (Fig. 22), situated on a rocky knoll, overlooking the B786

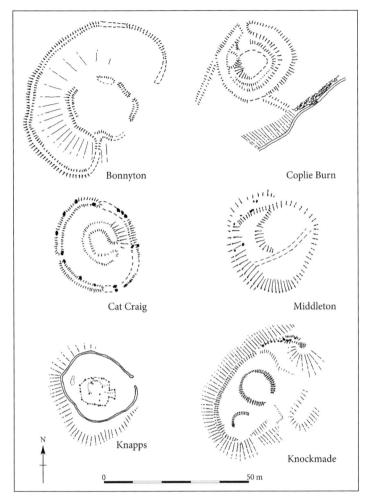

Figure 22   Plans of possible Bronze Age homesteads
(redrawn by Derek Alexander).

Lochwinnoch to Kilmacolm road. The site is located on the south-western shelf of the knoll and is overlooked by the summit which rises 4.6m higher to the north-east. The hill is protected on the south-east by a steep slope and a cliff on the south-west. An area 39m long, north-east to south-west, by 23m wide is enclosed by an earth and stone bank 1.5m wide and c.0.8m high. This bank consists of large stones revetting a core of smaller material. In the interior of the site are traces of two hut circles. The site was excavated in 1959–60, and again in 1967 by Robin Livens, then of the Hunterian Museum. In the northern part of the enclosure there was a large hut circle c.10.6m in

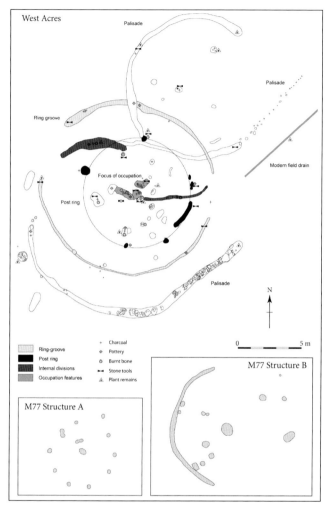

Figure 23   Plan of West Acres Bronze Age house and two
smaller structures found on the route of the M77
(AOC Archaeology Group).

diameter with an entrance gap 4.6m wide in the south-east. Excavation located
a central hearth, a stone-lined culvert (probably for drainage) and patches of
cobbles set in sand between outcrops of bedrock to form a level floor surface.
The wall of the hut circle consisted of large stones, was 1.5m wide and up to
0.3m high with as many as three courses of stonework preserved in places.
The smaller hut was c.6.1m in diameter and is less well preserved, and more
limited excavation of this feature revealed part of the stone wall. Finds from
the site included fragments of jet rings and part of a possible rotary quern. A

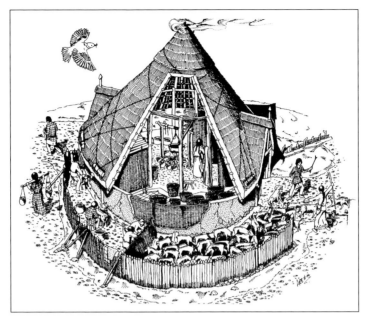

Figure 24   Reconstruction drawing by Alan Braby of West
Acres house (AOC Archaeology Group).

layer of occupation material, including sherds of coarse pottery, was found to continue under the enclosing bank and suggests that the site may originally have been unenclosed. Sherds of green glazed pottery and a number of later postholes may indicate medieval activity on the site.

At West Acres in Newton Mearns, archaeological trial trenching in advance of a new housing development located the truncated remains of a timber roundhouse and surrounding palisades (Figs 23 and 24). The site was fully excavated in 2002 by Ronan Toolis of AOC Archaeology Ltd. The main feature was a ring-groove house 12.5m in diameter with wide entrance gaps to the east and west. Pottery recovered from the roundhouse was of Bronze Age plain bucket-shaped type and radiocarbon dating (a total of 15 dates) provided a range between 1700 and 1100 BC. The excavator suggested that, much like Picketlaw, the site was probably not long-lived and may have functioned as part of a transhumance system where livestock (sheep and cattle) were moved around the landscape to make the best use of seasonally available pasture and to keep them away from ripening crops.

There was probably little difference in the size of the communities which occupied this settlement and the unenclosed hut circle at Picketlaw; both probably housed extended family groups and functioned as small farmsteads. A defended site which is a little larger than the homestead at Knockmade is the hill fort site at Craigmarloch, between Kilmacolm and Port Glasgow. The fort was excavated by Helen Nisbet, then of Paisley Museum, in the mid 1960s. It revealed two main phases of occupation. The first was a double line of palisades, which encircled the hill. An occupation layer associated with these palisades contained sherds of undecorated coarse pottery. Charcoal from the palisade trench produced a radiocarbon date of 790 BC, suggesting occupation in the Late Bronze Age. The second phase was a timber-laced stone rampart probably of Iron Age date (discussed in the next chapter)

Research methods that emphasise the environment of prehistoric peoples, rather than types of sites and finds, have revealed extensive clearance of mixed oak and hazel woodland to make way for cereals and rough grass; an expanding farming population and a temperate, warm, dry continental climate. The resultant period of population growth may have lasted from 4500 BC until about 1200 BC. About that time, the weather became markedly colder and wetter, with particular deteriorations around 1200 and 700 BC. The rise of the water table in the low land, and growth of peat on the high land, put considerable pressure on the remaining cultivatable terrain. These developments are reflected in the archaeological record by abandoned moorland Bronze Age sites and the introduction of 'fortified' farmsteads, enclosed by banks and ditches.

Some archaeologists have suggested that this environmental deterioration was a disaster even more dramatic than it first appeared. It has been argued that evidence from compacted ice in Greenland, tree rings in Ireland, minute particles of volcanic ash in Scottish peat, satellite photos of volcanic sulphur emissions and (more familiar) radiocarbon dating, all points to a volcanic eruption, c.1150 BC, at Mount Hekla on Iceland. Sulphur and ash from the eruption could have blocked out the sunlight, causing a 'volcanic winter' which covered the northern hemisphere for a period of up to two decades. The over-farmed uplands, already experiencing climatic deterioration, and possibly peat growth, became deserted. If this happened within a generation, what may exist in the moorlands in the west of Renfrewshire is a 'snapshot' of a Bronze Age community. Similarly, the evolution of the fortified Bronze Age farm site may be the result of pressure on arable land as well as the more traditional explanation of invasion and more sophisticated tribal weaponry. It should be noted, however, that others have suggested a much less rapid decline linked to longer-term environmental fluctuations.

6

Iron Age Renfrewshire

*c.*600 BC–AD 87

❖ ◆ ❖

The nature of the archaeological evidence for the Iron Age is completely different from earlier periods. Instead of isolated artefacts, burial sites or hoards of bronze objects, the evidence is formed by a wide variety of different types of settlements (Fig. 25). Many of the small settlements such as hut circles and homesteads that appeared in the later Bronze Age continue in use in the Iron Age. However, it is the appearance of larger settlements defended by stone walls and banks that characterises the Iron Age. The size and distribution of these hill forts may suggest the emergence of small tribal units. The deterioration in the climate, coupled with an increase in population may have led to pressure on resources and the need for communities to construct defences around settlements to protect both themselves and their possessions from attacks. However, excavation in other areas of Scotland has shown that many sites had undefended, open, phases of settlement, and there does not appear to have been a simple progression from undefended or unenclosed, to defended or enclosed settlements.

The hill fort of Craigmarloch (Fig. 26) is situated on the southern side of a series of rocky knolls lying between Kilmacolm and Port Glasgow. The site is hidden by mixed deciduous woodland, and it is only once the summit has been reached that the enclosing ramparts are readily visible. The defences consist of an earth and stone bank enclosing an oblong area *c.*64m by 35m (0.12ha). There is evidence of an annexe on both the north-west and southern sides. The ground within these annexes is relatively steep and must have been of limited value as an area of occupation. The site was excavated between 1963 and 1965 by Helen Nisbet, and the trenches were concentrated

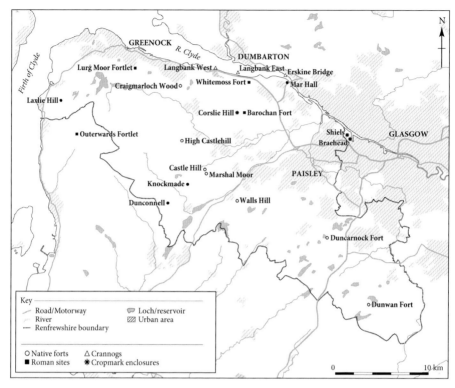

Figure 25   Map of major Iron Age and Roman
sites in Renfrewshire (Ingrid Shearer).

around the defences in the north-west end of the fort, since heavy tree cover
prevented excavation of the interior. Two phases of activity were identified.
The first was a double line of palisades which encircled the hill (discussed
in the previous chapter). An occupation layer associated with these palisades
contained sherds of undecorated coarse pottery. Charcoal from the palisade
trench produced a radiocarbon date of 810–530 BC. The second phase was a
timber-laced stone rampart, probably of Iron Age date, with an entrance at
either end. This timber-laced wall appears to have been destroyed by fire, and
the wall core has vitrified (Plate 2). Another radiocarbon date from charcoal
within the wall core gave a range of between 100 BC and AD 90. Artefacts
found in the interior include coarse-ware pottery, shale/cannel coal bracelets
and a small mould for a bronze stud.

Destruction of Craigmarloch's rampart by fire may be the result of an
accidental fire but is probably more likely a deliberate act of warfare. Indeed
the effort required to keep a timber-laced rampart alight has suggested to

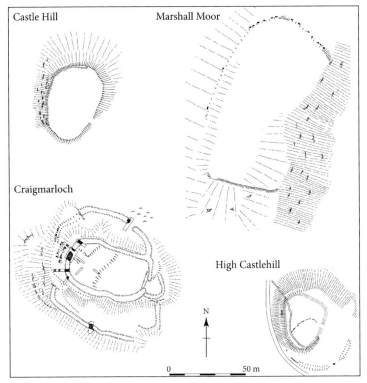

Figure 26   Plans of small Iron Age forts (redrawn by
Derek Alexander after Nisbet 1996 and MLS).

some experts that it was a deliberate act of destruction, akin to the slighting
of a medieval castle, making a major statement in the landscape. The warlike
nature of societies during the Iron Age is also reflected in the number of
other defended sites. Numerous similar hill forts are scattered across the hills
of Renfrewshire, including Dunwan, near Eaglesham, Marshall Moor, near
Bridge of Weir and Duncarnock, close to Newton Mearns.

The steep-sided green hill of Dunwan sits isolated on the southern side of
an expanse of moorland to the south of Eaglesham. Access to the site is along
the edge of a gently sloping ridge, which leads up to the entrance of the fort
(Fig. 27). The entrance is c.3m wide and has a slightly sunken approach about
16m long. The rampart enclosing the site consists of a turf-covered stone wall
and is c.3.5m wide. It appears as a level terrace around the summit of the hill
and encloses a roughly pear-shaped area of (78m × 48m) 0.2 hectares. Two
slightly sunken areas filled with patches of rushes may represent the remains
of house platforms. The rampart expands slightly at the terminals on either

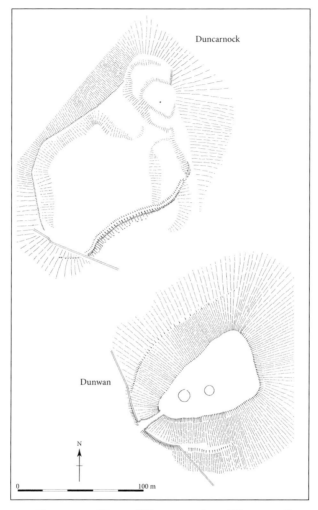

Figure 27   Plans of Duncarnock and Dunwan forts
(redrawn by Derek Alexander after MLS).

side of the entrance. A low terrace, curving down the west side to the foot of
the hill may be the remains of another rampart, although its location does not
immediately suggest a defensive line.

Known locally as The Craigie, the prominent hill of Duncarnock is
visible on the skyline when looking from the north (Plate 3). It has almost a
miniature 'Arthur's Seat' look to it; a wide flat back with a pronounced rocky
knoll at the north-east end (Fig. 27). It looks out over the Glanderston Dam.
Its name can be divided into three separate elements: *dun* (Gaelic for fortified

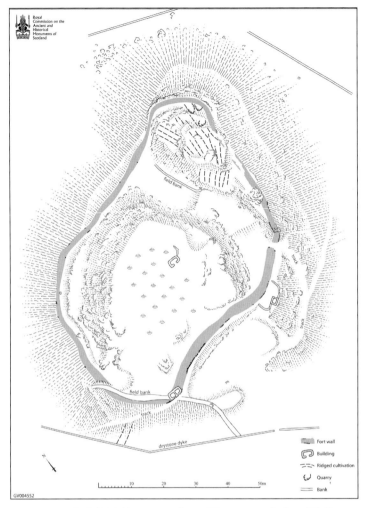

Figure 28   RCAHMS survey plan of Duncarnock fort (© Crown
Copyright: Licensor http://www.rcahms.gov.uk).

settlement); *car* (*caer* is Cumbric for fortified settlement); *nock* (*knock* or *cnoc* is
Scots or Gaelic for a small hill). The hill is steepest on the north–west where
rugged cliffs descend almost to the edge of the reservoir. The site has only
recently been planned by RCAHMS surveyors (Fig. 28). A single terraced
rampart encloses approximately five acres (1.1ha) and runs along the crest
of the slope. This rampart consists of a turf-covered stone-revetted terraced
wall 2m wide and 1m high. The easiest approach is from the south and the
stone-lined entrance leads into a natural hollow between the main enclosed

area and the rocky knoll at the north-east end. The large enclosed area makes this site the second largest hill fort in Renfrewshire. The rocky knoll at the north-eastern end may have been additionally defended forming a 'citadel' 24m by 34m. It was from this area that a sherd of coarse-ware pottery and a fragment of worked shale were recovered. Without excavation it is impossible to determine when this site was occupied, but it probably ranges from Late Bronze Age through to the Early Historic period.

Other prominent natural locations were easily defended such as at Dunconnel, near Lochwinnoch. The precipitous nature of this site can really only be appreciated close up, when it does not merge with the hills behind. The flat-topped hill is surrounded on all sides by bedrock outcrop and is most easily approached from the south-west, but even from this side there is no easy means of access. To the north-east the hill is steeper and drops down into a marshy area containing the head streams of the Garpel Burn that flows south-eastwards and joins the Calder Water, south-west of Lochwinnoch. As the name suggests, Dunconnel may have been a small fortified site but little remains visible on the surface. A previous survey suggested an inner enclosure c.13m in diameter (possibly a hut circle) surrounded by a larger enclosure c.40m in diameter. This enclosure is bisected by the line of a modern fence across the summit of the hill. After a fire on the hill a number of artefacts including fragments of shale bracelets and rings, and over 100 sherds of coarse pottery were recovered. The site commands extensive views along the Lochwinnoch Gap, and it is likely that many other forts used high vantage points simply for their commanding views.

Most of these fort sites sit in splendid isolation. However, to the south of Bridge of Weir there are two located quite close to each other: Marshall Moor (Fig. 26) and Castle Hill, East Barnaigh. Marshal Moor fort sits on part of a south-west to north-east ridge with steep cliffs defending the north-west side. A stone wall is clearly visible on the southern and western sides. The entrance may have been from the north-east end of the ridge where any access path would have to wind its way through large rounded outcrops of bedrock. The fort measures c.93m long by 48–51m wide and encloses an area of 0.4 hectares. Traces of a round hut have been reported in the north-east.

The earthwork enclosure at East Barnaigh is situated on the north-east end of a ridge to the south-east of the farm and looks over to the site of Marshall Moor fort. It is protected by steep natural slopes on the north and east sides, although these become less steep on the south side. The site is approached along the ridge from the south-west. The defences consist of a shallow ditch

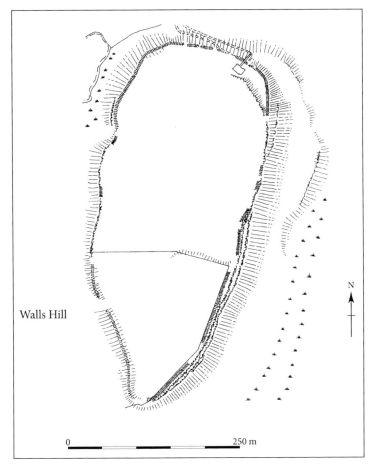

Figure 29   Renfrewshire's largest hill fort, Walls Hill, Howwood
(redrawn by Derek Alexander after Newall).

backed by a low rubble mound. The ditch is most prominent on the upslope, northern, side where it cuts through the lip of the natural scarp. The area enclosed measures *c.*80m by 40m. The form of this site suggests it may well be different from the other forts. No features are visible within the interior, and, although it is included in the later prehistoric section here, it could as easily be Early Historic or even Medieval in date. It is possible that the two sites were occupied sequentially, Marshal Moor being the earlier of the two.

Duncarnock is larger in area than Craigmarloch, but larger again is the site at Walls Hill, near Howwood (Fig. 29). A map of tribal territories in Scotland drawn by the geographer Ptolemy in the second century AD, probably based on the campaigns of the Roman general Agricola, marks the Damnonii as occupying the area that is now west central Scotland, central Strathclyde. The hill fort at Walls Hill has always been attributed to the Damnonii, possibly as their capital because of its size.

Walls Hill is the largest hill fort in Renfrewshire and consists of a large basaltic plateau surrounded by steep crags, which would have been defended by a rampart around the perimeter. The defences survive as a turf and earth bank *c.*1m high along the north and south-west sides. It encloses *c.*18.5 acres (7.5ha). The enclosed area is *c.*469m long from north to south and 198m wide from east to west. There are three possible original entrances through the perimeter: one at the north-west, one at the south-west and another at the north-east corner. The latter entrance was excavated along with a small area inside by Frank Newall in 1956. The rampart was found to be 3.0–3.5m thick and was faced with stone to the front and rear which revetted a core of mixed clay and earth. Evidence for a posthole at the front face of the rampart suggested that the wall face may have contained timber uprights or was preceded by a palisade. The entrance to the hill fort was found to be 1.5m wide and was also lined with opposed upright timbers perhaps supporting a timber gateway. The remains of a fourteenth–fifteenth century AD earth and stone walled structure with a clay floor was located to the south of the entrance. Underneath this were the remains of two earlier phases of occupation consisting of the possible remains of two huts. Sherds of coarse native pottery, Dunagoil Ware, then thought to date to the first century BC, were recovered along with some fragments of worked shale from a pit.

However, there is no absolute dating evidence from the excavations which could be directly attributed to the start of the first millennium AD. The large size of Walls Hill does not necessarily make it late in date. There are a number of different interpretations of how Walls Hill fits into the overall settlement pattern. One interpretation is that the smaller, dispersed communities amalgamated over time leading to fewer but larger forts, culminating ultimately in the occupation of Walls Hill. Alternatively, these different-sized settlements could be seen as being broadly contemporary, with the smaller settlements representing satellites around the central capital at Walls Hill, which itself may only have been fully occupied at certain times of year for ceremonies, hostings or fairs. Unfortunately, there is not enough dating evidence from any of the sites to be able to determine the relationships between these hilltop settlements.

The evidence for forts is not restricted to the upland areas of the county.

Figure 30   Crop-mark of three ditches around the summit of Corslie
Hill, Houston. The square feature in the centre is the base of
Barochan cross. (© Crown Copyright RCAHMS Licensor
http://www.rcahms.gov.uk).

At Corslie Hill, a triple-ditched enclosure surrounding the summit of the
hill was revealed by aerial photography (Fig. 30). Although nothing is visible
on the ground, differential crop growth over the infilled ditches produces a
pattern which is visible from the air, during favourable weather conditions.
The crop-mark on Corslie Hill shows sections of three concentric ditches
surrounding the summit of the hill. The area enclosed appears to be oval in
shape and measures c.100m long, north-east to south-west, by c.70m wide
externally. Unfortunately, the hill has been divided into four separate fields
and the clarity of the crop-mark varies between each, although in general it
is clearer on the north-eastern side. The width of each of the three ditches
also varies; the inner and outer ditches being noticeably broader than the
middle one. There is a break in the north-eastern arc of the outer ditch,
which is suggestive of an entrance. It is possible that the two broader ditches
are contemporary and represent the remains of a small Iron Age fort, while
the narrower middle ditch may be medieval in date.

    Another two crop-mark enclosure sites have been identified on the flood

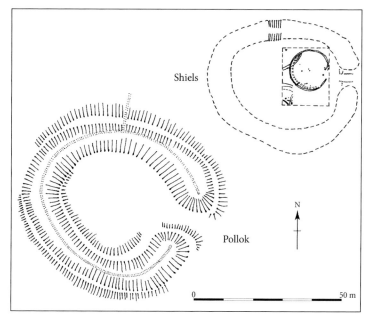

Figure 31   Crop-mark enclosure at Shiels and the earthwork
enclosure in North Wood, Pollok Park (redrawn
by Derek Alexander after Scott & MLS).

plain of the River Clyde. The first site was an oval Late Iron Age enclosure
surrounded by a wide and deep ditch at Shiels near Govan (Fig. 31). It
appeared as a crop-mark on an aerial photograph and was excavated in 1973
prior to the construction of a factory. The complex sequence of ditch fills
consisted of bands of clay, silt, sand and gravel with variable quantities of
organic remains, including insect remains, animal teeth, a mussel shell and
vegetation. A large amount of wood chips, twigs and bark was recovered
along with several larger worked stakes. Radiocarbon dates obtained for two
of these stakes indicated occupation during the Roman Iron Age into the
Early Historic period 400 BC – AD 400 and AD 330–540. Although local in
origin, the pollen assemblage from the ditch was very rich and indicated a
low level of trees, mainly alder, probably located along the edge of the river.
The evidence suggests that the enclosure was built and occupied in an open
landscape with a mixture of pastoral and arable farming, although there was
some suggestion that pollen associated with pastoral was more dominant than
arable at certain levels within the fill.

The second crop-mark was excavated in advance of building work and

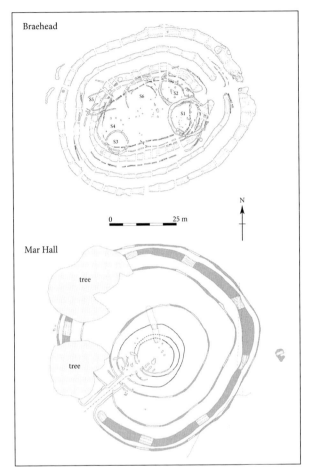

Figure 32   Ditched and palisaded enclosures at
Braehead and Mar Hall, Erskine
(AOC Archaeology Group).

was located immediately to the south of the IKEA store at Braehead in 2001
(Fig. 32). The site had originally appeared as a triple-ditched enclosure on
enlargements of vertical aerial photographs, and these three ditches were
confirmed by excavation. In addition to the ditches, there were the remains
of eight structures of which at least four were roundhouses. The location of
ring-groove houses at the eastern end of the enclosure just inside the entrance
has strong parallels with the site at Shiels. Multiple lengths of palisade were
recorded, in varying states of preservation. Some of these palisades may have
been associated with the ditches while others appear to have preceded them.
The definitive sequence has yet to be established and will be greatly aided

by radiocarbon dating, especially as the finds from the site were limited, comprising sherds of coarse pottery, rough-outs of cannel coal bracelets, coarse stone tools and lithics. Initial indications are that the earliest feature on the site may be a large roundhouse, which might not have been enclosed. The settlement then appears to have contracted over a period of time to within the area of the inner ditch before finally expanding back over the deliberately infilled inner and middle ditches.

A number of other enclosure sites have also been identified from crop-marks, and, undoubtedly, more are waiting to be discovered to fill the gaps on the distribution map. Most of these have been recorded in the arable fields along the southern side of the River Clyde around Erskine and Bishopton, such as the enclosures at Longhaugh Lodge, Richieston, Drumcross farm and Kirkton. There is also a large circular enclosure at Rosshall, near Paisley.

Only in 2007, a previously unknown ditched and palisaded enclosure was found at Mar Hall Hotel right beside the Erskine Bridge. This site, however, was not located by aerial photography as the field was not under crop but was only found during trial trenching for the new golf course by AOC Archaeology. A wide ditch enclosed an area 60–65m in diameter (Fig. 32). There was a fence or palisade on the outside edge of the ditch and two more widely spaced palisades in the interior. At the south-west there was a break in the ditch and the palisades all joined, forming a fenced avenue over 20m long (Fig. 33) leading to the door of a large timber roundhouse c.16m in diameter. Full publication of this excavation is ongoing, but its discovery clearly shows that there are still major sites to be found in Renfrewshire. It will be intriguing to see if the dates for the occupation of Mar Hall overlap with those from the crannog site that is located only 300m to the north-east right on the banks of the Clyde.

Crannogs are another type of site that contribute to the overall pattern of Iron Age settlement in Renfrewshire. A crannog is a wooden roundhouse built on stilts in water or on an artificial island. These are usually found in lochs, although there are the remains of a number of crannogs in the inter-tidal zone of the Clyde, on the mud flats.

The excavation of many of these structures, as at Langbank, on the southern bank of the Clyde, and at Dumbuck, opposite, was undertaken at the end of the nineteenth century. The crannog at Langbank West is one of at least three along the southern bank of the Clyde. This crannog is located 60m from the shore on the mud flats to the north-east of Langbank Church. It is almost circular in plan, 45m in diameter, and consists of a low mound

Figure 33   Mar Hall entrance to ditched and palisaded enclosure
with Erskine Bridge in background (Derek Alexander).

of seaweed-covered stones and gravels. Adjacent to the western edge of the
surface boulders are three small-diameter wooden piles. Cattle bones have
recently been recovered from the crannog site, and this may confirm that
it was from this site that investigations at the start of the century recorded
finding a midden, a spread of domestic rubbish. From this midden a small
bone comb decorated with circular patterns and a penannular bronze brooch
were recovered. The comb is thought on stylistic grounds to date to the
second century AD while the brooch is of a type found during the mid first
century AD. This comb is one of the few artefacts from Renfrewshire that
can be seen on display in the National Museum of Scotland in Edinburgh
(Fig. 34).

Langbank East crannog is located c.200m north-east of the M8–A8 junction
at Ferryhill Plantation. It sits c.150m out from the shore in an area of extensive
mud flats and consists of a prominent mound of large surface stones, often
covered in seaweed. It is an irregular oval mound, approximately 40m long,
north-west to south-east, by 30m wide. On the very uppermost part of the
site there is a low rectangular, stone feature, measuring 18m by 10m. Timber
piles can sometimes be seen protruding through the sand on the western side.

Figure 34   The small but perfectly formed
Langbank comb can now be seen in the
National Museum of Scotland (© The Trustees
of the National Museums of Scotland).

Between the site and the shoreline there are two, truncated, parallel lines of stones, although their association with the site is unclear.

The third crannog situated on the mud flats on the south side of the Clyde is at Erskine Bridge, to the north-east of Erskine Hospital, just below the site of the Mar Hall enclosure. The site consists of a low mound of stones and timber remains on the edge of a large sandbank immediately on the edge of the shipping channel. Due to this position close to the Mean Low Water Mark the site becomes submerged very quickly as the tide rises. The site is roughly oval in plan 40m long, north-west to south-east, and 20–30m wide. A plan of the site was made in the 1980s by using aerial photographs and ground survey and in several places jointed timbers were apparent. The broken topstone of a rotary quern was recovered. Samples taken from the timbers produced two radiocarbon dates; one between 400 and 65 BC and another between 45 BC and AD 200.

Although only a few Iron Age sites have been excavated, the difference in the artefactual evidence from earlier periods is clear. The pottery has changed from the more decorated vessels of the Bronze Age to plain coarse-ware vessels. These are large bucket-shaped vessels probably only for domestic use. Sherds of this pottery were identified on sites at Walls Hill, Craigmarloch

Figure 35   One of the Meikle Cloak Cave rotary querns (left) with modern replica at the NTS Weaver's Cottage, Kilbarchan (Colin Campbell).

and Knockmade. In addition, isolated sherds have been recovered from the sites at Duncarnock and Dunconnel Hill during field visits. However, the almost complete excavation of the enclosure at Braehead and extensive investigation at Mar Hall found only a very few sherds. It is possible that, during later prehistory, the role played by pottery in society changed. It may be that elaborate metalwork eventually replaced highly decorated pottery as a status symbol.

It is possible that many utensils and containers were in fact made from organic materials such as carved wooden bowls, wicker baskets and leather bags. However, because of acidic soils these artefacts only survive in waterlogged, anaerobic conditions, such as in bogs. However, a single piece of a possible wooden vessel was recovered from the excavations at Craigmarloch fort. Stone tools also continued to be used, and one typical find from Iron Age sites after around 300 BC is the rotary quern, which was adopted rapidly across the British Isles, replacing the saddle quern for grinding grain. Three quernstones were found in the small cave at Meikle Cloak, on the Calder River, above Lochwinnoch. Two were deposited in the Hunterian Museum, and the third can be seen at the Weaver's Cottage in Kilbarchan where the National Trust for Scotland's stonemason has made a working replica (Fig. 35).

Although this period is termed the Iron Age, very little ironwork actually survives from archaeological excavations. This is apparent in the excavations both at Craigmarloch and Knockmade, but is also true for other excavations throughout Scotland. Again, the problem is one of preservation: iron corrodes easily once buried in acidic soil. The evidence for the presence of metals on a site is usually more indirect. A mould for an ornamental bronze stud and metal slag were recovered from the excavations at Craigmarloch, which argue for metalworking on the site, while possible whetstones suggest that metal tools were being sharpened.

Materials such as jet, shale and cannel coal were used in the Bronze Age for the production of beads for segmented necklaces, such as the one found at the South Mound, or the disc bead from the ploughed field near Neilston. During the Iron Age, this resource appears to have been greatly exploited, and large numbers of shale/cannel coal bracelets have been recovered. Isolated finds have been made from Duncarnock fort and Dunconnel Hill. A number of pieces were recovered from the excavations on Knockmade, Walls Hill and two pieces came from the homestead at Knapps. A large assemblage of bracelets was recovered from the excavations at Craigmarloch and at Braehead. These have invariably been interpreted as bracelets or arm rings, although some are of very small diameter and may have belonged to children. A major problem in interpreting the use of shale rings is the absence of contemporary burials which would perhaps reveal where these items were worn on the body.

There is little evidence for funerary activity in the Iron Age. It is possible that excarnation or cremation may have been the most common funerary rites in the Iron Age. There are very few burials in Scotland that can be attributed to the Iron Age, and those that can reveal no single funerary tradition, cremation and inhumation in long cists being equally used. In Renfrewshire, there is no evidence for any Iron Age funerary rites, although a rock-cut cist at Laxlie Hill, above Inverkip, has been attributed to this period. The site is on the north-east side of the upper reaches of the Beatock Burn, south-east of Inverkip and consists of a long cist cut into a small natural rock outcrop. It is aligned north to south and measures c.1.7m long by 0.9m wide and 0.6m deep. No artefacts have been recovered from the fill of this cist, and its size suggests it is unlikely to be of Bronze Age date. Perhaps it belongs to the Iron Age or later.

Iron Age ritual is little understood. A change from rituals based around ancestor worship to ones based around the agricultural cycle may be evident in the Iron Age, and domestic settlement sites may have been the focus for everyday ritual activity. The small scale of many enclosure walls indicates they were not primarily defensive, and it has been suggested that boundaries may have played a significant role in Iron Age rituals. It is possible that such boundaries were constantly rebuilt and maintained, perhaps by a communal workforce under the orders of the political and social elite. It is through such work that social divisions could have been re-emphasised and confirmed. Often special ritual deposits have been found under or included within these boundaries. A piece of quernstone found reused in the walls of the hut circle at Knockmade may be just such a deposit. It is possible that natural boundaries such as rivers and bogs were also treated in the same way as manmade boundaries.

Evidence from pollen preserved in the peat bog at Whittliemuir dam, beside Walls Hill fort, shows that between 400 and 0 BC there was a sharp decline in tree pollen, indicating extensive woodland clearance, perhaps to improve areas of grazing as there is little evidence in the pollen record for arable crops. By the first century AD the landscape of Renfrewshire would have been a patchwork of open fields and grazed land mixed with areas of lochs and bogs and clumps of woodland. It was into this varied landscape that the Roman army marched in around AD 80.

7

Roman Renfrewshire

AD 82–c.160/170

On the face of it, Roman Renfrewshire was a very brief interlude, consisting of the Agricolan invasion (represented by the fort at Barochan) and the Antonine frontier, constructed some 60 years later, of which the fort at Whitemoss and the fortlets at Lurg Moor and Outerwards constituted the western flank (Fig. 25). This frontier was abandoned about 20 years later (within the decade AD 160–70).

Although concerted military action only lasted a brief 80 years, it is reasonable to assume occasional Roman influence in the area, until the final withdrawal of troops from the province in the early years of the fifth century AD.

Caesar invaded Britain in 55 BC, and the full-scale conquest of the island commenced almost a century later under the Emperor Claudius. The Romans advanced northwards throughout the first century, meeting particular resistance from the Iceni in the south, the tribes of North Wales and the Brigantes in the north of England. Gnaeus Julius Agricola was governor of Britain from AD 77 to 84 when the Roman army advanced into Scotland. It is our good fortune that Agricola's daughter married the Roman historian Cornelius Tacitus, and it was Tacitus who wrote an account of his father-in-law's campaign.

This is why we have a written account of a consul of Rome, former governor of Aquitania and friend of the Flavian emperors, campaigning in the area around Renfrewshire and the Forth and Clyde valleys in the summers of AD 80, 81 and 82. From this account, it appears that Agricola's army spent three summers campaigning and building forts in southern Scotland as far north as the Tay. By this means lowland Scotland, including Renfrewshire, was secured.

Who were they fighting? It is assumed that the cartographer Ptolemy based his map of the British Isles on information gathered during Agricola's campaign. He names four tribes in southern Scotland – the Votadini in the Lothians; the Selgovae in the upper Tweed valley; the Novantae in the south-west; and, in our area – stretching from Ayrshire, through Renfrewshire to the central lowlands – the Damnonii.

What is it possible to find out about the Damnonii in Renfrewshire? If the Romans saw them as a distinct tribal group, are there any distinctive monuments or artefacts that could be called Damnonian? Frank Newall described a rough type of pottery found in Iron Age contexts at Dunagoil hill fort on Bute and Walls Hill, near Howwood, Renfrewshire, as 'Damnonian', but it has few distinguishing features. It appears from Newall's excavation at Walls Hill and recent pollen analysis from nearby Whittliemuir that the fort was abandoned several centuries before the Roman advance and must have belonged to an earlier phase of the 'Damnonian' Iron Age. In fact, there is little evidence at present to link the known Renfrewshire hill forts to the Roman period and they may already have been abandoned.

The crannogs at Langbank and Erskine are some of the native monuments in this area that can be dated to this time. The presence of the Roman fort at Barochan, however, suggests that there was some concentration of native settlement in the area. The proximity of the crop-mark enclosure on Corslie Hill to Barochan Hill, and the discovery of a Roman patera of the first century AD at the foot of the former, may indicate a contemporary native settlement. The patera, a bronze handled-cup (Fig. 36), was found in autumn 1886 while digging in the field, along with two handles possibly for a cauldron or bucket. It measures 24cm in diameter at the mouth, 16cm high, with the 20cm long handle which is stamped with the word 'OLIBI', the maker having been Publius Cipius Polibius in the Naples area of Italy.

We are told by Tacitus that Agricola was very particular about the selection of sites. Tacitus wrote, 'He himself always chose the ground for encamping; the salt marshes, firths and woods he himself always first examined.' The fort at Barochan is situated on the top of the hill. The Agricolan fort (with an eastern annexe) on Barochan Hill was first located from the air in 1955 and excavated in 1972 and 1984–85 (Fig. 37). It lies within the Barochan Estate 2km north of Houston but the partially wooded hill which marks the site can be seen from the B789 Houston–Langbank road. Small-scale excavation on

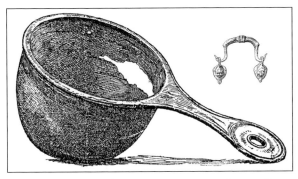

Figure 36   Barochan Roman patera and one of two
bronze handles found at the same time in
1886 (Society of Antiquaries of Scotland).

the site revealed that the fort was 3.5 acres (1.4 ha) in extent and located two
gateways and a number of internal buildings (Fig. 38). Material recovered
suggests that it was a Flavian foundation and may therefore be associated
(along with the small fort at Mollins, near Cumbernauld) with the work
of Agricola in AD 80. The hill on which the fort sits rises to 73m above
sea level and commands an excellent view southwards across the Cart and
Gryffe valleys to the hills beyond. Frank Newall likened its situation to the
Agricolan forts in the Angus glens, which also overlook valleys. If we compare
its situation to the forts associated with the Agricolan advance in Angus and
Kincardine, its strategic purpose becomes more apparent. The northern forts
were intended to command the glens. Standing on Barochan Hill, it is clear
that the fort was meant to overlook most of central Renfrewshire and the
surrounding countryside.

Its connections with the rest of the Agricolan network have been obliterated
by time. When the site was excavated in the 1980s, a road was found heading
south-west from the western gate of the fort. The nearest Flavian forts are
at Bothwellhaugh, near Motherwell, or Loudon Hill in the Irvine valley. It
has been suggested that there should be a Roman road linking Barochan and
Loudon across the Gleniffer or Fereneze Braes above Paisley, but it still awaits
discovery. A section of possible Roman road, however, was excavated by
Frank Newall on the Eaglesham Moors.

Agricola was withdrawn shortly after his victory at Mons Graupius in AD 83,
and the Emperor Domitian reduced the garrison in Britain and consolidated
the frontier further south. Sometime around AD 100, the frontier forts as far

Figure 37 Diggers take a rest beside the excavated west gate of Barochan Roman fort. Note the upright markers in the trench indicating postholes (Frank Newall).

south as Corbridge were destroyed. The forts were restored, but the ultimate response was the construction, between AD 120 and 125, on the initiative of the Emperor Hadrian, of a 73-mile-long defensive wall stretching from the Tyne to the Solway. Several forts and signal stations were held to the north of Hadrian's Wall. Hadrian's death in AD 138 marked another change in policy. The governor mounted a full-scale invasion, advancing once again as far as the Forth–Clyde line. The reasons for this change of policy are not clear. It is possible that the Hadrianic solution was as much to secure the frontier from internal revolt as external attack. This danger may by then have receded. There may have been a desire to hold the shorter Forth–Clyde line to reduce the number of troops required. There is some inscriptional evidence to suggest that the German frontier was manned at this time by soldiers from the southern uplands of Scotland, so recruitment could have been a motive, or a result. Finally, a new emperor would approve a scheme which would add glory to his name.

The frontier was moved north, and Hadrian's Wall fell into disuse. A new wall was constructed c. AD 143 along 37 miles from Bridgeness, on the Forth, to Old Kilpatrick, on the Clyde. To the east, it overlooked the Carse of Falkirk and, to the west, it was overlooked by the Campsie and Kilpatrick

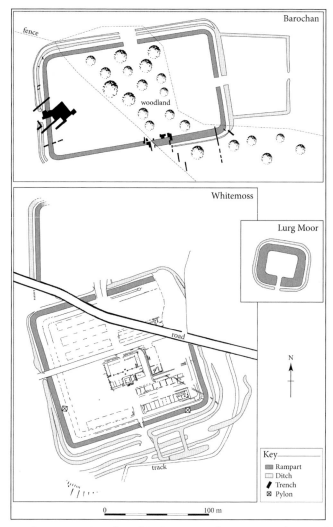

Figure 38 Renfrewshire's Roman forts at Barochan and
Whitemoss and the Lurg Moor fortlet (redrawn by
Ingrid Shearer after Keppie & Newall and Newall).

Hills. The western half of the Antonine Wall was constructed of turf and the
eastern half of rammed clay. The turf or clay was set on a stone base up to 4m
in width and probably had a superstructure of wood. There was a 12m gap or
berm north of the wall, between it and a 12m wide by 3.5m deep, U-shaped
ditch. A military road ran behind the wall, linking the forts and fortlets
which housed the garrison.

As with Barochan in the Agricolan system, the strategic importance of Renfrewshire, which constituted the western flank of the Antonine frontier, was reaffirmed. The most westerly fort on the turf wall was situated at Old Kilpatrick, north of the river. A fort was constructed south of the Clyde at Whitemoss farm, west of Bishopton overlooking the end of the wall and the lowest fording point on the River Clyde at Dumbuck. It was discovered by aerial photography in 1949 and excavated in the years 1951–54 and 1957. Situated about 1.5km west of Bishopton on the B789, the 4.9 acre (2.04ha) Antonine fort has been ploughed flat, and there are no visible surface features.

The fort site occupies a prominent position as the ground falls steeply to the north and south-west, with a basalt escarpment to the west and a depression to the north-east. It has good views to the east and from it can be seen the other Antonine forts at Old Kilpatrick, Duntocher and Castlehill on the north side of the Clyde. It measures 127m by 135m internally and at 1.72 hectares is only slightly larger than Old Kilpatrick. The defences consisted of a turf rampart, 6m wide, separated by a berm from a ditch 3.6m wide (Fig. 38). Entrances were identified in the north, west and south sides. At least three phases of ditches were apparent on the southern approach, which was the weakest defensively. To the north of the fort, there was an annexe, defended by a rampart and ditch, which may have enclosed a bath-house. Excavations within the interior located the principia (or headquarters building) in the centre of the fort with a granary to the east, and a stables block opposite a barracks block to the south-east. The numerous finds from the site include large quantities of Roman pottery such as mortaria, grey ware and Samian (Plate 4). They are stored in the Hunterian Museum at Glasgow University but many can be seen on their website.

Newall identified three phases of use. Phase 1 probably corresponds with the Antonine I period from AD 142 to 155. Following a period of abandonment, Phase 2 corresponds to the Antonine II period reoccupation of southern Scotland from AD 158 to 165. After a longer abandonment phase, there was a final Phase 3 use, which Newall felt might belong to the Severan campaigns of the early third century. The structural evidence was slightly different in each of the phases. The earliest buildings appear to have been of sleeper beam construction, set in foundation trenches. These trenches were then reused in the second phase for inserting upright posts into. The final phase made more use of clay, cobble and stone sill foundations for timber superstructures.

The only fully stone-built structure appears to have been the central shrine (Aedes) at the core of the headquarters building, which also appears to have had three phases of construction, being rebuilt on the same spot following each phase of abandonment. Large quantities of charcoal and burnt daub spread across the site indicate that following both Phase 1 and Phase 2 the site was destroyed by fire. It is unclear, however, whether this fire was the result of an attack, was a deliberate destruction by the retreating Roman army, or whether it occurred shortly after the site was abandoned. Certainly, there is evidence from other Roman military sites in Scotland for deliberate dismantling and burial of resources as part of their withdrawal.

Further west of Whitemoss, an aerial survey in 1952 located a fortlet at Lurg Moor, above Port Glasgow (Plate 5). This probably housed a cavalry patrol and overlooks the firth, as well as the hills to the north and west. With a commanding view over the Clyde estuary and the hills on the other shore, this fortlet is worth trekking across the open moorland to see. The only visible Roman work in the county (apart from a section of the ditch at Barochan), it is best approached from the B788. Park near the Knocknairshill Reservoir. Follow the Devol Burn (which enters the southern end of the reservoir) up onto the moor until it is intersected by a line of pylons. Follow the pylons roughly northwards until they are intersected by an east–west wall. Follow this westward and you will come to the fortlet, which is perched on the edge of the steep slope to the south of Greenock. The small fortlet measures 44m by 39m, over a 10m wide rampart which stands 1.6m high (Fig. 38) The rampart is surrounded by a rock cut ditch 2.5m wide and up to 0.8m deep. A causeway on the southern side leads to the gate into the fortlet. A length of Roman road leads southwards away from the fortlet and probably ran to the fortlet at Outerwards, north of Largs, Ayrshire. The site of Lurg Moor has never been excavated, but surface finds include pottery of Antonine date. Standing on the site it is easy to imagine the Roman troops who were sent here, perhaps from the larger forts at Whitemoss or Old Kilpatrick, to undertake a short stint of guard duty in this outpost. In 1970, Frank Newall discovered a similar small fort near Outerwards farm, north of Largs, just over the border into Ayrshire. The ditch is clearly visible, although a modern roadway runs through the site. The fort contained two buildings, which were probably rebuilt during its occupation. As at Lurg Moor, the fortlet was probably a base for a small cavalry patrol.

The Antonine frontier was attacked *c.* AD 155–57, and forts were destroyed or abandoned and then re-occupied. The new emperor Marcus Aurelius re-established Hadrian's Wall (with some northern outliers) as the frontier.

Perceptive readers will be beginning to establish a pattern. The frontier was at the mercy of native uprisings and upheavals and changes in imperial policies and ambitions. The position is further complicated by the fact that the frontier was not always where the line of fortification was established. There was also what some writers have called the 'hidden frontier', beyond the physical frontier, but just as real. It constituted an area of influence exerted through spies, patrols, occasional punitive expeditions, alliances and payments of money. Because of its strategic position at the western end of the lowlands, near to the seaways, Renfrewshire was an important part of the hidden frontier long after it was beyond the physical frontier.

The roads and forts associated with the frontier, did not simply mark the 'limes' or limit, of Roman military occupation, but, as Hadrian's Wall divided the Brigantes and the tribes of the southern uplands, it was used to divide and subject the native peoples of the frontier area. It is also worth considering that there is some evidence (for example, with the Votadini) that the Romans used the southern Scottish tribes themselves as a barrier to the less amenable tribes further north.

The Roman province of Britannia long survived the abandonment of the Antonine Wall and the representatives of the imperial government, from their viewpoint in the productive and prosperous south, adopted many strategies in dealing with the problem of the northern frontier. These strategies are hard to define because of the lack of evidence. The general history of the northern frontier, of which our area is a part, has to be assembled from coins, inscriptions recording the rebuilding of forts and chance references to Britain by late classical writers such as Dio Cassius, Zozimus, Orosius and Ammianus Marcellinus.

Another problem is that it is never clear whether the names mentioned are reliable or refer to particular tribal groups or alliances, for example, the Maeatae or the Picts. Although the Damnonii, which the Romans may have called the inhabitants of Renfrewshire, were never mentioned again, they were part of the events that took place along the 'hidden frontier'

Punitive campaigns were undertaken on several occasions, normally in response to incursions into southern Britain. The army marched north under Septimus Severus (AD 208–211); possibly under Constantius Chlorus in AD 306; and under Theodosius and Stilicho at the end of the fourth century. These campaigns were in response to increasingly effective raids by the northern tribes, often in conjunction with the Scots and Saxons.

Dio Cassius describes a typical situation:

Since the Caledonians did not remain true to their promises and had made preparation to assist the Maeatae and since at that time Severus was embroiled elsewhere, Lupus [the governor] was forced to buy peace from the Maeatae and in exchange recovered a few captives.

The pattern was repeated throughout the third and fourth centuries. The Picts were mentioned by Roman writers for the first time in AD 297, and, from AD 360 onwards, the northern tribes combined their attacks on the province with the seaborne assaults of the Scots and Saxons. Roman spies or agents known as *areani*, who worked among the native tribes, were implicated in these 'barbarian conspiracies' and were disbanded.

There is evidence that the Romans had a continued strategic interest in the area. After the withdrawal of imperial troops from Britannia in AD 410, the British tribes in the south offered resistance to the invaders for a further 150 years. This was based on the model of late Roman field armies and the reoccupation of hill forts. The Proto-Historic British kingdom of Strathclyde based on the hill fort of Dumbarton Rock, which encompassed the adjacent area of Renfrewshire, probably grew out of this 'sub-Roman' political situation.

8

Early Historic Renfrewshire

FIFTH TO ELEVENTH CENTURY AD

———◆———

The Early Historic Period was previously called the Dark Ages by scholars when it was felt that the withdrawal of the Roman army from Britain must have resulted in a decline in classical civilization in Britain and a return to barbarism. It is unlikely that anyone would hold such a view today, but this period is certainly marked by a limited amount of both historical and archaeological evidence; but if this is to be considered as 'dark' then it was no darker than the periods that preceded it. In the third and fourth centuries AD, the plethora of tribal names mentioned by Ptolemy had been reduced to two groupings north of the Forth, the Maeatae and the Caledones, and the survival of the Votadini in Lothian. Whether these represent larger confederations of small tribal groups remains unknown. By the mid sixth century, however, those groups north of the Forth were known as the Picts while in Argyll the Scots of Dalriada, originally from Ireland, had taken control. In Scotland to the south of the Forth and Clyde, there were three British kingdoms: Gododdin in Lothian, Rheged in Dumfries and Galloway and the Kingdom of Strathclyde.

Of the peoples who inhabited Scotland during this period (the Picts, the Scots, the Britons, the Angles and later the Norse), the Britons have had the least written about them. There are a number of reasons for this. They are probably less attractive for study than the Angles, who have quite good historical records, while they also have fewer readily identifiable archaeological remains than the Picts, with their symbol stones, and the Norse, with their well-preserved settlements of longhouses. The Scots of Dalriada, although having similarly limited historical records and few immediately identifiable archaeological remains, have eclipsed their southern neighbours in study by virtue of having united these disparate groups and providing their name to the country we live in today.

The British were the indigenous occupants of Britain prior to the Anglo-Saxon invasions of England in the fifth century AD and spoke Brythonic or Cumbric, a P-Celtic language (similar to Welsh). Although they originally occupied the majority of the mainland down to the south coast of England, the Britons were never a single uniform culture and displayed different regional patterns of settlement and material culture. The northern limits of the British Kingdom of Strathclyde stretched from the Firth of Forth westwards to Glenfalloch, south of Crianlarich, where there is a rock with the Gaelic name 'Clach nam Breatann' – stone of the Britons. The southern boundary appears to have varied greatly as large chunks were taken over by the Angles of Northumbria, but at one time it extended into Cumbria.

Our knowledge of Strathclyde comes from a range of historical sources and includes lists of kings, some entries in annals and a number of recorded poems. Their history can be tentatively pieced together from the fifth century AD onwards, when St Patrick wrote a letter to Ceredig (or Coroticus), king of the Strathclyde Britons, complaining that his warbands had been raiding Ireland. In this letter, he denounces Ceredig as not being Roman or a fellow Christian – an insult that may have contained just a little sting.

It was during the sixth century that Christianity came to Renfrewshire when Rhydderch Hael, king of Strathclyde, encouraged the British saint, Kentigern (or St Mungo), to establish a church at Glasgow. It is likely that another British saint, of whom we know a lot less, Mirin, also established an ecclesiastical settlement close to Seedhill in Paisley during the sixth century. Also, Saint Conval, probably a Scot from Ireland, established an ecclesiastical site at Inchinnan where he died in 612. Nothing survives of any of these early ecclesiastical sites, although it is likely that the decorated carved stones of tenth–twelfth century date from Inchinnan came from the old churchyard that may also have been the location of St Conval's establishment (Fig. 39). In Barrhead, on the lower south-eastern slopes of the Ferenze Hills, is the former location of a holy well known as St Connel's Well and the site of a former chapel. Nothing, however, remains and the foundation date of this chapel remains unknown.

By the end of the seventh century AD, the neighbouring kingdom of the Gododdin in the Lothians had fallen, having never recovered from their defeat at Catterick in northern England at the hands of the Angles. Although

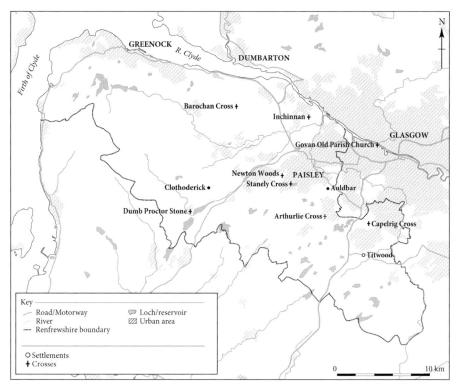

Figure 39   Map of Early Historic sites in Renfrewshire (Ingrid Shearer).

the Britons of Strathclyde also gradually lost territory in southern Scotland to the Angles, who set up a bishopric at Whithorn in AD 730, they managed to hold them off, while simultaneously fending off incursions from the Picts and Scots to the north.

Oddly, there is a record that a considerable number of Northumbrian coins, known as stycas, were found at Paisley in 1782 and bore the names of numerous Anglian kings of the seventh–eighth century AD. Unfortunately these coins have subsequently been lost. Although there is a record of the Anglians over-running the plains of Kyle in AD 750, it is usually thought that Paisley lay beyond their limit but, given the fact that Dumbarton was besieged and captured by a joint army of Angles and Picts in AD 756, then it is possible that the area remained under Anglian influence for a short period of time. Perhaps the coins came from an early chapel site dedicated to St Mirren, or could they have been booty from a raid against the Angles by the Britons of Strathclyde? The Kingdom of Strathclyde appears to have regained some of its former land and power under the rule of Arthgal in the ninth century only to be attacked by the Norse Kings, Olaf and Ivar, of Dublin in AD 870. After a four-month siege of Dumbarton, the occupants of the fort had to surrender through lack of food and water. Arthgal was among the large numbers of prisoners who were carried off in a fleet of 200 longships back to Dublin where he was eventually put to death, perhaps at the instigation of Constantine I, king of the Dalriadic Scots. This allowed Constantine to put Arthgal's son, Rhun, on the throne of Strathclyde and, in effect, made it into a client kingship. It is possible that the foundation of the church at Govan, dedicated to St Constantine, may have taken place during this period. It is probable that the men of Strathclyde refused to join with the Scots and many left in 890 and fled to Gwynedd in Wales.

Archaeological excavations were carried out on several areas of Dumbarton Rock in 1974–75, and the report is the principal source of archaeological evidence for the rulers of Proto-Historic Renfrewshire so far uncovered. Two admittedly small groups of early pottery fragments are of particular significance. The first consists of sherds of late Roman vessels, which may indicate relations between the hill fort's rulers and the Empire, and the second is the so-called 'E-ware', belonging to the later sixth–seventh century, which indicate the presence of imported Mediterranean goods at the court of the Proto-Historic British kings.

The next 120 years of the Kingdom of Strathclyde were much as before; a succession of kings came and went, and battles were fought, lost and won. In this period, a number of them can be highlighted. A king named Rhydderch appears to have killed Culen, king of Scots, in AD 971 and subsequently routed the forces of his successor, Kenneth II, at a place called Moin Vacomar.

Few Viking or Norse objects and sites have so far been identified in Renfrewshire but, from the literary and place-name evidence, it is clear that, for a period of almost 300 years, they were a political and cultural force in the area.

To understand the Viking world, you have to turn the map of Europe upside down and look at the continent from the perspective of the Scandinavian peninsula (which helps to explain the recorded Viking incursions at the beginning and end of the period), and you also have to remember that most Vikings were settlers and farmers and raids largely took place in the early part of the period.

Excavations identified a destruction level at Dumbarton Rock which contained an iron sword pommel of a type found in ninth-century Viking sites in Dublin, although whether this relates to the siege of AD 871 is debatable. It has been suggested that these Norse besiegers were trying to establish a route between the Viking kingdoms of Dublin and York which did not involve crossing the Pennines, although it may simply have been part of a raid into central Scotland.

Evidence of Viking settlement in the area is also scarce and relies on place names, the hogbacks at Govan and a hoard found at Port Glasgow in the nineteenth century. The Scandinavian place-name element -bie or -by, which, according to Professor Nicolaisen, means a farm or a village, may be present in the Renfrewshire place names 'Busby' and 'Humbie'. These names, however, may be much later (eleventh or twelfth century) and Danish in origin, in which case, they may indicate influence from the south rather than the west.

Recent excavation work in advance of the Eaglesham by-pass (Glasgow Southern Orbital road) in 2002 located the remains of a large circular enclosure at Titwood, less than a kilometre south-east of Humbie House (Fig. 40). The near circular enclosure measured 36m (north–south) by 41m (east–west) and

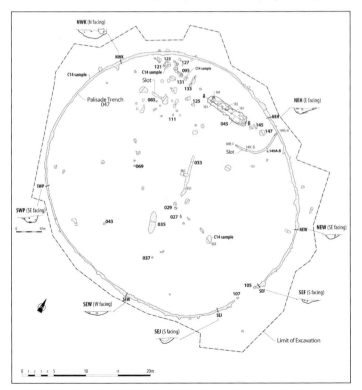

Figure 40   Titwood palisaded enclosure dating to eighth–
tenth century AD (CFA Archaeology Ltd).

was defined by a slot for a timber fence. The slot was 0.3–0.6m wide and up to 0.4m deep in places. The best-preserved section of the palisade slot was in the west and contained lots of packing stones, which indicated that it had been built of continuous upright posts. Another interesting feature was that the circuit appeared to be made up of straight sections c.5m long. There was a single entrance in the south-east marked by a large post on either side. Internally there was a concentration of features within the north side of the enclosure where a series of scoops, postholes and gulleys may represent the remains of a sub-rectangular building up to 20m long by 9m wide. Almost no artefacts were recovered during the excavation, although two radiocarbon dates did indicate that one pit contained Neolithic material. Six other radiocarbon dates, however, gave a range for the palisade and postholes as falling between the eighth and tenth centuries AD. The main occupation of the site appears, therefore, to have belonged to the Early Historic period. It is notable that had the site not been named Titwood it probably would have been called after the farm to the east, Humbie. The place name Humbie is probably of Scandinavian (Norse) derivation and could therefore belong to the late first millennium AD. Could this site represent the original farm of Humbie and be a Scandinavian settlement? The place name Humbie could be derived from 'hund', which would therefore mean the 'farm of the dog'. Unfortunately this site was destroyed during the road building, but at least archaeologists were given the chance to excavate and thoroughly record it.

The only other sign of a Scandinavian presence in Renfrewshire is a silver hoard discovered near Port Glasgow in the nineteenth century. It contained arm-rings and coins and has been dated very tentatively to around AD 970 (Fig 41).

Following the sack of Dumbarton in AD 871 the power centre in Strathclyde appears to have moved up river to Govan, just outside the limits of Renfrewshire. At Govan Old Parish Church, there is a wonderful collection of carved stones, including five tenth-century hogback gravestones which are clearly of Scandinavian influence. The collection of stones at Govan appears to represent an early church site, with surrounding circular ditch, and a high status secular burial ground. It is likely the church was founded as early as the ninth century AD, though radiocarbon dates from some skeletons suggest there may have been an earlier ecclesiastical site there, dating back to the fifth century. This earlier site may have been associated with St Kentigern. The commonest motifs on the cross slabs at Govan are mounted figures. These are usually riding from right to left and often carry spears. The majority of

Figure 41   Two Norse silver armlets found in Port Glasgow
(© The Trustees of the National Museums of Scotland).

these figures appear to be secular rather than ecclesiastical. There is very little evidence of monastic influence behind the Strathclyde sculpture. Recent work has shown that the majority of the free-standing crosses are of similar dimensions, suggesting they were all made to standard measurements. It is possible that Govan represents the burial ground of a secular aristocracy, perhaps explaining the dominance of the armed horseman rather than religious iconography.

It is likely that the site at Govan also functioned as a secular meeting place since, prior to the nineteenth century, there was a moot hill called the Doomster Hill, which, although now disappeared, is shown on early maps of the area and in a drawing of the site from across the river at Partick. This hill had a stepped profile perhaps due to being partly manmade and could be compared to the moot hill at Scone which, from the early tenth century, was used as the place to crown the kings of Alba.

The tenth-century hogbacks are so called as they have high arched ridges like the back of a hog. They are likely to have been commissioned by the ruling elite of Strathclyde, which at this time had strong links with the north of England, especially Cumbria. The decoration on the stones included detailed interlace work, and the ridges tend to be covered in rows of off-set tegulae, which are thought to mimic roof-tiles or shingles. In general, the arched roofs with animals at each end are believed to represent timber halls.

It was during these later years of the Kingdom of Strathclyde that the series of carved stone crosses and cross slabs was constructed in the area around Paisley. Definitely the finest cross of the Govan School is Barochan Cross (Fig. 42) which originally stood south of the mill of Barochan before being moved to the top of Corslie Hill c.350m to the south (Fig. 30). The cross was again moved to Paisley Abbey where it is still dramatically displayed in the

Figure 42   Barochan Cross: the finest of
Renfrewshire's crosses (Stuart 1856).

south-west corner of the nave beneath the stained glass window of William Wallace. The socket stone, however, can still be seen in its position on Corslie Hill. The cross stands 3.4m high, with the lower 0.9m inserted into the socket stone. Unlike all the other cross-shafts in the area, the Barochan example still has its head complete. This can be described as a ring-headed cross head with circular armpits and a style more familiar in the Hiberno-Scottish crosses of the West Highlands. The interlace on the cross head continues across from one arm to another and is enclosed within a circle in the centre. This feature is similar to the detail on a cross head from Kilwinning, Ayrshire. The lower panel on the front of the cross shows three sets of figures above each other. The topmost shows a horseman carrying a spear riding, from left to right, towards an inward-looking figure. In the middle there are two figures facing inwards with a smaller figure in between, the figure on the left appears to be holding an axe. Below this are two inward-facing animals, perhaps dogs or wolves. The sides of the cross-shaft are decorated with interlace and incised swastikas. The exact date of the cross is unknown, but it seems likely to be early in the Govan/Strathclyde series and may be as early as the eighth century AD but certainly the ninth century.

The other crosses (Fig. 43) of which there is enough left to estimate a date (Arthurlie and Inchinnan) appear to belong to the tenth–eleventh centuries AD. Originally the Arthurlie cross-shaft was located in a field c.200m south-east of the Kirkton Burn but was knocked over and rescued in the nineteenth

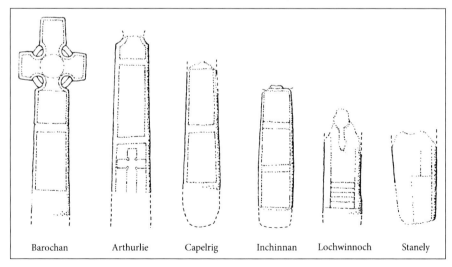

| Barochan | Arthurlie | Capelrig | Inchinnan | Lochwinnoch | Stanely |

Figure 43   Surviving cross-shafts in Renfrewshire (redrawn by Ingrid Shearer after Ian Scott in Craig 1994).

Figure 44 Two of the three early historic sculptured stones
at Inchinnan: the possible shrine lid in the foreground
with the recumbent cross slab behind (Ingrid Shearer).

century from use as a bridge over a burn. It now stands, surrounded by a
protective railing, in the middle of a housing estate on Springhill Road,
Barrhead (Plate 6). It measures 2.2m high, 0.5m wide and 0.2m thick. The
cross-shaft is mostly decorated with a number of panels filled with interlace.
Although the head has broken off, the circular armpits at the top of the shaft
suggest it may have been similar to the complete example from Barochan.
Three fine examples of the Govan School of sculptured stones are located
beside the main door of Inchinnan Parish Church (Fig. 44). They were
moved to this location from the churchyard of the old Parish Church, which
sat close to the confluence of the White and Black Carts but was demolished
in 1965 because it lay at the end of Glasgow Airport's runway. The site of
the old church is a Scheduled Ancient Monument. The recumbent cross-slab
decorated with a large cross surrounded by interlace is thought to be of tenth
to early twelfth century origin. The second is also a recumbent monument,
perhaps a lid of a shrine decorated with animal and figural patterns and may
belong to the early tenth century. The third and final piece of sculpture at
Inchinnan is a cross-shaft, decorated with interlace and probably of tenth–

eleventh century AD. Unfortunately, the latter has been displayed lying on its back so the other side is obscured.

The remainder of the crosses are less well preserved but may also date to this period. Part of a cross-shaft, including the boss, is located in the new cemetery, Calder Glen, Lochwinnoch. The cross-shaft is known locally as the 'Dumb Proctor'. The stone is c.1.3m high (above its socket stone), 0.52m wide and 0.16m thick. Unfortunately, the carving is extremely worn and almost impossible to make out, although it reputedly had the figure of a man on horseback with a border of interlace work. It is also thought to have had at one time writing (described as 'Saxon' letters) on it and the lower part of a crucifixion scene. The original location of the stone is unknown, but it is believed to have been found during ploughing close to Crook Hill.

The Stanely Cross originally stood in the vicinity of Camphill High School, Paisley, but was moved c.200m to the south-east into the grounds of Stanely Reservoir in an effort to protect it. This cross-shaft was 0.95m high, 0.5m wide and 0.2m thick, set in a pedestal 1.1m long by 1.0m wide. The front displayed an incised cross, a mounted warrior and a figure flanked by two beasts. Unfortunately, the stone seems to have been forgotten for some time, and it was only recently that fragments of what was left of the cross-shaft had to be transferred to a storage shed at the reservoir. It is thought to be of tenth-century date.

Another cross-shaft and its base were originally situated on the eastern end of a low ridge to the north of Barcapel Holm Farm above the Auldhouse Burn before it was moved to Kelvingrove Museum in 1926, although now no longer on display. The sandstone shaft, missing its cross head, is 2.35m high, the lower 0.3m of which slotted into the socket stone and is known as the Capelrig Cross. During the excavation a series of flat stones, perhaps paving, were noted around the base. Although the cross-shaft appears to have been decorated with interlace in panels on all four faces, one of the sides and the rear face are extremely worn. A small cross with expanded terminals had been incised onto the sandstone boulder which formed the base.

Other crosses in this group, however, have not been so fortunate. A sculptured stone reputedly stood in Newton Woods (Fig. 45), between Foxbar and Elderslie in the eighteenth and nineteenth century and only two fragments now survive in Paisley Museum. This monument appears to have been dominated by sculptured beasts with no interlace. The Steed Stone (Fig. 45) once stood beside the road at Auldbar, between Barrhead and Dykebar, but its present whereabouts is unknown. It is reported to have been 1.35m

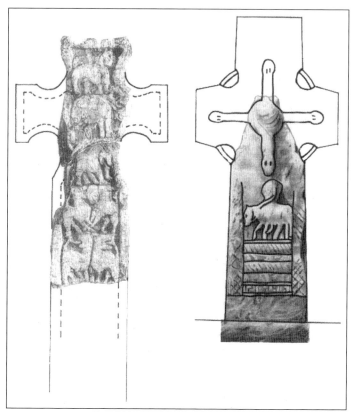

Figure 45   Reconstructed outline of the cross found at Newton
Woods, Elderslie, and the Dumb Proctor cross at Lochwinnoch
(redrawn by Ingrid Shearer after A. MacQuarrie 2006 and with
permission of the Committee of the Friends of Govan Old).

long, 0.4m wide and 0.2m thick. It stood in a base 1.35m long, 0.9m wide and
0.45m high. It is reported to have lain in a gravel pit for a long time before
being re-erected. Although one report suggests it was decorated only with
wreathed knotwork another mentions a figure of a man or a horse. Certainly,
the latter decorative motif may explain the name of this sculptured stone,
which is thought to have been a cross-shaft. Part of the stone, perhaps the
base, was incorporated into a set of gateposts, which have also gone missing. It
is likely that there were others across Renfrewshire which have not survived,
but may have been located where there are 'cross' elements in place names.

As at Govan, the most common motifs on the cross-shafts are mounted
figures, usually riding from right to left and often carrying spears. The

majority of these figures appear to be secular rather than ecclesiastical and there is very little evidence of monastic influence behind the Strathclyde sculpture. Recent work has shown that the majority of the free-standing crosses are of similar dimensions, suggesting they were all made to standard measurements. It is possible that Govan represents the burial ground of a secular aristocracy, the last of the kings of Strathclyde, perhaps explaining the dominance of the armed horseman rather than religious iconography.

If the secular origin of these crosses is accepted, it appears likely that they marked either estate boundaries or were placed close to settlement sites. The kings of Strathclyde, such as Ceredig or Rhydderch Hael, would have undoubtedly been able to call on men from Renfrewshire to man their war galleys or fight in their armies, but where did these men live? Early Historic settlement sites are notoriously difficult to identify, perhaps because many were timber-built halls similar to the structure identified under the earthen mound, possibly a motte, at Courthill, Dalry in Ayrshire. It is likely that many later medieval castles may overlie settlements of this earlier period, as was discovered in excavations at Cruggleton Castle, in Galloway, or at Dundonald, in Ayrshire. It is possible, therefore, that some of the earlier castle sites, especially some of the earthwork sites, overlie Early Historic settlements. The naturally well-defended promontory on which Duchal Castle stands may have been an ideal site for a settlement. In addition to these underlying sites, Early Historic settlement may have continued to use, or reuse earlier hill fort sites such as Duncarnock or Dunwan, and it is possible that the outworks at Craigmarloch fort were added in this period.

Place-name evidence may also help to identify settlement sites. If the earliest written form of a place name can be traced, it is often possible to deduce the meaning of the parts or elements of the name. Since old names very rarely change from generation to generation, they preserve the description of the place in the language of the people who first named it. In order to do this, you have to know the original and subsequent languages of the area and the way that language and, in particular place names, changes with the passage of time. Certain elements of names which are mainly confined to the area to the south of the Forth–Clyde valley are taken to indicate the extent of the Cumbric speaking area, including elements like *cair* (meaning fort), *tref* (homestead or village) and *penn* (meaning end or head). There are some telling names in Renfrewshire, which suggest possible settlement during this period. Renfrew itself can be broken down into *ren* (*rhyn* – old Welsh for a point) and *frew* (*frwd* or *friu*, meaning flow or current) and probably refers to the area where the Black and White Carts meet and flow into the Clyde. Clochoderick is the name of a large glacial erratic boulder situated between Howwood and Kilbarchan; this place-name can be broken down into *cloch* (meaning stone) and *roderick* (perhaps referring to the Strathclyde king, Rhydderch). The stone may represent a boundary marker of an Early Historic estate, although an alternative explanation has been suggested that it refers to a Boderick rather than a Rhydderch and may in fact be of twelfth century date. Govan itself may derive from Brittonic *gwovan*, which means 'the small hill', possibly referring to the Doomster Hill. Without detailed historical documents, only archaeological excavations will be able to shed more light on the Dark Age of Renfrewshire.

9

Early Medieval Renfrewshire

Eleventh to Fourteenth Century AD

The Kingdom of Strathclyde had become a client kingship of the Scots MacAlpin kings based at Scone during the later ninth century AD. The last of the original line of the Kings of Strathclyde was Ywain the Bald, who in 1018 led a contingent of the men of Strathclyde in the army of Malcolm II (1005–34) and aided in the victory at Carham, Northumbria, that secured the annexation of Lothian as part of the Kingdom of the Scots. The success was short-lived, for after Malcolm's death and the crowning of his grandson Duncan (1034–40), the country fell into civil war after he was deposed by MacBeth (1040–57), another of Malcolm's grandsons. After a relatively peaceful reign, MacBeth was killed in battle at Lumphanan by Duncan's son, Malcolm III (1057–93). There is little recorded evidence of what effect this period of Scottish history had in Renfrewshire. Only after Malcolm's sixth son, David, and the third to be crowned King of Scots, had succeeded to the throne, is there a sudden increase in both the historical and archaeological evidence.

King David succeeded to the throne of Scotland in 1124, following the death of his brother Alexander I. David had spent much of his youth at the court of the English king Henry I and was obviously influenced greatly by his experiences there. As King of Scots, he was responsible for many far-reaching changes. It was during his reign, for example, that numerous Royal burghs, such as Haddington and Peebles, were established; he introduced a new type of sheriffdom based on the English model; he was the first Scottish king to strike his own coinage; and he was a pious man who, following the example of his mother Margaret, introduced new religious orders into the country. David was also responsible for introducing the process of feudalisation into

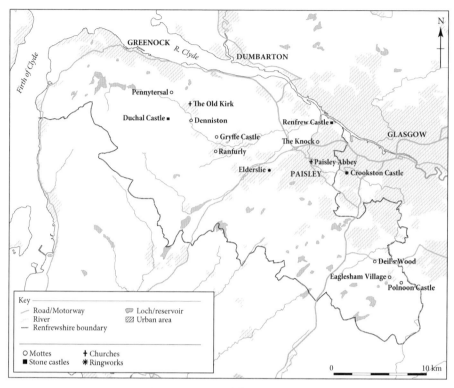

Figure 46   Feudal sites in Renfrewshire (Ingrid Shearer).

Scotland, a process which changed the nature of landholding in many parts of the country. The results of feudalisation are visible both in historical documents and in the archaeological record. It is during this period, and in the subsequent reigns of Malcolm IV and William the Lion, that the castle, in the form of the earthwork motte, the archetypal feudal symbol, spread across Scotland. As part of the process of feudalisation, David I introduced many new offices, to the majority of which he appointed men who had come up from England with him. For example, the Norman Hugh de Morville was appointed the first hereditary Constable of Scotland, while the Breton Walter fitz Alan became the first King's Steward. Walter fitz Alan was part of the family who had been stewards to the lords of Dol in Brittany and his father had entered the service of William the Conqueror's son, Henry I. Walter fitz Alan (1136–77) must have entered the service of David I around 1136 when he witnessed the foundation charter of Melrose Abbey. Along with small parcels of land in eastern Scotland, David granted Walter extensive lands in western Scotland, including the northern half of Kyle in Ayrshire and most of what was to become the sherrifdom of Renfrewshire, consisting of Renfrew, Mearns and Strathgryffe. Apart from land around their major castles at Renfrew (Fig. 46) and Dundonald, only a small part of this feudal lordship actually remained in the hands of the Stewards. The majority was let out to numerous tenants who in return had to fulfil their feudal duties of providing rents (usually in kind as food and accommodation) and military service (providing an appropriate number of knights and accompanying men-at-arms).

In 1164, a battle apparently took place at the Knock (a small hill between Renfrew and Paisley). The protagonists were Somerled, Norse Lord of the Isles, and King Malcolm. Somerled was killed in the encounter. More than 100 years later, in October 1263, King Haakon led an expedition against the Scots. After much prevarication by the Scots, who took advantage of the lateness of the month and the Norwegians' distance from home, a rather indecisive battle at Largs led to the Scots claiming victory and the retreat of the Norwegian king.

Throughout the twelfth and thirteenth centuries, the Stewards accumulated more land on Bute and Cowal and gradually became one of the most powerful noble families in western Scotland. During the Wars of Independence, the Stewards played an important role. One married Marjorie, daughter of Robert the Bruce, and their son went on to become King Robert II, first of the royal Stewart line, in 1371.

The historical evidence is fragmentary, and it is only possible to provide a partial reconstruction of the organisation of the Stewart fief in the twelfth and thirteenth centuries. Renfrew remained in the hands of the Stewards, as did the greater part of Paisley, although a large portion was granted by Walter I to the Cluniac monks who had first been established at Renfrew but moved to Paisley in 1169. A number of smaller landholders at the time of the first three stewards (1136–1241) are known. Arkleston was held in the twelfth century by Grimketil who may have been succeeded by Arknel. Both names are Scandinavian and may reflect the continuation of the Norse/Irish influence in the area, which had been so prevalent in the later years of the kingdom of Strathclyde, as witnessed at Govan. The aptly named Ingleston (Englishtown) to the west of Arkleston was held by Adam of Kent, and Ralston possibly by Ralph of Kent (a predecessor of Alan). However, one of the best-known tenants of the first two Stewards was Robert Croc who most likely had a castle and settlement at Crookston, but also had lands in Neilston and Cowglen in Mearns. Some of the rest of Mearns was part of the feu of Peter, son of Fulbert, who also held Upper Pollok with his brother Robert, while another portion of Mearns was held by Roland of Mearns. Cathcart was the feu of Reginald of Cathcart, and Eaglesham was most likely held by Robert Montgomery. Although Walter the Steward granted the lands of Houston to Baldwin of Biggar, he in turn granted them to Hugh of Pettinain. Baldwin may also have held part of Inverkip. Little is known of who held the land in the parish of Kilmacolm, but Duchal is likely to have belonged to Ralph de Lyle, although the origins of the name Dennistoun (or Danielstoun), also near Kilmacolm, remain unknown.

The relatively plentiful written evidence available for this period is supplemented by the archaeological record. Earthwork fortifications in the form of mounds (or mottes), circular enclosures (called ring-works) or combinations of both (known as motte and baileys) are the monuments most associated with the earliest phases of Anglo-Norman settlement. A motte and bailey consisted of a stockade on top of an earth mound associated with a larger, lower, stockaded enclosure. The Bayeux Tapestry depicts the Norman invaders constructing a motte, and there are many examples to be found in the south (e.g. Cliffords Tower, York) and in other parts of Scotland.

Mottes, however, present the fieldworker with a problem of identification. In the 1980s, there was a controversy in the archaeological journals about the interpretation of mounds. Nineteenth-century antiquarians and surveyors had interpreted mounds in neighbouring north Ayrshire as 'tumuli' or 'barrows' when, in fact, they may have been mottes. The controversy centred on a mound called Court Hill in Dalry, excavated by Cochrane-Patrick in 1872. In this case, the mound was constructed on the site of an earlier wooden structure and was variously interpreted as a prehistoric timber building under a barrow or a Dark Age hall covered by a motte. These arguments tend to confirm the problems of interpreting mounds from surface indications alone.

Without the kind of evidence that excavation can provide, the field archaeologist has to decide whether a particular mound is natural, prehistoric, medieval or the result of industrial or agricultural activity. It could, for example, be a glacial feature, a burial mound, a cairn, a motte, a limeworking, the result of mining or clearance for cultivation, or a combination of any of these. The way the mound was described in the past may also be suspect, in that it reflected the preconceptions of the observers.

There are the remains of a series of mottes scattered across Renfrewshire (Fig. 47). In general these are small sites, around 20–35m in diameter (at the base) and up to 4–5m high. Very few of the mottes appear to have

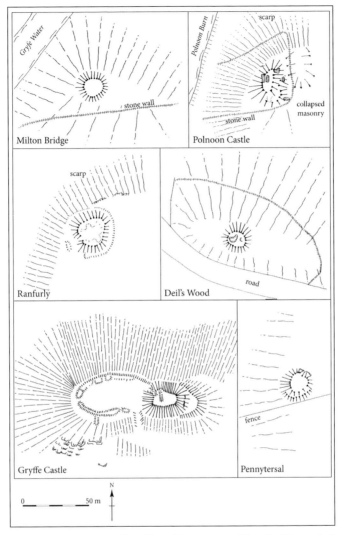

Figure 47   Renfrewshire mottes (Derek Alexander).

associated baileys. Most of the sites take advantage of natural scarps to provide additional defence and height to the mound, often located above streams or rivers. The distribution map of earthwork castles in Renfrewshire shows two concentrations of mottes: in Eastwood (East Renfrewshire) around Eaglesham, and in Strathgryffe, around Kilmacolm and Bridge of Weir (Inverclyde).

In Strathgryffe, there are four possible motte sites: Denniston, Pennytersal, Ranfurly and Gryffe Castle (Fig. 47). The most noticeable is Denniston or Milton Bridge motte located on the end of a natural ridge overlooking the

Figure 48   Sherd of twelfth–thirteenth century white gritty pottery
and a fifteenth–sixteenth century 'jetton' found at Denniston
motte, Milton Bridge, near Kilmacolm (Derek Alexander).

Gryffe Water (Plate 7). The conspicuous grass-covered mound measures *c*.25–
26m in diameter at the base and has an almost circular flat top measuring
13m east to west by 12m north to south. Its height varies from *c*.4m on the
west to *c*.2m on the east. This site was partially excavated in the nineteenth
century when a local antiquarian cut a trench from east to west through
the centre down to the natural subsoil. This revealed that the mound was
made up of clay. Just over a metre from the surface were four rows of rough
boulders overlying a layer of charcoal (perhaps evidence of a structure on top
of the mound). More recently a sherd of white gritty ware, probably dating
to the twelfth–thirteenth century was recovered from an erosion scar on the
north side of the motte (Fig. 48). In addition a fifteenth-century copper alloy
'jetton' or counting piece, probably of German manufacture, was also found
and is indicative of even later continued use of the site (Fig. 48). Later when
they were no longer used as settlements, many mottes were used as law hills
or moot hills where justice was dispensed and taxes gathered. It is possible
that the Denniston site belonged to a knight, Hugh de Danielstoun, who was
one of the individuals listed on the Ragman Roll. The mound at Pennytersal
is very similar to that at Denniston. It is situated on the edge of a natural slope
down to a burn and is a flat-topped earthen mound, *c*.27m in diameter and
2–3m high. There is a slight indentation at the north side of the mound, and a
number of large stones visible at the base of the mound at this point may be an
original kerb or a part of a later structure (perhaps a kiln) cut into the mound.

The southern edge of the mound has been damaged by cattle trampling. As at Denniston there is no sign of a ditch at the base of the mound or a bailey.

Castle Hill motte is situated on Ranfurly Golf Course and is undoubtedly the best example of a motte in Renfrewshire (Fig. 47). It is located on the edge of a steep natural scarp which overlooks the remains of the later sixteenth-century stone castle of Ranfurly and the burn beyond. The mound measures 35m in diameter at the base, with a flat top 15–19m by 20m. It stands over 4–5m high and is surrounded by a rock-cut ditch, 3–4m wide and 0.5–1.0m deep. A flagpole constructed on top of the motte has probably disturbed the archaeological deposits, and there are faint indications that a trench was excavated through the top. It was reported that a Mr Bonar had a trench dug through the motte to solid rock, but no relics were found, although Samian pottery, a bronze key, green glazed pottery, bones, charcoal and whitening material, found in the Mote Hill, Ranfurly were exhibited in Glasgow in 1911. It is surprising that although this is the best-preserved motte in the county nothing is known of whom it belonged to; the Knoxes of Ranfurly are not mentioned until the fifteenth century. This motte is situated in the grounds of a golf course and permission should be sought before going to visit it.

On the opposite side of the river from Ranfurly motte, to the north, are the remains of a site called Gryffe Castle (Fig. 47). The site is located on the north-west end of a ridge tellingly called Law Hill, north of Gryffe Children's Home. Covered in mature trees, the prominent location of this site is slightly masked. The summit of the hill is c.50m long by 18m wide and is best approached from the south, the northern and western sides being very steep. At the eastern end there is a turf-covered sub-rectangular motte c.17m long, 14m wide and 2m high. To the east of the mound, the summit of the hill is a relatively flat terrace surrounded by a stone and earth bank, best visible at the south-west. This enclosure may represent the remains of a bailey. Remains of a possible entrance are visible on the southern side between the motte and the bailey. This is the only possible motte and bailey castle in Renfrewshire.

In East Renfrewshire, there is a cluster of motte sites around Eaglesham. Strikingly the road between Mearns and Eaglesham bends sharply around this tree-covered natural ridge called Deil's Wood or Castlehill Plantation (Fig. 47). Situated roughly in the middle of the ridge is a grass-covered mound, c.23m in diameter, 2m high on the south and 3m high on the north side. The summit is oval in shape 14m long, east to west, by 10m wide. This feature has variously been interpreted as a tumulus, a cairn or a motte. Two depressions on the summit may be from when the son of the laird dug into the top of the mound looking for gold. Although without excavation it is impossible to be certain about the function of this mound, its shape, size and position are closely comparable with the two mounds at Denniston and Pennytersal, which are considered to be mottes.

In the middle of Eaglesham itself, situated on the northern side of the burn running down the village common, there is a large mound now obscured by young trees. 'The Mote' or 'Moat Hill' is shown on a map made by John Ainslie in 1789, but unfortunately the construction of a nineteenth-century cotton mill on the south-east side must have removed at least 5m of the mound. It has been suggested that the motte was originally oval in shape, 31m by 24m at the base, 20m by 16m on top and 2–3m high. There are indications that a later rectangular mound, 12m by 10m by 1.5m high, was built on top. Local tradition has it that the mound was used for festivals and public meetings, although it remains possible that this mound may be a motte, possibly the first castle of the Montgomeries in the twelfth century. It has also been suggested that Montgomery's later stone castle of Polnoon may be sitting on an earlier motte site (Fig. 47). Underneath the remains of the stone castle is a steep conical mound overlooking the Polnoon Water. This roughly elongated oval mound measures *c.*28m long, south-west to north-east, by 14m wide at the base and 16m by 6m on top. The mound stands between 3–4m high and may have partly incorporated an existing natural mound. Masked by tumbled masonry, it is difficult to determine whether this mound was constructed as part of the later stone castle, or was an earlier motte that also belonged to the Montgomeries.

There are a number of other possible motte sites throughout the county, but many are less well preserved than those discussed above, while others such as Knock Hill (possibly the original castle of the Knoxes) near Renfrew were cleared away during the course of agricultural improvements. This large mound which sat on the north-west side of the road between Paisley and Renfrew must originally had a good view over the White Cart and the low-lying ground beyond to Inchinnan. The mound known both as the Knock and Kemp Knowe was partly levelled in the late eighteenth century, and the site is now built over by Moorpark housing estate. However, it was described as having been a circular mound of earth, about 20 yards in diameter surrounded by a moat 5 yards broad and 4 feet deep. From this description, it sounds like a typical motte.

The other type of earthwork castle that has been identified in Renfrewshire is the ring-work. This consists of a small area surrounded by a defensive ditch and bank; the latter would have been topped with a wooden palisade. Free-standing structures in the interior would have provided the necessary accommodation, and often a timber gatehouse would form a major element. Ring-works have been interpreted as a cheaper and quicker alternative to motte construction, although they appear to have provided a larger defended area. Another interpretation suggests that they were constructed in areas where topsoil was thin and the subsoil often consisted of bedrock, precluding the construction of a large mound. The area to the south of the Clyde, southern Glasgow, is said to have been characterised by the construction of ring-works rather than mottes on the basis of evidence recovered from excavations on the series of earthworks at Queens Park, Pollok Park, Crookston Castle and Castlehead, Paisley. However, the dating evidence from these sites has often proved inconclusive.

The most impressive of these ring-works is the one at Crookston, which, although outside the county boundary, would have been inside in the thirteenth and fourteenth centuries. The remains of the impressive fifteenth-century stone tower are surrounded by a single deep ditch with a slight internal bank set on the top of a low hill overlooking the Levern Water (Fig. 49). The area enclosed by the bank and ditch is pear-shaped and is *c.*80m long by 60m wide. The tower was subsequently constructed in the centre of the site. Excavation undertaken in the 1970s, and recently published, recovered pottery from the bank that confirmed the ring-work's twelfth-century date. As mentioned above, this earthwork, or ring-work, was the castle of Robert Croc who lived there before 1180. As well as the ditch, the site would have been defended by a palisade or wooden rampart, enclosing an area of around 0.5 hectares. The ring-work was probably entered over a wooden bridge across the ditch to the west and would have originally contained numerous timber structures including a hall, domestic quarters, stables, kitchen, bakehouse and brewhouse. Mention has been specifically made of a chapel on the site.

Historical evidence, although far from complete, provides a detailed insight into the land tenure in Renfrewshire in the twelfth century. Crookston is often cited as an example of archaeological confirmation of feudal landholding and an example of the residence of one of Walter the Steward's vassals. During the Wars of Independence, the earthwork castle probably belonged to Aleynd Glasfrith (Glassford). The site was the first property to be owned by The National Trust for Scotland and is now managed on their behalf by Historic Scotland.

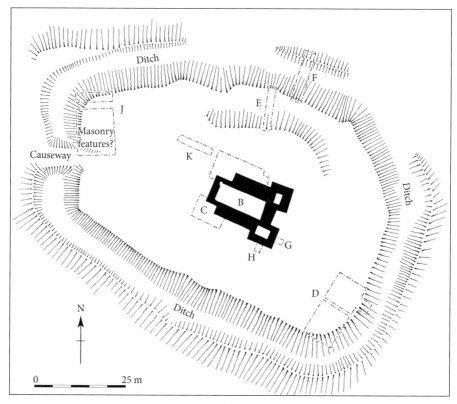

Figure 49   The earthen ring-work of Robert Croc around the
later stone tower of Crookston Castle (John Lewis 2003).

The earthwork in the North Wood of Pollok Park is another example of
a possible ring-work. It is 30m in diameter and is enclosed by a ditch 9m
wide. Entrance to the site is by an 8m wide causeway from the east. The site
was excavated in the 1950s by Glasgow Archaeology Society but was never
fully published. Summaries of the work suggest that the entrance causeway
was paved and there was a circular house 5m in diameter in the centre of the
enclosure, with a central posthole. The enclosing bank was found to have a
stone kerb on its inner edge. Few finds were recovered from this work but
included two perforated shale discs and the upper stone of a rotary quern. The
lack of medieval pottery from the finds assemblage is notable, and it is possible
that this site belongs to the Early Historic period in the first millennium AD.
In 2007 further excavation work was carried out by the society, the results
of which may be able to date the site. It is possible that the early castle site

at Pollok stood on the summit of the hill to the east of Pollok House where a huge sycamore sits atop a large earthen mound that looks very motte-like. Certainly the medieval tower-house of the Laigh (low) castle at Pollok stood below this hill, beside the river White Cart, and a fragment of its wall can still be seen in the exterior of the eastern corner of the stable block complex.

Perhaps a better comparison to the Crookston ring-work is the larger earthwork on the western slope of Camphill that forms the core of Queen's Park. This site is enclosed by a bank and ditch and measures 120m across north-west to south-east by 98m. The bank is best preserved on the east and south-east where it is 1.8–2.4m high and 7.5–9.0m wide. The site was excavated in 1867 when an area of paving covered with fragments of oak charcoal and charred oat grains was found in the interior. The site was excavated once again by Jack Scott and Horace Fairhurst in 1951 when the ditch was located, and sherds of medieval pottery (pre-fourteenth century) were recovered from the lower fill.

The crop-mark site on Corslie Hill, north of Houston, described in the Iron Age chapter, reveals three ditches defending an oval area on the summit (Fig. 30). The two broad ditches on the aerial photograph may be contemporary and could be of Iron Age date, while the third narrower ditch may be a defensive feature, representing the remains of a single-ditched ring-work constructed over an earlier fort. This site is mentioned as the location of the early castle of the Flemings, which was allegedly burnt down by Edward I during the Wars of Independence. Sherds of green-glazed medieval pottery have been recovered from the plough-soil.

These sites, coupled with the results from Crookston, have led to the impression that Renfrewshire was characterised by ring-works in the feudal period, and as a result many other enclosures, of unknown date, are often attributed to this class of monument, although there is very little evidence for this. The remains of an earthwork on Byres Hill, in Barshaw Park, for example, shown on the first-edition Ordnance Survey map and now destroyed by a golf course, have been described as a possible ring-work. The crop-mark of an enclosure at Ross Hall may be another.

In general, such ring-works are likely to have provided a more common means of protection than is otherwise thought, but their less substantial construction has meant that, over time, they have been more easily destroyed than their better-known counterpart, the motte.

Not all early castles in Scotland were earthworks; there were a number of stone castles. These consisted of large courtyards surrounded by high stone curtain walls linking large round towers, and incorporating drum towers at the gatehouse. The central courtyard often contained ancillary structures such as stables, bakehouse, brewhouse and stores, with accommodation for the lord in the towers. Rothesay Castle is a good west of Scotland example which also belonged to the Stewards.

In 1997, three trial trenches were dug at Castlehill Gardens, Renfrew in an effort to identify remains of the thirteenth–fourteenth century castle. From the twelfth to the sixteenth centuries there appear to have been no fewer than three separate castle sites in Renfrew. The first castle was probably a motte or a ring-work built on the King's Inch after Walter, Steward of Scotland, was confirmed in possession of the lands in a charter of King Malcolm IV in 1161–62, but an archaeological excavation in advance of the construction of Braehead shopping centre found no trace of it. This castle was replaced in the thirteenth century by a new structure on rising ground on the site now occupied by Castlehill Gardens. This new castle was probably built by James, the fifth Steward, sometime after the Battle of Largs and the cession of the Western Isles to Scotland in 1266. The site was supposedly adjacent to the River Clyde, the course of which has since changed, and on the west side of the road leading to the ferry. It was partly surrounded by a large and deep ditch, which was reputedly faced with stone on the inside. Traces of this ditch were said to have been visible until 1775. The third castle was built by John Ross, sometime before his death in 1474, again on the King's Inch, and was a stone-built three-storied tower, which stood on the spot until the eighteenth century.

The site of the second castle, belonging to the thirteenth century, was investigated by an archaeological project. Desk-based research, geophysical survey and test pitting suggested that the site had been greatly disturbed. Following dismantling of the castle much of the stone had been removed from the site and used in the construction of a soap works in the nineteenth century. The site was subsequently built over by the Castlehill House and its extensive gardens. Demolition of this structure, its levelling and creation of a playground led to further disturbance, while repeated development on the fringes of the site has gradually removed traces of the original castle mound and ditch. Excavation of three trenches confirmed this disturbance and located the brick-built foundation of the large bay window at the north-western corner of Castlehill House. One trench located in the southern part of the park recovered a line of stone paving. In front of and below this stone paving there were the remains of what can be interpreted as either a rubble-filled foundation trench or the rubble core of a wall, the facing stones of which had been robbed. A layer of clay to the south of the stone paving contained sherds of twelfth–fourteenth century cooking vessels. It is possible that these remains represent traces of the royal castle of Renfrew. Only larger-scale excavation would be able to determine which part of the castle, whether an inner structure or part of the defences, these features represent. Although nothing survives above ground of the castle at Renfrew, in which Robert II was born, it must have been an imposing structure if their other castles at Rothesay and Dundonald are anything to go by. It is likely that this castle would have been a courtyard castle consisting of curtain walls with circular towers.

The only surviving remnant of a curtain wall castle within Renfrewshire is Duchal Castle near Kilmacolm. The heavily overgrown remains of the castle are located on a promontory between two rivers, the Blacketty and the Green Waters (Fig. 50). The steep, cliff-faced, river gullies provide natural defence on all but the north-west side, which is in turn protected by a ditch of which only the northern half survives. Traces of an enclosure wall form a rectilinear courtyard c.55m long by up to 25m wide. The wall is c.1.5m thick and built of uncoursed rubble. The remains of a window embrasure are visible in the largest upstanding section of the northern wall. Further east is a stone-lined hole, 3–4m deep, which leads down through a cleft in the bedrock to the level of the Green Water. It is likely that a set of stairs provided access down to the river from where water could be drawn. The most spectacular part of the castle are the remains of the tower, located at the south-eastern end, built upon an outcrop of bedrock 2–3m high (Fig. 51). The tower is 11.5m long and 9m wide. The interior of the courtyard is divided into two halves by the foundations of a rectangular structure, which may be a later addition. Duchal Castle belonged to the Lyle family from the thirteenth century until 1544. The castle was besieged by James IV in 1489. Be very careful when visiting this site as many of the walls are undermined and in a very unstable condition. Do not stand on the edge of any of the walls, especially at the south-west end.

Another landscape feature that would have been present in the late thirteenth and early fourteenth centuries is the medieval forest used for hunting game. Historical research has identified a number of mottes in north-east Scotland which may have been associated with managed hunting reserves; the mottes perhaps acting as hunting lodges. In Renfrewshire, the main area for hunting was Paisley Forest, which belonged to Paisley Abbey. This forest extended

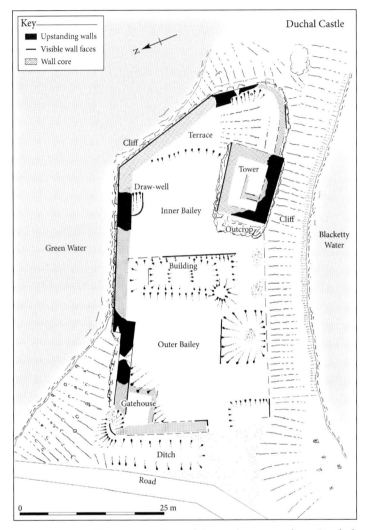

Figure 50   Plan of the enclosure castle at Duchal,
near Kilmacolm (Derek Alexander).

across the Gleniffer Braes, although its precise limits are unknown. Often such forests were given defined boundaries, either natural ones, such as rivers, or artificial ones were constructed, in the form of banks and ditches. Although no banks and ditches relating to Paisley Forest are known, perhaps detailed examination of early map evidence, coupled with field survey, may help identify them. There was also a hunting forest in Strathgryffe, and possibly some of the small mottes around Kilmacolm and Bridge of Weir were therefore used as hunting lodges.

Figure 51   Reconstruction sketch of Duchal Castle on its
promontory between two rivers (Derek Alexander).

In addition to the secular castles sites, the feudal period witnessed a
major expansion of the church in Scotland. The principal surviving early
church in Renfrewshire is Paisley Abbey. It was founded in 1164 by Walter
fitz Alan who came up from Shropshire and became Steward to David I.
Walter granted lands in Renfrew to a prior and 12 monks from the Cluniac
Priory of Much Wenlock, Shropshire. Nothing survives of the priory at
Renfrew, but shortly after the monks moved upstream to a more favourable
location in Paisley, and the construction work on the abbey commenced.
It became an abbey in 1245 and was endowed with considerable farm and
church rents. Under the patronage of the Stewarts it eventually controlled
the churches of Neilston, Kilbarchan, Eastwood, Houston, Kilellan, Erskine,
Kilmacolm, Largs, Prestwick, Monkton, Dundonald, Riccarton, Auchinleck,
Lochgilphead, Buchannan, Innerwick, Legerwood, Cathcart, Inverkip,
Mearns, Rutherglen, Kingarth, Kilpatrick, Roseneath, Kilfinan, Turnberry,
Straiton, Lochwinnoch and Skipness. In 1177, Walter fitz Alan's wife and
daughter were buried in the chapter house.

Like many of the early castle sites, the majority of ecclesiastical sites, mainly
parish churches and chapels, have been removed by constant reuse. Thus many
of the current parish churches probably occupy the sites of earlier structures.
A thirteenth-century charter shows that Paisley Abbey was assigned revenues
from the chapel of Lochwinnoch and the parish churches at Cathcart, Mearns,
Neilston, Kilbarchan, Houston, Kilellan, Erskine, Kilmacolm and Inverkip,

along with others outside the county. Few remains of these early medieval churches in Renfrewshire survive, although the parish church at Kilmacolm incorporates thirteenth-century stonework in what is now the Murray Chapel. The early construction is still visible as a piscina and three lancet windows. In addition to the removal of the remains of early parish churches by later rebuilding, many small chapels were probably destroyed during the Reformation. The site of the church at St Fillan's, Kilellan, may be located on a site used as a place of worship since the eighth century AD.

By far the most impressive remains are of Paisley Abbey, located on the east bank of the White Cart (Plate 8). It sits surrounded by a sanitised landscaped area of paving slabs, cut grass and young trees that belie the historical importance of the site throughout Renfrewshire's history. Although the majority of the surrounding monastic structures have been demolished it has been possible through comparison with other sites, coupled with information gleaned from old maps and historical references and limited archaeological investigation, to construct a possible plan of the site. This process has been made easier by the rediscovery of the stone-built drain which would have linked many of the structures in the monastic complex. As it survives today the abbey church is the result of a number of rebuilds. Like all churches of the period it is aligned east to west. It consists of an aisled nave at the west end with an aisle-less chancel at the east. The abbey would have had a range of buildings around the cloistered courtyard to the south-west of church, including the chapter house to the east and the refectory to the south, with an adjacent kitchen. The monks' dormitory is thought to have extended southwards from the south-east corner of the cloister. Other buildings may have included a smithy and an infirmary, while a bakehouse and brewhouse are also likely to have been present.

During the Wars of Independence the abbey was burnt by English troops in 1307, perhaps in retaliation to support given by the abbot to Robert Bruce. Although destroyed and subsequently rebuilt, the fabric of the building still contains sections of thirteenth-century stonework. The most obvious of these sections is the west front, which, although it had three traceried windows cut through at a later date, is substantially complete. Other noticeable sections of thirteenth-century date are the arcade of the chapel off the south transept and the south aisle wall. Recent archaeological investigations have revealed little of the thirteenth–fourteenth century buildings of the Abbey, and the artefactual material recovered from the abbey drain appears to date from the fifteenth century onwards, suggesting it was either a late construction or that it was cleaned out prior to this date. However, a general plan of the site can be constructed from old maps, and other monastic sites to reveal a complex of structures including church, cloisters, drain and chapter house all enclosed within a precinct wall.

Elderslie, near Johnstone in Renfrewshire, has long been suggested as the birthplace of the Scottish hero William Wallace. Arguments remain however over whether he was born there or in Ayrshire, although it is unlikely this will ever be confirmed one way or another. The site in Elderslie has a monument dedicated to Wallace built in 1912 and was also the site of a building known as Wallace's House. Unfortunately, this crow-stepped building was demolished in 1974, but it appears to have been a sixteenth- or seventeenth-century building rather than belonging to the thirteenth century. It appears that this structure had been an outbuilding for a tower-house that had stood on the site. The tower, and the farm which replaced it, have also disappeared. However, map research revealed that there had been a large enclosure 100m long by 75m wide around the site (Fig. 52). Archaeological excavation work, undertaken in 1998 prior to re-landscaping around the monument, located the remains of a flat-bottomed ditch over 5m wide and 1.5m deep. The inside face of the ditch was revetted by a mortared and battered stone wall. The base of the ditch was filled by a grey-sticky clay, which suggested it may have at some time formed a wet moat. A sherd of thirteenth-century green-glazed pottery was recovered from the ditch fill, and radiocarbon dating of hazel twigs suggested it had already begun to fill up in the mid fifteenth century. It is possible therefore that this unusual moated enclosure could date back to the thirteenth or fourteenth century and could be contemporary with Wallace. Such moated sites are relatively rare in Scotland although they must have been more common once; recently another has been identified at Perceton near Irvine while the outer ditches around Craigie Castle, also in Ayrshire, may have had a similar origin. They would have formed the lightly defended centres of landed estates probably acting as large farms. Within the ditch and probably a defensive bank, there would have been a mixture of domestic and agricultural buildings, animal pens, orchards and even small patches of arable land. Interpretation panels are now available on the site explaining its complicated history. As well as the monument, there is a yew tree, again known as 'Wallace's Yew', but which is probably around 300 years old. The location of the site of 'Wallace's House' on the end of a slight ridge and above a burn, the Aldpatrick Water, is in keeping with the settlement locations of other thirteenth–fourteenth century settlements, such as mottes.

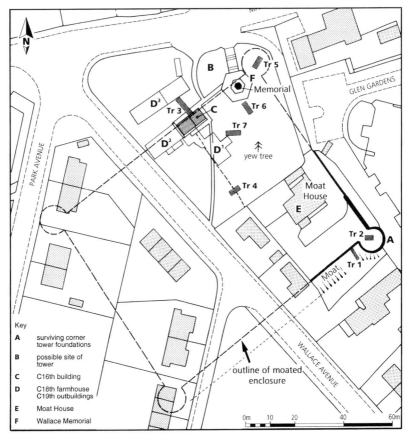

Figure 52   Plan showing original extent of Elderslie moated site,
location of buildings and excavation trenches (Derek
Alexander & Centre for Field Archaeology).

Archaeologists look on coin hoards as evidence of unsettled times. There
are three major coin hoards from Renfrewshire which span the period of
the Wars of Independence. In 1791 a hoard consisting of 515 silver pennies
of Edward I, II and III, and 5 pennies of Alexander III was discovered near
Paisley. In 1879, a pot containing 455 pennies of Edward I, II and III and 3
Scots coins of Alexander III was found in Giffnock. This collection of coins
is thought to date between 1292 and 1360. More recently, in 1963, workmen
digging a trench for an electricity cable in Bell Street, Renfrew, recovered a
green glazed jug, a few inches below the surface, containing over 674 coins
(Plate 9). The majority were English coins dating from 1299 to 1321, although
148 Scots coins were also recovered including coins of Alexander III, Robert I

and Balliol. It is possible that this hoard of coins was originally placed within garden plots associated with the buildings in the town. The coins have now been dispersed among the collections of the National Museum, the Hunterian Museum, Paisley Museum, the British Museum, Renfrew Town Council and a private collection. Just why these collections of coins were hoarded away and not recovered we will never know. They do appear to reflect the unstable times during the Wars between England and Scotland and may simply be a result of people amassing and hiding monetary resources.

The Stewards and their vassals would have needed ample monetary resources to support the Bruce cause. Partly as a reward for this support and also to cement his power in the west, Robert the Bruce married his daughter, Marjorie, to Walter the Steward (the son of James the Steward who had died in 1309) in 1315. There is a tale that she died in 1316–17 after falling from her horse, while heavily pregnant, somewhere on the road between Paisley and Renfrew and that her son was born in Paisley Abbey; alternatively it has been suggested that she may have died in childbirth at Renfrew Castle. It has recently been suggested by Sylvia Clark that the monument erected 'to mark where she fell off her horse' in Renfrew Road, Paisley is a bit of myth-making and wishful thinking by Paisley local historians back in the nineteenth century.

When Robert the Bruce died in 1329 at his manor house of Cardross, just a short sail down the Clyde from Renfrew, he left a five-year-old son, David, as heir to the Scottish throne. During the minority of David II, the kingdom was once again thrown into turmoil. The English king, Edward III, secretly encouraged a group of Scottish landowners who had been disinherited by Bruce to support Edward Balliol, son of John Balliol, in an attempt for the Scottish throne. This group invaded Scotland in 1332 and defeated the Scots army at Dupplin, near Perth. Although Balliol was crowned king, he and his supporters were forced to flee back to England. When in 1333 they returned with support from Edward III, they again defeated the Scots at Halidon Hill in Berwickshire, and David II fled to France. David returned to a far from united Scotland in 1341 when Edward III was engaged in war with France, and in 1346 he invaded England but was defeated at the Battle of Neville's Cross, during which he was captured. In his absence, the kingdom was ruled by Robert Stewart, the son of Walter and Marjorie. It was to take until 1357 for David to be released for the handsome sum of 100,000 merks over 10 years and 23 hostages to be submitted to ensure this ransom was paid. Perhaps some of the coin hoards, described above, were being gathered for this ransom but were never handed over. The Stewards who were effectively in control of Scotland in David's absence may not have been that keen to have him come back.

On returning to Scotland, David had to re-establish royal authority, especially in order to increase the royal revenues in an attempt to meet the ransom demand. He seems to have been very successful in achieving this, through increasing custom duties on exports and raising taxes, and the crown was obviously wealthy enough to enhance its prestige by the construction of a large L-shaped tower, subsequently called David's Tower, on Edinburgh Castle in 1368. This tower consisted of a vaulted basement for storage, with a hall on the first floor, the king's chamber above and the queen's chamber above that. It is unclear where these ideas for the tower design came from; perhaps David was influenced by his time in France or England. More importantly, this construction is often regarded as the progenitor of that ubiquitous Scottish castle form: the tower-house. When David had returned to Scotland, he had rewarded a number of nobles for running the kingdom in his absence, the foremost of these being Robert the Steward, son of Walter Steward and Marjorie Bruce, who was made Earl of Carrick. In spite of the fact that he rebelled against David in 1363, Robert remained heir-presumptive, and in the event of David's unexpected death in 1371 was crowned king Robert II at Scone; the first of the Stewart dynasty.

Robert II, who as discussed above, was probably born at Renfrew Castle in 1316–17, was Guardian of Scotland between 1346 and 1357 and was in his mid fifties when crowned king of Scots in 1371. Many historians have painted him as a weak senile king, but the first part of his reign was very successful: he managed not to be drawn into the Hundred Years War between England and France; he continued to increase the royal revenues; and he managed, unlike the house of Bruce, to produce five legitimate sons to whom the crown could be passed. By 1384, however, Robert had been replaced as effective ruler by his eldest son John, Earl of Carrick. Carrick favoured war with England, and in 1388 a raid into Northumbria defeated an English army at Otterburn but his political ally, James, Earl of Douglas, was killed in the battle. Carrick was lamed after being kicked by a horse, and effective rule of the realm was given over to his brother, the Earl of Fife, who became Guardian of Scotland, but it was John, Earl of Carrick, who, on the death of their father in 1390, changed his name and was crowned King Robert III.

Robert II and III, partly due to the age of the former and the invalidity of the latter, did not move around the kingdom much. They appear to have preferred to stay in central Scotland allowing and encouraging their numerous offspring and the major noble families to rule the other parts of the country. With the focus of the traditional Stewart lands in Renfrew, Cunningham, Kyle and Carrick these two kings spent more time in Renfrewshire than any previous or subsequent Scottish monarchs. Robert II is recorded as issuing five acts from Renfrew (the Castle), one from Inverkip and one from Chrisswell Chapel (between Gourock and Inverkip). In addition to acts from Renfrew and Chrisswell, Robert III issued acts from Finlayston, Elliston, Erskine and Renfrew.

10

Later Medieval Renfrewshire

FIFTEENTH AND SIXTEENTH CENTURIES AD

———— ◆ ————

The later medieval period, from 1400 to 1600, was as unsettled as any of the preceding periods and can be characterised by the construction of large numbers of tower-houses (Fig. 53). These small castles, developed from the form of David II's tower at Edinburgh, were built to confirm the owner's status. They could, on occasion, withstand raids from neighbours, and were in even rarer circumstances involved in more protracted sieges. This was a time when landowners and their retainers fought with their fellow landowners over territory, religion and the monarchy.

Perhaps the most impressive of all the towers in the old county of Renfrewshire is the magnificent Crookston Castle, built around 1400, within the earlier twelfth-century ring-work, by Alexander Stewart, Lord of Crookston from 1374 to 1406. Here the main tower is 18m by 12m and has a rounded barrel-vaulted basement with a two-storey-high vaulted hall above (Fig. 54). There was a square tower at each corner of the main block. The entrance is on the ground floor beside the north-east corner tower and was protected by a portcullis raised from an intramural chamber off the hall above. The basement would have been used for storage and was lit by high slit windows. There was also a well within the thickness of the north wall, and access could be gained to the basements of the corner towers, the north-western of which may have been the kitchen. The basement of the north-eastern tower contained a pit prison. Unfortunately the tower was heavily damaged during a siege by James IV in 1489 when the royal artillery, possibly including the mighty bombard Mons Meg, pounded the castle into submission and caused the substantial collapse of the two western towers. After this the

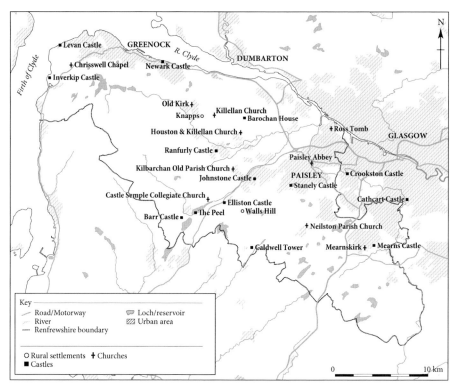

Figure 53   Map of medieval castles, churches and other sites in Renfrewshire.

castle became a secondary residence when the Earl of Lennox built a palace at Inchinnan in 1506 (another Renfrewshire building that has vanished). In 1758, the ruin came into the possession of the Maxwells of Pollok, and Sir John Stirling Maxwell gifted it to the National Trust for Scotland in 1931 as their first property. Although still owned by NTS it became a Guardianship site in 1964 managed by Historic Scotland. A yew tree which stood to the west of the castle fell in the nineteenth century, and some of the wood was used to make a model of the castle which can still be seen in Pollok House.

When the site was excavated in 1973–75, five trenches were opened around and within the tower (see Fig. 49). This located a clay floor, which may have been the foundation for stone flags within the basement of the tower. A trench over the position of the north-west tower found large quantities of medieval pottery and two coins, one of James II and one of James IV. An earlier coin, a silver groat of Robert III (issued 1393–1406), was found in the trench outside the south-eastern tower. A small patch of copper alloy chain

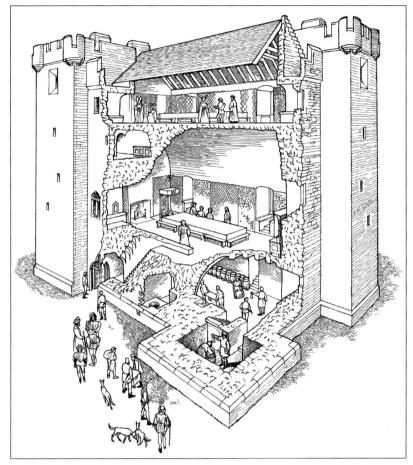

Figure 54   Reconstruction drawing of Crookston Castle fifteenth
century tower – cut away to show storage cellar, great
hall, and chambers above (© Crown Copyright Historic
Scotland. http://www.historicscotlandimages.gov.uk).

mail armour was found in the outer enclosure close to the entrance and may
date to before 1500 AD.

The periodic weakness of the Stewart dynasty and the endemic lawlessness
of the Scottish landowners meant that there was no effective way of resolving
long-running disputes. For example, a disagreement over the relatively minor
office of baillie of the Barony of Cunningham in 1366 led to a feud between
the Montgomeries and the Cunninghams which lasted, off and on, for two
and a half centuries before it was resolved in 1609.

James IV had to work hard to achieve order, having himself come to power in 1488 as a result of a revolt which had seen his father defeated at Sauchieburn, near Stirling, and murdered in the aftermath of the battle. There were two major risings against James IV in 1489, one of which was focused in the old seat of Stewart power, Renfrewshire. The revolt had been led by John Stewart, the Earl of Lennox, and Sir Robert Lyle. As a result, their lands were declared forfeit but a number of the revolt leaders, including Lyle, locked themselves in their castles of Dumbarton, Crookston and Duchal. James then instigated a quick campaign to reduce these castles and brought with him the royal artillery, which included the massive bombard 'Mons Meg'. This was a considerable task, given the primitive state of the roads and pathways linking east and west.

At Crookston, the siege was over very quickly once the artillery was brought to bear, and it has been suggested that the loss of the western towers may have been a direct result of this siege. The siege at Duchal may have been supervised by Sir John Semple, sheriff of Renfrew, and John Sandilands, laird of Hillhouse. The former had to provide the oxen to pull the artillery, and the latter hired workmen in Paisley who had to level the road for the guns with spades and shovels. The deep ravines on either side of the Duchal castle and its ditch, although good defence against an assault on foot, would have been of limited use against a prolonged artillery bombardment (Fig. 51). The surrounding landscape provides plenty of practical gun sites that would easily be within range and elevation for firing directly at the walls. It is no wonder, therefore, that the siege was over within a couple of days. An interesting note about the siege is that earlier that summer a Danish pirate called Lutkyn Mere had been captured by the navy of James IV, and while 36 of the pirate crew were executed 9 others (presumably gunners) volunteered for the siege of Duchal. In addition to Mons Meg, one of the guns was named Duchal after the siege. These guns caused such severe damage during the siege that masons had to be employed to effect repairs early in September 1489. Across the Clyde at Dumbarton, it was more difficult to bring the guns to bear on the walls of the rock-girt castle, and Lord Darnley, the son of the Earl of Lennox, held the castle twice against the king until it was finally forced to surrender.

The burgh of Dumbarton was then used for building and equipping James IV's new navy, which he then used in campaigns along the western coast against the Lord of the Isles. It is recorded that the king was again at Duchal on 16 March 1498 where he celebrated his twenty-fifth birthday and passed an act revoking all grants made by him during his legal minority.

Figure 55   East elevation of Cathcart Castle with inset
of moulded plaster heraldic shield found during the
excavations (main photo courtesy Paisley Art Gallery
and Museum; inset courtesy Brian Kerr).

Another of the early Renfrewshire families was the Cathcarts, who are
recorded in the area from the twelfth century. It is likely that their early
castle stood on the site of the later stone tower on the rocky knoll high above
the White Cart. Earliest mention of the castle is, however, not until 1507 in
a charter of James IV when John Cathcart gave it as a wedding present to his
son Allan. It was this Allan who then sold it in 1546 to Gabriel Semple of
Ladymuir. It remained with the Semples until 1720 but in the 1740s was sold
for its materials to a Glasgow merchant who removed the roof and the timber.
Unfortunately the tower fell into disrepair (Fig. 55), and in 1980 Glasgow City
Council had it demolished. At least detailed floor plans and early photographs

survive to show what the castle was like, and an archaeological excavation was undertaken of the surrounding courtyard and buildings.

Heavily overgrown foundations of the northern and western walls of the tower can still be seen on the site. The tower, which was probably built after 1450, had a vaulted basement with three floors above and sat within a barmkin enclosure 22m, east to west, by 15m with small round turrets at the corners. Excavation, supervised by Brian Kerr, found that the south-east turret had been built on a steep rock scarp that was the inner face of a rock-cut ditch 7m wide and 3.5m deep. Part of the corner turret was preserved in the cellar of a seventeenth-century building that had been built across the ditch. This building was partly demolished when the internal timber was stripped out in the eighteenth century, and the infill included debris from the castle including ornamental moulded plasterwork. One of the best pieces was the complete heraldic shield of the arms of Bryce Sempill and his wife Jean who owned the castle in 1627 (Fig. 55 inset). Artefacts also included large amounts of late medieval green glazed pottery, seventeenth- and eighteenth-century ceramics and glass.

The Cathcarts were among a number of Renfrewshire landowners who were involved closely in the politics of the reign of Mary, Queen of Scots. At the Battle of Carberry (1567), Mary was not confronted by a group composed of Protestant revolutionaries but also a number of Catholic lords, including Lord Semple of Castle Semple. Following Mary's imprisonment in Loch Leven, the Earl of Glencairn, another Renfrewshire noble based at Finlayston, and a zealous Protestant, destroyed the furnishings of Mary's private chapel in Holyrood. It is likely that a number of small chapels in Renfrewshire may also have been destroyed at this time. Like Semple and Glencairn, Lord Cathcart was also a supporter of James VI. In opposition to these were the Queen's men, who in Renfrewshire consisted of the Earl of Eglinton (who owned Polnoon Castle, Eaglesham) and Lord Ross of Hawkhead. In addition, she had the support of John Hamilton, Abbot of Paisley Abbey (illegitimate son of James, first Earl of Arran). Following the Reformation, in 1563, Abbot Hamilton had been imprisoned in Edinburgh Castle for illegally celebrating Mass. In the immediate aftermath of the Battle of Langside (1568), he unsuccessfully tried to dissuade Mary, Queen of Scots, from fleeing to England and was eventually hanged in 1571 for supporting her. He was buried in Paisley Abbey. Claud Hamilton, nephew of John, was appointed as commendator of the abbey in 1553 and was also a strong supporter of Mary, accompanying her at the Battle of Langside, following which he was forfeited, fled the country and only returned in 1584. absence, Lord Semple was made commendator.

The Semples were a powerful local family and had a strong castle at the north-east end of Lochwinnoch. The third Lord Semple was active in Scottish politics between the 1540s and the 1570s. He was taken prisoner by the English in 1547 and took the side of Mary of Guise against the Protestant Lords of the Congregation. In 1560, Castle Semple was besieged by a group of these lords under the Earl of Arran. Semple supported Mary, Queen of Scots until the murder of Darnley and changed sides before the Battle of Langside. He was also involved in local feuds with other members of the Hamilton family and with the Montgomeries. He was taken prisoner by Hamilton after the murder of the regent in 1570 and died in 1572.

The particularly violent feud between the Cunningham and Montgomery families in North Ayrshire and Renfrewshire came to a head at the end of the sixteenth century. James IV had raised each of the heads of the families to the status of earl, the Earldom of Glencairn for the Cunninghams and the Earldom of Eglinton for the Montgomeries. Although there had been a minor feud between the families in the 1520s, they surprisingly stayed at peace with each other throughout the Reformation and the Marian Civil War, despite the fourth Earl of Glencairn being a staunch Protestant and supporter of King James VI and the third Earl of Eglinton being a Catholic who supported Queen Mary. The feud was rekindled over the appointment of commendator of Kilwinning Abbey in North Ayrshire, which had in the past been a Montgomery post but which was granted to a Cunningham in 1571. In 1583, some of the Cunninghams attacked the Montgomeries at church on a Sunday morning and wounded one of them. However, one of the Cunninghams was killed in this fight; that family then plotted their revenge and in the last week of April 1586, the Earl of Eglinton and a small party of his servants were ambushed while journeying to Stirling and murdered. Although a large number of the families were located in northern Ayrshire, there were also branches and allies in west Renfrewshire. The Cunninghams, for example, could count on the support of the Maxwells of Stanely who had a separate feud with the Montgomeries. The feud between the Maxwells and the Montgomeries had led to the murder of Stanely and the reprisal deaths of Lord Montgomery and his son. The Maxwells had sought protection from Glencairn. The Montgomeries had some support from the Boyds of Kilmarnock, while the Semples were also allied by marriage to them and had a history of feuding with Glencairn.

Given this history of endemic feuding, it is not surprising that the typical laird's, or small landowner's, house of this period was the tower-house. In the case of smaller holdings, the tower itself was little more than a slightly grander, defensible farm and the laird little more than a slightly grander farmer.

Tower-houses are probably the most conspicuous survivals from medieval times. With the construction of David's Tower on Edinburgh Castle rock in 1368, many nobles aspired to this new architectural style. The classic example of this is the tower built by Archibald Douglas, better known as Archibald the Grim, at Threave soon after he became Lord of Galloway in 1369. It is likely that the tower built by Sir John Montgomery at Polnoon, near Eaglesham, with the ransom money he obtained from capturing Henry Percy at the Battle of Otterburn in 1388, may have been a similar structure, although very little now remains (see Fig. 47). The remains of the fourteenth-century tower of Polnoon stand on a knoll, possibly the remains of a motte (see above), overlooking the burn of the same name. A very steep slope down to the burn protected the north and west sides of the castle, while the south was defended by a length of ditch, c.30m long by 18m wide, now mostly infilled. A description of the Battle of Otterburn, which took place during the reign of King Robert II, is contained in the English ballad 'Chevy Chase' and specifically mentions Renfrewshire landowner Sir John Montgomery who engaged the English leader Earl Percy

Now yield thee, Percy, he said,
Or else I'll vow I'll lay thee low
To whom must I yield, quoth Earl Percy,
Now that I see it must be so? . . .
As soon as he knew it was Montgomery
he struck his sword's point in the gronde;
The Montgomery was a courteous knight
And quickly took him by the honde
The deed was done at Otterbourne
About the breaking of the day;
Earl Douglas was buried at the braken bush
And the Percy led captive away.

Although the surviving plan of the site is by no means clear, it is likely to have consisted of a simple rectangular tower, similar to other contemporary (late fourteenth century) castles at Threave and Lochnaw. By 1789 the castle had clearly fallen into disrepair, and it appears on one of John Ainslie's sketches as a silhouetted ruin. The remains have been substantially robbed for stone. Very little in situ structure survives, although a number of large collapsed fragments of masonry lie around the site, and one of these may be part of a rounded stair well.

Tower-houses were constructed between c.1350 and c.1600 as defensible residences. Typical examples consist or three to five storeys with a stone vaulted floor on the lowest level, which supported the stone floor of the great hall on the first floor above. This was a single chamber with a large fireplace and corner stairs leading up to smaller chambers in the upper storeys. Rooms, presses and spiral staircases were often set into the walls, which could be several feet thick. Windows were small in the earlier periods, then enlarged and embellished in later times. Attics had crow-stepped gables, and there was generally a corbelled or machicolated walkway round the edge of the roof. Early examples were simple towers, sometimes entered by a wooden stairway to a door at the first floor level. The plans of later towers are more elaborate: L- and T-planned towers gave way to Z-plan towers. An additional wing was called a 'jamb', and these often developed into courtyards incorporating other single-storey buildings. In the more peaceful years which followed the seventeenth century, gun loops gave way to ornamental windows, and towers which were still the centre of estates became the core of mansion houses.

Renfrewshire has many examples of tower-houses in all states of development and survival. Early examples include Inverkip (also called Ardgowan); Stanely (where the jamb is clearly an addition to the original tower) and Levan, at Gourock, which is an early L-shaped tower.

Four of the best examples of towers are Stanely, Barr Castle, Castle Levan and Mearns Castle. The tower-house at Stanely (built c.1500) unfortunately sits in the middle of a reservoir built in 1837 and can, therefore, only be viewed from a distance (Fig. 56). It consists of a rectangular block 14m long by 7.2m wide with a wing, 6m by 6m, added on to the north-east corner. The main spiral stair is located in the south-west corner and provides access to both the main block and the later wing. The main block contained a vaulted cellar (now largely collapsed) and a kitchen at one end. A service stair led from the cellar up to a small room at one end of the hall on the first floor. There are two floors of bedrooms above the hall. Traces of the continuous corbelling, which would have supported the parapets, can still be seen. The internal layout is remarkably similar to Fairlie, Law and Skelmorlie castles in Ayrshire. The windows on the ground and first floor have been blocked, but the consolidation work carried out when the reservoir was built, most notably

Figure 56   Stanely Castle sitting in middle of the reservoir
built in 1838 and with the stump of the Stanely Cross in the
foreground (courtesy Paisley Art Gallery and Museum).

the addition of an internal buttress supporting the remains of the spiral stair
well, has prevented any major structural collapse. The tower was constructed
by the Maxwells of Newark, but prior to that the barony (estate) belonged
to the Calderwood Maxwells and before them, in the fourteenth century, to
the Dennistouns.

The tower-house of Barr Castle at least can be approached on foot. Barr
Castle was drawn by MacGibbon and Ross in the 1880s when the remains were
more extensive. It is a standard tower-house with four storeys, battlements, a
courtyard and a wing on the south side (now gone). It is dated to *c*.1520 and

was owned by the Ferguslie Hamiltons until the eighteenth century when it passed to the MacDowalls of Castle Semple. The Hamilton ownership is reflected in the lintel inscriptions (LH IC 1680 at the foot of the stair and IW MH on the porch). The tower measures 10.8m long by 7.9m wide and is complete to the height of the four continuously corbelled courses, which would have originally supported the breastwork. The basement is divided into a cellar and kitchen with the main spiral staircase in the north-west corner giving access to the hall on the first floor and leading to the rooms on the second and third floors. The hall contains a large fireplace in the west wall. A small stair in the south-west corner reached through a window embrasure also leads up to the rooms on the second and third floors. The original entrance was at first floor level in the north wall but a later door was knocked through at ground level from the west. Outside the tower are the faint traces of a rectangular enclosure, which extended to the west and south. Traces of a roof raggle on the southern gable end indicate that a two-storey structure was built against this side. This excellent example of a sixteenth-century tower-house is in need of repair with its windows and doors bricked up. Access into the interior is therefore currently impossible.

Castle Levan is more readily accessible as it was restored and converted into a Bed and Breakfast. Located in Gourock, looking out over the waters of the Firth of Clyde, it was built c.1500 by the Morton family and was passed to the Semples in 1547. It consists of a large rectangular tower, 10.6m by 7.9m, which is attached at its south-east corner to a smaller block, 8m by 6.3m. The main stair is in the south-east corner of the larger block. The ground floor of both contained barrel-vaulted cellars. The main block contains a first-floor hall with an access stair down to the two cellars below in the south-west corner and an additional spiral stair (in the same corner) which provides access to the westernmost of two bedrooms on the floor above. The smaller wing contained a kitchen on the first floor with a bedroom above. Both ranges are provided with additional rooms in the attic space. When the castle was restored in the 1970s, a small archaeological excavation was carried out around the exterior. This revealed that the surrounding barmkin courtyard had been over 13m wide and that the smaller, southern, tower was built over the robbed out line of the east side of the barmkin. On the east side of this tower, excavation found the kitchen midden with over 5,000 fragments of bone and sea shells, and sherds of late medieval pottery.

The impressive stone tower of Mearns Castle, on a hill with good prospects over the land to the north-west, is slightly obscured by the round modern church and Mearns Castle High School. It was constructed by Herbert, Lord Maxwell, in 1449. It fell into disrepair in the nineteenth century but has been restored with a flat roof, and is used as rooms adjoining the church. The ground floor contained a cellar with two slit windows and a service stair to the hall above in the northern corner. A door was knocked through the north-eastern wall in the seventeenth century. Another later door knocked through the north-western wall links the tower, via a corridor, to the modern church; an arrangement repeated on the first floor above. The original doorway in the north-eastern wall was at hall level and had a rounded arch (now partially blocked). The hall also has a high vaulted ceiling with traces of a musicians' gallery. A spiral stair in the northern corner provides access to the bedroom above. Excavations were undertaken around the tower which confirmed the date of the earlier ringwork as twelfth century.

Other towers across the county are less well-preserved. For example, the remains of the castle at Ranfurly, Bridge of Weir, are ruins located on a tree-covered scarp above the Ranfurly Burn on the west side of the golf course. It is overlooked by the remains of the motte, which is located c.150m to the south-east. The tower measures c.7.8m by 6.7m and probably dates to the sixteenth century, although the lack of a vaulted basement may suggest an earlier date. The two doorways positioned directly above each other, one on the ground floor and one on the first floor, give the north-east façade a peculiar look. It is likely that the upper one was original, with the other having been knocked through the 1.4m thick wall when a later wing was added to this corner. A spiral stair provided access from the first floor to the upper stories. This staircase was located in the north-east corner beside the entrance, which may suggest that this was the earlier of the two doorways. As well as the later structure, which projects from the east of the tower, there was a further range, with three cellars (perhaps with a hall above), located to the south-east of the tower. The castle belonged to the Knox family from the fifteenth century until 1665 when it was taken over by William Cochrane, first Earl of Dundonald, before later passing to the Aikenheads.

Also in a ruinous state are the remains of the Semples' early castle at Elliston. The stump of masonry which once formed the south-west corner of Elliston Castle is located in the garden of a private house. The remains are located close to a small burn that runs past it and down into the Black Cart Water. The castle probably dates to the early sixteenth century and would originally have been 11.5m long by 9.6m wide. The basement, once reported to have been vaulted, is now completely filled with collapsed wall material.

The surviving fragment of the hall above includes a shot-hole and a window embrasure. Between the castle and the modern house are the remains of a possible courtyard, of which the south-east and north-east walls still survive as foundations. This is believed to be the original Semple feu. A Robert de Semple was chamberlain at the royal castle at Renfrew in the reign of Alexander III. His son also held that office and called himself William de Semple of Elliotstoun or Ellieston in a charter of 1344. In a charter of 1474, Sir William Sempill is called baron of Elliotston and Castleton. The first Lord Sempill (who was created a peer by King James IV) erected or, more likely, rebuilt, at or near the eastern end of the loch, the castle of Castleton which he called Castle Semple. This building was in turn demolished in 1727 to make way for the construction of the Castle Semple Mansion House.

Some of the towers that survive have clearly either been part of a larger complex of buildings or have been added to in later periods. For example, Caldwell Tower is all that remains of a once more extensive sixteenth-century structure belonging to the Mures of Caldwell. It sits in pasture land above a steep gorse-covered hillside looking southwards across Lochlibo to the village of Uplawmoor. The two-storey tower has been much altered, with renewed breastwork resting upon original chequered corbelling. A ground floor door leads into the barrel-vaulted basement from the north-west. This basement has blocked windows in both the south-east and south-west walls, while there is a dumb-bell gun loop in the north-east wall. A later external stair has been added to the north-east façade and provides access to both the first and second floors. The first floor is also barrel vaulted and has a fireplace in the north-west. On the second floor, there is also a fireplace in the north-west and two of the windows have blocked shot holes below them. There are also the remains of a heraldic panel on the exterior of the north-west façade. When William Mure of Caldwell was involved in the Covenanters' rebellion of 1666, the estate was forfeited and the castle fell into disrepair. The remaining tower seems to have been rebuilt for some reason during the eighteenth century, by which time the Mures had recovered the estate and built and extended the Hall of Caldwell.

Johnstone castle has also been much changed over the years. This L-shaped fifteenth-century tower is located within a housing estate on the south-west side of Johnstone. It was originally called Easter Cochrane but was renamed Quarrella House after 1519. When acquired by the Houstouns of Johnston in 1733 they changed its name once again to Johnstone House. The new owners developed the site, eventually adding a large mansion completed in the early nineteenth century. This mansion was subsequently demolished in the 1950s. The original tower has survived all these changes and bears the marks of the later additions. Signs of the mansion walls can be seen abutting the north side. Alterations made by the Houstouns in the eighteenth century, when all the windows were changed to a Gothic style and given pointed, arched surrounds, are visible.

Recently the tower again changed hands when it was sold by Renfrewshire Council, who had used the remaining structure as a store. This historic building once visited by Frederick Chopin is now being converted once more into private living accommodation. During restoration work, original windows and fireplaces have been rediscovered, sealed behind rough stonework and Victorian concrete. The continuing structural restoration work and historical research by the new owners is expected to reveal further details of the early history of the site.

At Newark Castle, the south end of the east wing of this well-preserved site is the original four-storey fifteenth-century tower, which has been incorporated in the later mansion (discussed below). At Inverkip, by contrast, the later mansion house was located away from the old tower. This tower, built around 1500, is located within the grounds of the modern mansion house of Ardgowan, on a promontory overlooking Inverkip Marina. Although this structure is later it may overlie or be close to the site of the thirteenth–fourteenth century stronghold which is recorded as having been used by English troops during the Scottish Wars of Independence. The surviving tower is of later construction and is substantially complete to the level of the battlements. The original entrance was at ground floor level in the south-west corner providing access to a small, barrel-vaulted cellar lit by three narrow slit windows; the one close to the southern corner was an inverted keyhole gun loop. A spiral staircase, also in the southern corner, led to the first-floor hall while another spiral staircase in the western corner provided access from the hall to the bedroom and battlements above. Current access is provided by a stone stair to a door knocked through at hall level beside the main stair. The seventeenth-century wing to which this door led has since been demolished. The parapet is supported on chequer corbelling, and there appears to have been bartizans or roundels at three of the corners. This castle belonged to the Stewart of Ardgowan, descended from John of Ardgowan, an illegitimate son of Robert III.

Other small castles in Renfrewshire have disappeared completely. A similar dated small castle site was excavated at Old Bar Castle, 150m west of Rashielee

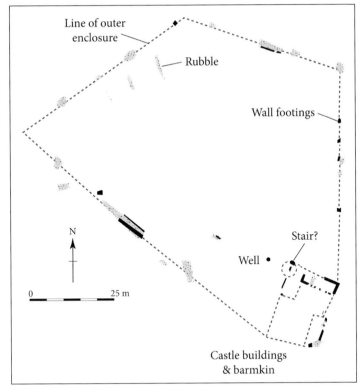

Figure 57   Plan of Old Bar Castle, Erskine, showing castle
buildings in south-east and outer courtyard beyond (redrawn
by Ingrid Shearer from plans supplied by Jim Hunter).

Farm, in 1973 by Jim Hunter of Paisley Museum, prior to the expansion of
the new town of Erskine. This was the site of a house which belonged to the
Stewarts of Barscube from around 1490 to 1673. Although the site had been
robbed of most of its stonework and heavily ploughed, the rough outline was
recorded (Fig. 57). An L-shaped building formed by two wings 11m long by
4.4m wide formed the northern corner of a quadrangular courtyard. There
were indications of the base of a spiral stair at the external northern angle.
There was a larger walled rectilinear enclosure to the north-west, which took
in much of the slope above the castle. Perhaps the most remarkable discovery
was made once the developers moved in when a beautifully preserved stone-
lined well (Fig. 58) was hit by a gas main. This was located within the larger
enclosure 6m west of the possible stair tower. The well was choked full of
stone and included window rybats with bar holes and several steps from a spiral

Figure 58   Fine ashlar stonework of well
found at Old Bar Castle (Jim Hunter).

newel stair. The well was emptied down to a depth of 4.5m but unfortunately due to the rising water was not bottomed. The site is now covered by North Bar housing estate.

Also of interest, though ruinous, is Auchenbothie, where the remains of the surrounding fermtoun can still be distinguished. Newark, at Port Glasgow, developed into a mansion house, as did Johnstone Castle. In other cases, the estate centre moved and the tower-house has all but disappeared, as at Polnoon, near Eaglesham, and Craigends in Houston.

The search for tower-houses is made easier by the Poll Tax Roll of 1695, which records the tax assessment of landowners and notes the estate centres where a tower, if it existed, may have been sited. The early seventeenth-century maps of Blaeu and Speed also indicate the houses of prominent landowners. Pont's map of 1590s also shows many of the locations of Renfrewshire castles and many with small sketches. One of the largest of these is Castle Semple at the north-eastern end of the loch. Unfortunately nothing survives of this large castle, which was demolished around 1730 and replaced by a large mansion. However, in the loch on a small island there is another smaller castle marked on Pont's map. Called The Peel, it is one of Renfrewshire's most unusual castles.

Figure 59   Nineteenth-century drawing of Peel Tower remains at Castle Semple
Loch showing stairs to first floor and inner rebates of gun loops in
basement (Hector 1890). Inset shows bronze canon found in loch.

The foundations of the Peel are located on a peninsula within the RSPB
bird sanctuary at the current west end of Castle Semple Loch. The position
would formerly have been an island in the middle of a more extensive loch.
The site is heavily overgrown with shrubs, and the remains are difficult to
make out. However, the site was cleared out in the late nineteenth century
and a plan and elevations drawn (Fig. 59). This revealed the foundations
of an ashlar-faced tower dating to *c*.1550–60. It was built by Robert, third
Lord Semple. The tower measured 10.3m long, south-west to north-east, by
8.3m wide and walls *c*.2.4m thick. The south-west end of the structure was
pointed, but the other end was flat and had an entrance at ground floor level,
which led into a vaulted basement. Just inside the door on the left-hand side
there was a turnpike stair leading to the small hall on the first floor. The
ground-floor basement was *c*.7.5m long by 2.9m wide and had a fireplace at
the north-east end beside the door. Two horizontal wide-mouthed gun loops,

0.9m wide, protect both long sides of the tower. The embrasures had recesses for wooden sills to which the guns would have been attached on a pivot to let them swing back and forth covering wide angles of fire. A sixteenth-century cast bronze gun recovered from within the loch near the ruin may be one of the guns used to defend the site (Fig. 59 inset). The Semples were involved in a number of local feuds and in the Marian Civil Wars. Following a brief siege in October 1560, the Semples' other castle at the other end of the Loch (Castle Semple) was captured and damaged. Although the small tower in the loch was destroyed at the same time, enough must have survived for Robert, fourth Lord Semple, to use it as a prison in 1575. This unusual artillery work is now a Scheduled Ancient Monument and a remarkable testament to the power of the Semples. Another statement of their power and status as sheriffs of the county can be seen in the huge ceremonial sword on display in the National Museum of Scotland. Known as the 'Sempill Sword', this magnificent sword is too large to have been a practical weapon: it is 2.55m long and weighs over 10.5kg. It was reputedly carried before Mary Queen of Scots at the Battle of Langside in 1568.

Most accounts of medieval Renfrewshire concentrate on the family histories of the Stewarts, Hamiltons, Montgomeries, Cunninghams, Maxwells and Semples (and their castles). This is because previous Renfrewshire historians lived in a more paternalistic age, when many of the estates and families were still extant. While it is true that some of the events in which these families were involved were of more than local significance and many individual landowners played a significant role in the story of the county, other things were happening which may have left less trace in the documents or the landscape but which were, in the long run, of greater importance in the history of Renfrewshire.

The foundation of the burghs and the Reformation settlement were without doubt the two most important events of the later medieval period. Prior to the twelfth century, there were very few urban settlements in Scotland apart from around the castles of Stirling and Edinburgh. David I created some burghs in the mid twelfth century, with trading rights and other privileges. Some were based on small existing settlements, while others were totally new foundations. David also permitted his major nobles and churchmen to found their own burghs, for example, at St Andrews and Glasgow based on the bishoprics. By the death of William the Lion in 1214, there were around 30 royal burghs throughout Scotland. Although little more than the size of a modern village, these centres flourished and were the heart of Scotland's commerce. The burghs of both Renfrew and Paisley grew markedly in the late medieval period.

There is a long-standing debate among historians whether commerce creates towns or towns create commerce. The medieval development of Paisley and Renfrew are good examples of the two sides of the town origin debate. Renfrew is described as a burgh in a charter of King David, dated 1141, and was designated a Royal Burgh in a charter granted by King Robert III on 10 November 1396. Its rights were confirmed in charters of 1575 and 1614. The later charter, granted by King James VI, confirmed the burgh's market and fishing rights and made additional provisions to protect Renfrew's position as a Clyde port (the significance of this will become apparent in a later chapter). However, throughout the later Middle Ages many of the surviving documents record Renfrew quarrelling with surrounding burghs in order to protect its privileges rather than extending and exploiting them like Glasgow and Paisley. The Royal Burgh of Renfrew was a creation of the early Stewarts who moved on to greater things. In the later Middle Ages, the neighbouring township of Paisley had more effective patronage and its inhabitants a more expansive approach. It was also situated at the lowest fording place on the River Cart, a greater stimulation to trade than any Royal Charter.

By the later Middle Ages, the Abbey had a considerable rental income which, when added to the proceeds of the abbey as a place of pilgrimage, income from the adjacent township of Paisley and donations from local landowners, made it a very wealthy establishment. It was frequently visited by Stewart monarchs. Its wealth was reflected in the abbey buildings (though little remains of the original abbey which was burnt by the English in 1307) (Fig. 60), and it was exploited by a series of very able abbots who held office from the end of the fourteenth century to the Reformation.

The most notable of these were Abbot Tervas (1444–59) and Abbot George Shaw (1471–98). They protected Paisley's interests against the attentions of the Bishops of Glasgow, rebuilt the Abbey several times, and played their part in the affairs of the kingdom. Abbot George Shaw built a great precinct wall 5m high around the abbey policies and was instrumental in gaining a charter which raised Paisley to the status of a Burgh of Barony in 1488.

The little township was already a Burgh of Regality by virtue of a charter granted by King Robert III (who is buried in the Abbey) but its elevation to a Burgh of Barony meant that it no longer had to pay dues or defer to the Royal Burgh of Renfrew. This was an affront, and a considerable loss of revenue, to Renfrew. Abbot Shaw, however, meant business. He built a tollbooth,

Figure 60   Four-seater sedilia in the south choir wall, Paisley Abbey, thought on
stylistic grounds to be late fourteenth century (MacGibbon and Ross 1896–7).

which was a council office and jail, appointed magistrates and burgesses, and
erected a market cross as an indication of Paisley's new status. This provoked
a midnight raid in 1495 from the inhabitants of Renfrew to 'ding doon' the
cross, which led to a reprisal raid by the men of Paisley. Court action by the
Royal Burgh was robustly opposed and defeated on appeal. The Abbot had
established Paisley as a burgh beside the wall of the great Abbey church.

The St Mirin Chapel, which forms an extension to the south transept, was
endowed at this time. An inscription records the name of the benefactor, James
Crawford of Kilwynet, and the altar screen, which was moved to the chapel
from another part of the abbey, dates from the same period. Though thought
to depict the life of St Mirin, the costumes and buildings are contemporary
in style and belong to the fifteenth century. There are 10 screens in all, and
there have been various theories about what they represent. The most likely
is that they correspond to a passage in the contemporary manuscript book of

daily readings known as the Aberdeen Breviary and possibly represent: Mirin as a child being brought to St Congal's monastery in Bangor; St Congal investing Mirin; Mirin becoming Prior; Mirin going to preach to an Irish king but being sent away; Pains of his wife's childbirth visited in the king; Child bring born; King asking Mirin for forgiveness; King and Queen and Mirin reconciled; Mirin in his cell with a heavenly light; Mirin restoring a dead man to life. The chapel is well worth a visit to get some idea of late medieval sculpture. It is our good fortune that it survived the upheaval of the Reformation since it is one of the few surviving intricate decorations from the great years of the Abbey's power and wealth.

One of the most remarkable rediscoveries of Renfrewshire's archaeology in recent years, in November 1991, has to be the Paisley Abbey Drain. It runs in an east–west direction south of the present abbey, between it and the River Cart (Fig. 61). It was constructed in the fourteenth century as the main drain for the abbey buildings, which were more extensive than the present reconstruction and included a chapter house, cloister, mill, gatehouse, etc., all enclosed by a stone wall.

The drain, which varies in height from 1.5m to 2m, is made of finely dressed stone with a pointed arched roof. Howell's guide to the Abbey of 1929 refers to the drain as an 'underground passage . . . apparently leading from the Abbey to the river. It is solidly built. During an exploration of the passage in 1888, 120 carts of rubbish were taken out, among which several articles were found, including fragments of stained glass.'

Thirty cubic metres of silt were removed in the 1990–91 exercise, mainly from the western part of the drain. Notable finds included a complete early sixteenth-century chamber pot, the matrix of an Abbot's seal, a bone dice, lead seals from cloth imported from Europe, fragments of slate covered in graffiti and the earliest polyphonic music notation to be discovered in Scotland. The finds were probably deposited in the drain in the early part of the fifteenth century. The largest category of finds was enough medieval pottery to fill 35 large boxes. Represented were a wide variety of vessels, clays and glazes. Identification of this pottery from the unstratified mud of the drain could reveal much about the life and contacts of the late medieval Abbey. The results of the excavation were outlined in a major conference organised by the Renfrewshire Local History Forum and published in a book edited by John Malden.

By the later Middle Ages, the whole abbey complex would have been enclosed by a high precinct wall (Fig. 61), probably built sometime after 1473

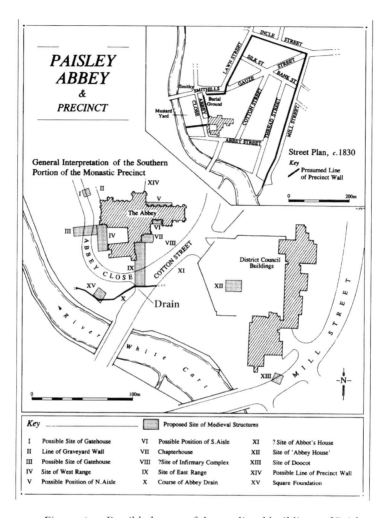

Figure 61   Possible layout of the medieval buildings of Paisley
Abbey and its Precinct showing the line of the
now famous drain (courtesy GUARD).

by Abbot George Shaw, which, although its exact position is unknown, is
believed to have followed the line of Lawn Street (forming the north-west
side), Incle Street (forming the north-east side) and Mill Street (forming the
south-east side). The south-west side of the abbey precinct would have been
the banks of the White Cart and would have thus enclosed an area of around
48 hectares. Water from the river is likely to have been channelled off by means
of a lade from up stream, above the falls, to a mill and then perhaps passed

Plate 1   Jet beads and spacer plates from South
Mound necklace, Houston (Derek Alexander)

Plate 2   Craigmarloch vitrified wall showing inner and outer stone
wall faces with mass of vitrified wall core in between (Helen Nisbet).

Plate 3   Duncarnock hill fort with rampart visible from
the north-west across Glanderston dam (Ingrid Shearer).

Plate 4   Samian bowl from the Antonine period Roman fort at Whitemoss near Bishopton (© Hunterian Museum and Art Gallery, University of Glasgow).

Plate 5   Lurg Moor Roman fortlet from the north–west
(© Crown Copyright: RCAHMS (RCAHMS Aerial Photography).
Licensor http://www.rcahms.gov.uk).

Plate 6   Arthurlie Cross in Barrhead (Ingrid Shearer).

Plate 7   Denniston motte, Milton Bridge, on ridge
above Gryffe Water near Kilmacolm (Ingrid Shearer).

Plate 8   West front of Paisley Abbey with its original twelfth-
century door and later lancet windows (Ingrid Shearer).

Plate 9   Silver coins from the hoard found in Bell Street, Renfrew (©
Hunterian Museum and Art Gallery, University of Glasgow).

Plate 10   Finely carved tomb recess of Sir Robert Sempill, First Lord
Semple, in the Collegiate Church, Castle Semple (Derek Alexander).

Plate 11   Coffins found during rebuilding of graveyard wall at
Kilbarchan Old Parish Church (© Addyman Archaeology).

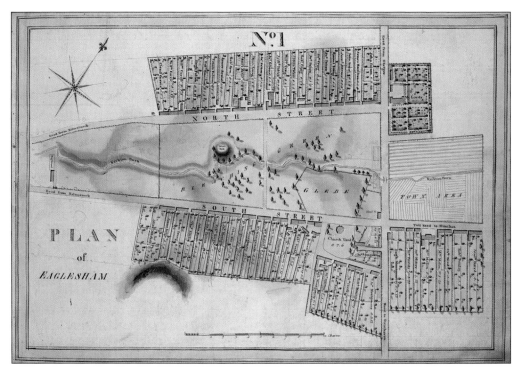

Plate 12   Plan of Eaglesham village by John Ainslie in 1789 including
Moat Hill in centre of village green. (National Archives of Scotland
© Earl of Eglinton and Winton).

Plate 13 Busby waterfall and mill foundations (© Stuart Nisbet).

Plate 14 Crofthead Mill and Neilston village (Ingrid Shearer).

Plate 15   One of the octagonal gun positions at East
Yonderton anti-aircraft battery, Houston (Derek Alexander).

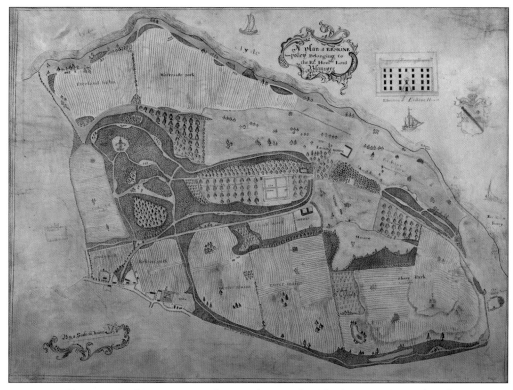

Plate 16   Erskine House and grounds, 1774 by Charles Ross (reproduced
courtesy of the National Archives of Scotland – RHP1043).

via the Abbot's house through the abbey drain before re-entering the White Cart. The recent archaeological investigations, however, revealed little of the thirteenth–fourteenth century buildings of the Abbey, and the artefactual material recovered from the abbey drain appears to date from the fifteenth century onwards, suggesting the drain was either a late construction or that silt had previously been cleaned out prior to this date. The latter explanation seems more likely.

There is a wealth of historical records relating to the abbey and, although those most often quoted are the early ones, there is a great deal of information on the fourteenth–sixteenth centuries as well. Following the destructive raid by the English in 1307, the abbey appears to have fallen on hard times, despite having acquired money from a number of new churches. One of the benefactors who helped towards the reconstruction of the abbey was Alan Cathcart. In the later fourteenth century, there are still reports of building work at the abbey, including work by John Morow who had also worked on Melrose Abbey. Robert II had tombs built for his mother and father in 1379, and in 1406 Robert III, who died probably following a heart attack on hearing his son had been captured by the English, was buried in front of the high altar. There is now a memorial to Robert III, constructed in 1888, in the choir. In the early fifteenth century, the abbey appears to have had two rival abbots, John de Lithgow and Thomas Morow (the latter was heavily involved in the negotiations for the release of James I). Only in 1432 was the matter decided in favour of Morow, but during this time the abbey buildings appear to have been neglected and fallen into disrepair. This was probably when the drain silted up.

Later in the mid fifteenth century, Thomas Tarvas, a Tironesian monk (not a Cluniac) was appointed abbot and during his period of office the finances and care of the buildings appear to have improved greatly. During the reign of James IV, the monastery appears to have prospered since its Abbot, George Shaw, was the teacher of James and his brother. It was in Paisley Abbey that James IV was absolved of any connection with the death of his father after the Battle of Sauchieburn. George Shaw was succeeded by his nephew Robert Shaw, who in turn was replaced in 1525 by John Hamilton, illegitimate son of James, first Earl of Arran. Hamilton was a powerful man who was appointed a King's Councillor in 1540 and Treasurer of Scotland in 1543, and eventually Archbishop of St Andrews and Legate of Scotland in 1547. He was a supporter of Mary, Queen of Scots and, following the Reformation, was imprisoned for a period for celebrating Mass. He was with Mary at Langside in 1568 and was eventually hanged in 1571 for supporting her. After the Battle of Langside, Lord Semple was made commendator of the abbey, although it was restored to Claud Hamilton in 1587, and he was created Lord Paisley in 1594. Although during the Reformation the abbey buildings may have suffered, the greatest destruction at this time was caused by the collapse of the central tower, which almost completely destroyed the choir and the north transept.

Little archaeological work has been undertaken in either Paisley or Renfrew to examine the remains of the medieval towns. It is unlikely that either would have been large, like Edinburgh or Perth, and they do not appear to have been defended by stone town walls. A straggle of houses and shops would probably have existed along the main thoroughfares, probably backed by plots of land enclosed by hedges and fences.

Another type of structure which would have formed a characteristic feature of the medieval landscape is the mill. Although mill sites are often mentioned in historical records – Paisley Abbey, for example, is described as having two mills, at Ardgowan and Drumgrain – they have proved very elusive to archaeologists. The main problem in identifying sites is that the constant feature in the history of the mill site is the fall of water that produces the power. This does not change over the years, so succeeding generations rebuild mills on the same sites. Another difficulty is the likelihood that most mill structures would have been of timber rather than stone construction. A vertical wheeled mill, of timber, was found during excavations beside the Poldrait Burn in Glasgow but was dated to after the fifteenth century. It is not known exactly when vertical wheeled mills were first introduced into Scotland, and it is probable that any mills constructed prior to the early fourteenth century may have been horizontal mills, similar to the twelfth-century example excavated at Orphir, Orkney. It is likely, however, that most mills would have been located close to the towns and throughout the surrounding countryside often associated with earthwork or stone castles, churches or villages.

The majority of the inhabitants of late medieval Renfrewshire lived off the land. The abbey gained a great deal of its income from farm rents. The market of the new burgh dealt mainly in agricultural produce. Given the importance of farming, what were the farms of this time like and are there any surviving remains? While it is possible to identify some sites from place-name and charter evidence, the problem is the familiar one that good farm land and sheltered, dry house sites are the same now as then – with the result that medieval farms were probably in the same position occupied by some twentieth-century farm houses.

The countryside around the small towns would have been scattered with small farmsteads. There are a number of sites which can be interpreted as medieval farmsteads. Excavation last century at Castlehill, Dalry, Ayrshire, revealed the remains of a timber hall sealed below an earthen mound. These remains have been interpreted as a twelfth-century timber hall which was replaced by a small motte. It is probable that that a large number of similar undefended timber halls formed the focus of many small farming settlements in Renfrewshire.

There are, however, one site and two excavation reports that give us some idea of late medieval farms in this area. At Knapps, close to Kilmacolm golf course, Frank Newall excavated a stone-walled circular enclosure. This revealed traces of a medieval farmstead with a number of stone and timber-built structures overlying an earlier, prehistoric settlement. Pottery from the medieval occupation suggested a fourteenth-century date. The reoccupation was certainly at a period before 1635 when stones were removed to rebuild the manse beside Killellan church.

Knapps raises an interesting question about farmhouses at this period. Although it is circular by virtue of the fact that it reuses an existing structure, when were circular farms superseded by rectangular buildings, of which there are many examples from later centuries? The site at Laggan Hill (discussed below), which consists of circular and rectangular structures, may provide some answers.

Sherds of medieval green glazed pottery, possibly fourteenth century in date, were recovered from the excavations at the large Iron Age fort on Walls Hill. This was a more significant site than Knapps, as Newall interpreted the structure as the earliest local example of the typical post-medieval farmhouse – with all of the chambers in a single range.

The cobbled area was the byre; the living area is identified by a hearth and a scatter of pottery and a third chamber whose presence was indicated by postholes. The building made use of the surviving prehistoric walls. It is difficult to identify this site on the ground at Walls Hill today, but it is undoubtedly an example of an important stage in the development of farmhouse types.

It is probable that this site was situated within the Forest of Paisley and would have formed an ideal base for the actions of James Douglas in 1307, during the Wars of Independence. This evidence for reuse of the site at Walls Hill may be supported by the pollen evidence, which can be used to detect changes in the surrounding vegetation and, by inference, changes in land use.

Figure 62   Castle Semple Collegiate Church built in 1504
by John, first Lord Semple (Derek Alexander).

A recent study of a pollen core from Whittliemuir Dam, immediately to the east of Walls Hill, reveals a period of major decline in tree cover after 1200 AD, which may reflect the clearance of woodland to provide land for both pastoral and arable farming.

There were a number of chapels spread throughout Renfrewshire prior to the Reformation, of which the Castle Semple Collegiate Church is the most remarkable survivor (Fig. 62). The remains of this early sixteenth-century church stand, roofless, at the northern end of Castle Semple Loch close to the location of Castle Semple. It was only briefly occupied as a collegiate church. Built and endowed by the first Lord Semple in 1505, the tower and the blocked off windows are original. It was remodelled by the addition at the east end of an apse and pointed style windows following the death of Lord Semple at Flodden in 1513. Of particular note is the tomb of the first Lord Semple set into the north wall (Plate 10). The Reformation in 1560 and the eclipse of the Semples led to its abandonment as a collegiate church in the mid sixteenth century when it was divided internally by cross walls for use as burial vaults.

Few of Renfrewshire's later medieval parish churches survive. At Neilston Parish Church there is a Gothic window incorporated into the rear of the present structure, while Mearnskirk contains part of an earlier sixteenth-century structure. Likewise when Kilbarchan Old Parish was rebuilt in 1724 it incorporated the north aisle which was associated with the Cunninghames of Craigends and was part of an earlier medieval church. At the Old Kirk, Kilmacolm, the present church dates from 1831 but contains the remains of thirteenth-century lancet windows and piscine, and the Murray Chapel contains the Porterfield Tomb dated to around 1560.

Other Renfrewshire churches contain late medieval sculptures. The mid Victorian Renfrew Old Parish Church contains the early fifteenth-century tomb that commemorates Sir John Ross of Hawkhead and his wife. Despite some repairs to the figures and canopy, the heraldic panels are well preserved (Fig. 63). The church also contains the (possibly fifteenth-century) altar/tomb known as the Motherwell monument. The church at Houston was built in 1874–75 on the site of an earlier eighteenth-century church. The interior contains a fifteenth-century memorial to Sir Patrick Houston (Fig. 64). This consists of the recumbent effigies of man and wife. Although St Fillan's Church is a simple rectangular, unroofed structure with a lintel dated 1635, it is probably on the site of an earlier church since the graveyard contains medieval gravestones with sword decorations. There is a similar fifteenth-century gravestone with sword and cross built into the wall beside the gateway into Kilbarchan Old Parish Church.

Many ecclesiastical sites would have been private family chapels, although some may also have acted as parish churches, while others would have marked local burial grounds. Unfortunately, after the Reformation many of these were abandoned, fell into disrepair and were subsequently robbed of their stone for building purposes. Of over 20 reported chapel sites in Renfrewshire, none survive. Many of the former chapel sites are indicated by place names, for example, Chapel farm (NS 325 695) stands close to the location of a chapel endowed by the Lyle family, near Duchal Castle. A hermit of the chapel, a Master David Stanyer, witnessed a deed in 1555. Close to Chapell House, in West Arthurlie, Barrhead, there was a chapel and a well dedicated to St Connal or St Conval (NS4930 5887) which had fallen into decline by 1450. Other chapels appear to have been associated with parish churches. St Catherine's Chapel, Kilbarchan, was built in the graveyard of the parish

Figure 63   Fifteenth-century burial tomb of Sir John Ross of Hawkhead and his
wife in Renfrew Old Parish Church (MacGibbon and Ross 1896–7).

church, and records reveal that Robert III confirmed a grant of land in 1401
to provide a chaplain for both church and chapel. In Eaglesham, prior to the
construction of the church in 1790, a small chapel was used as the main place
of worship in the village, probably under the patronage of the Montgomeries
(later the Eglingtons).

Historical records also reveal the existence of a number of other chapel sites
including one at Newark Castle, Port Glasgow (perhaps in the courtyard) and
one at the Steward's manor of Blackhall in Paisley can be inferred, since its
chaplain witnessed a charter in 1272. It is clear that lay patronage of chapels was
very common, and many of the sites are associated with the major landholding
families in the area, often located close to castle sites; chapels close to Duchal,
Newark and Blackhall castles have already been mentioned. The Knoxes of
Ranfurly, Bridge of Weir, had a chapel beside the Pow Burn (NS3850 6533),
c.200m north of their tower-house, while a possible site at Chapel farm, near
Houston (NS 410 682), may have belonged to the Flemings of Barochan. The
sites of many other chapels have been built over by the expansion of towns,

Figure 64   Effigy of Sir Patrick Houston
(d.1450) within Houston Parish
Church (Derek Alexander).

such as St Lawrence's Chapel and burial ground in Greenock (NS2834 7587); a chapel and burial ground at Chapelton farm, Port Glasgow (NS 312 729); St Roque's Chapel (NS 4756 6389) in Paisley, which belonged to the Abbey; and another in School Wynd, Paisley, dedicated to St Nicholas.

In addition to the recurrent association of chapels and graveyards, there were also numerous holy wells. Holy wells are recorded at the site of two possible chapels at Warlock Gates (NS3637 6054) and St Bryde's (NS 385 609), both endowed by the Semple family prior to the construction of the Collegiate Church. The chapel dedicated to St Conval in Barrhead was also supposed to have a well, and the name of Chrisswell Chapel is also telling.

The remains of Chrisswell Chapel were located on the south-east side of the A78 Greenock to Inverkip road, just to the south-west of the IBM factory.

Old map evidence suggests that the building originally measured 20m long, north-west to south-east, by 12m wide. Only parts of the two side walls survived until the 1970s. The walls were constructed of mortared rubble held together by rubble and contain small slit windows. The chapel appears to have been founded with the support of Robert II (1371–90) and Robert III (1390–1406) who both issued an act from there. Unfortunately, like many of Renfrewshire's medieval chapels, nothing survives of this site today.

11

Early Modern Renfrewshire

AN INTRODUCTION

The passage of time destroys the remains of earlier ways of life. If a building becomes redundant, there is very little reason for subsequent generations to preserve it. The archaeologist's task is made more tantalising, but in some respects easier, when only a few monuments arbitrarily survive from a bygone age. When enough survive for them to be casually destroyed, he or she is drawn into more pressing debates about significance and preservation. However, it is interesting to note that a mere three centuries after the events, it is difficult to find sites relating to the earliest stages in the development of trade, mining and agricultural improvement in Renfrewshire.

This is only one of the problems facing the post-medieval, or industrial archaeologist. Another is lack of perspective. Students of earlier ages can identify significant changes in society that have left their mark on the archaeological record. Often they occurred hundreds or even thousands of years apart. The industrial archaeologist, on the other hand, has to identify which monuments are most important from a great many more examples, all created in a relatively recent period of dramatic social and economic change. In a densely populated area like Renfrewshire, there is the additional problem that many of the sites have been built over several times during the period.

Despite these problems, it might be said that the landscape of Renfrewshire has undergone at least four periods of fundamental change in the last 300 years. The causes of these changes are relatively easy to identify from the written sources. If we take the late medieval landscape described in the Poll Tax Roll of 1695 as the starting point, the first period of change took place in the early eighteenth century. The agents of change were the growth of trade, the development of the textile industry, agricultural improvement and mining. The second stage was triggered by the application of water power to large-scale textile manufacture, in particular the construction of cotton mills. It is described by contemporary witnesses in the *Old Statistical Account* and recorded on Ainslie's Map of Renfrewshire. The third stage followed shortly afterwards and was facilitated (in the county of his birth as elsewhere) by James Watt's refinement of the steam engine. This, with other factors, led to an exponential growth in engineering (including shipbuilding) and the extraction of iron, coal and clay. It also made possible the building of railways, which, once again, affected the distribution of population and the location of industry. All of these changes greatly influenced population density and distribution – towns and villages grew in size, as did their attendant works, such as roads and reservoirs. This landscape is depicted on the first-edition Ordnance Survey maps of the county, which were surveyed in the 1850s. The last fundamental change to people's living and working patterns was brought about, within the twentieth century, by the motor car, the aeroplane, electricity and more pervasive state planning.

Each of the changes outlined above resulted in the establishment of a pattern of land use (for example, cotton and shipbuilding did much to industrialise riverside and shoreline areas of the county). Our aim is therefore to identify surviving monuments that illustrate the first, or subsequent important, phases in land use changes, which will allow us, in turn, to construct a coherent post-medieval archaeology of the county and begin to understand why the landscape looks as it does today.

In medieval times, the landowners controlled the production of the countryside and small urban communities were controlled by the organisation of burghs. This too broke down during this period. Renfrew, the Royal Burgh with most rights, did not develop at the rate of the smaller burghs of barony. Port Glasgow was established to give Glasgow burgesses a seaport. But, as the career of James Watt shows, the burgesses system of control broke down as industry developed and the guilds could no longer control the burgeoning demands of the developing economy.

The old and new systems evolved as they interacted with one another. For example, the landed families in the area obviously controlled the rights to the land. Landowners who were willing to work with commercial interests (which was one of the principal reasons for the initial success of the textile industry) could at various times sell land for industrial development; sell water rights; feu land for housing; exploit minerals on their land; finance the construction of mills; finance turnpikes and canals and later railways. It is important to emphasise that these activities (though pursued by landowners all over the country) were new to the feudal landowning class. This group itself was not static – some families like the Shaws and the Maxwells of Pollok persisted; some like the Maxwells of Stanely and the Semples failed; and new, sometimes short-lived dynasties who derived their capital from trade, like the MacDowalls and Millikens joined the group. Their importance for our purposes is not biographical but how their use of landed capital promoted change.

Another constant feature is geography, and here we have to confront an unpalatable truth – especially for Paisley people. The history of Renfrewshire, especially from the seventeenth century onwards, is part of the history of what much later became the Glasgow 'region'. While local historians may close their eyes to the influence of Glasgow and look on it as a 'rivalry', which first raised its head in the disagreements between the Bishops of Glasgow and the Abbots of Paisley, in fact the industrial development of Renfrewshire can only be seen as part of the development of the trade of the Glasgow area. Glasgow provided the impetus for the development of international trade. Grangemouth, as well as Port Glasgow, was sustained by this. Glasgow was the nexus for the exploitation of the resources of the area. Renfrewshire provided coal for the Lanarkshire iron works, and the Lanarkshire iron works provided the raw material for Renfrewshire ship-building and engineering. The Johnstone canal and the Monkland canal were part of the same regional economy. The need of this regional economy to have a deep water west coast port resulted at various times in the establishment of Port Glasgow, the Renfrew railway, the Greenock Turnpike, the Johnstone canal, the Greenock railway, the development of Greenock itself, and the various (ultimately successful schemes) to deepen the Clyde to Glasgow.

Despite this being a local guide, it is also wise to remember that the West of Scotland was itself part of a larger picture. Throughout the period, developments were influenced by English capital and inventions (especially the textile industry). American and French wars were at times crucial stimuli – and barriers – to trade, and contacts with Ireland and the Caribbean produced raw materials, labour and wealth.

A second geographical consideration is the importance of rivers. They have relatively declined in the contemporary consciousness since they are no longer a significant source of power or barriers or aids to travel and trade. The widespread use of motor cars and the level tarred roads they require, conspire to make most rivers, for most of the time, unseen. As Sylvia Clark noted in *The Industrial Archaeology of Paisley*:

> Most [industrial sites] have been determined by the transport provided by the river, canal or railways; but there is also in Paisley a distinct category of industries based on water supply – bleaching, dyeing and printing cloth and yarn, with the attendant industries of soap, starch and chemical manufacture, and also brewing, distilling and tanning.

A third geographical consideration is the importance of geology. Previous writers have inserted geological maps at the start of their accounts of the county, but it is more appropriate to consider the underlying geology in terms of its exploitation in the period 1700 to the Second World War. The maps make sense of the widespread distribution of mineral sites (particularly coal and limeworking) and draw attention to their important role in the economic development of the area, which, for many Renfrewshire communities, rivalled that of the textile industry. The significance of mining is often forgotten, since the mining villages of Inkerman, Quarrelton and Hurlet have now disappeared.

With these factors in mind (and acknowledging that historical development is a continuous process, and all divisions are, in some senses, artificial), we turn to the first of these periods.

12

Post-Medieval Renfrewshire

*c.*1600–1750

It is possible to describe the years roughly between the Union of the Crowns in 1603 and the last Jacobite rebellion in 1745 as a single era in the social economic and archaeological history of Renfrewshire (Fig. 65). The county only featured occasionally in national political and religious upheavals, but there were considerable changes in trade, industry, mining and agriculture. Of particular note was the growth of the communities of Paisley and Port Glasgow.

It may seem on the face of it ridiculous to call the mid sixteenth century to the early eighteenth century 'more peaceful times'. Metcalfe, for example, in his history of the county devotes over 150 pages to this period describing (among other events) the violent feuds and manoeuvring which took place in the area during the reign of Mary Queen of Scots; the Cunningham/ Glencairn Semple/Hamilton struggle for Abbey lands; the disruption caused by the proximity of Dumbarton, which was a potential landing place for French aid: the survival of the old religion in Paisley and the resistance to the Reformed church; the Union of the Crowns; the National Covenant; the Civil War; the Cromwellian Union; Covenanting times; the Revolution Settlement and the events leading up to the Union of 1707. But Metcalfe, like all historians, was a product of his times and his sources. He had access to presbytery records (for church history, witchcraft and Covenanters) and to the documents and charters of the landed gentry – and there certainly are Renfrewshire sites which can be identified with the events he describes. For example, the Gallow Green in the west end of Paisley was where four women and two men were hanged on 9 June 1697 as a result of the Bargarran

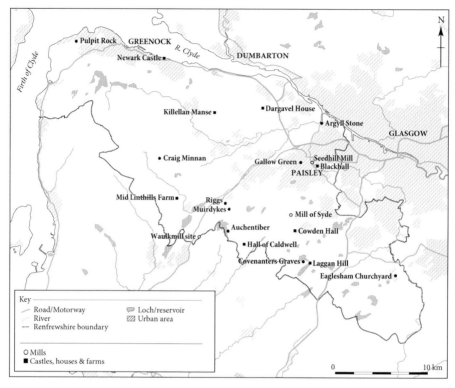

Figure 65   Map of post-medieval sites in Renfrewshire (Ingrid Shearer).

witch trial when they were accused by the 12-year-old Christian Shaw. The presbytery records only mention that the victims were burnt. The Gallow Green is now entirely surrounded by buildings but can be accessed by a path opposite Tannahill's Cottages in Queen Street.

Muirdykes Farm, near Howwood, was the scene of a skirmish in the abortive rising led by the Earl of Argyll in 1685 in support of the Duke of Monmouth's revolt against the succession of King James II. The battle of Muirdykes was fought on 18 June 1685 between troops under the command of Sir John Cochran for the Earl of Argyll against the forces of James VII and II. Argyll had raised an army to support the Duke of Monmouth's rising in southern England but following an ineffectual campaign on the north of the Clyde most of his force melted away. Argyll, separated from his troops, was captured near Inchinnan (see below), while Cochran and around 70 followers pressed on into the Renfrewshire hills. Cochran's progress was blocked by a large party of loyalist soldiers, and he took up a defensive position from which he apparently beat off attacks on both the left and right sides, including

Figure 66   The Argyll Stone (also known as St Conval's Chair) at Inchinnan
close to the spot where The Duke of Argyll was captured after his
failed rebellion in 1685 (Derek Alexander).

some hand-to-hand fighting. The skirmishing appears to have continued
until nightfall when Cochran and his force slipped away. On hearing of
the capture of Argyll, the force disbanded and dispersed. Cochran was later
captured but escaped execution after a bribe was paid by his father. The site
of the skirmish is located on Muirdykes Mount *c*.1.5km south of Howwood.
A number of bullets were reported to have been found on the site in the
nineteenth century.

The Argyll Stone, at Renfrew, is really *two* large boulders enclosed by a
metal railing and marks the spot where the ninth Earl of Argyll, Archibald
Campbell, was captured on 18 June at the close of his rebellion in 1685. This
stone (Fig. 66) is actually an Early Historic cross base that must have had a
close association with Inchinnan Parish Church on the other side of the river
and may even have stood beside the road leading to the fording point of the
river. Argyll had only returned to Scotland at the start of May from Holland
after spending three years abroad. His aim was to start a revolt to topple the
Catholic King James VII of Scotland who had succeeded his brother Charles II

to the throne of Great Britain as James II. Having left what remained of his army, the Earl with a single follower was stopped from crossing the river by a troop of mounted militiamen. While trying to escape, Argyll was struck down by a drunken weaver, John Riddell, who came out of a nearby cottage and hit the Earl on the head with the flat of a broadsword. Riddell was awarded £50 for his action. Argyll was taken first to Glasgow and then to Edinburgh Castle under a guard of militiamen commanded by Sir John Shaw of Greenock. He was beheaded by the Maiden on 30 June.

Finally, there is a memorial in Eaglesham Churchyard to Covenanters Gabriel Thomson and Robert Lockhart.

These sites are significant, but the dynastic and religious struggles of the period produced only spasmodic violent episodes. Although these are well documented in a large number of contemporary sources and emphasised in previous histories, we would suggest that the experience of most people, for most of this time, was of more peaceful conditions. Is there archaeological evidence to support this view?

LAIRDS' HOUSES

The main evidence of peace comes from a small group of domestic buildings dating from the seventeenth century, which very clearly indicate the changed character of the times. They are in the main lairds' houses, which by their broader windows, undefended doors and lack of thick defensive walls and gun loops, suggest a more peaceful era. Good examples of such houses include Cowden Hall, Killellan Manse and Blackhall. MacGibbon and Ross's drawing of Blackhall shows a three-storey hall with large windows and a ground floor door, suggesting a rebuilding in this period. Less than half a mile away is the largely sixteenth-century Place of Paisley, restored in the twentieth century as part of the Abbey buildings. Originally the conventual buildings of the medieval abbey, they were transformed after the Reformation by Lord Claud Hamilton into a mansion or town-house. The building was purchased by Lord Dundonald in 1673, and he made further additions and alterations. The Hall of Caldwell also dates from this period.

Newark Castle is located on the shoreline of the Clyde at Port Glasgow but is dwarfed by the large dockyard sheds to the west. The oldest part of this site, which is in the care of Historic Scotland, is the four-storey tower built in 1478 by George Maxwell (after having been given the barony of Finlayston).

Figure 67   The fifteenth-century tower of Newark Castle on the far left with
the late sixteenth-century ornate wing added by Patrick Maxwell
in the foreground (MacGibbon and Ross 1887–92).

The tower is 8.7m by 6.9m with a cellar on the ground floor and a hall on
the first and bedrooms on the third and fourth floors. Original access to the
tower was via a door in the north wall at ground level. A spiral staircase in
the north-east corner led up to the battlements; the parapet is supported on
simple chequered corbelling. The tower would originally have sat at the east
side of a courtyard, access to which was on the west side via a stone gatehouse,
with stone arched entrance and rooms above. Access to the gatehouse was
defended by a number of inverted keyhole-shaped gun loops.

   In the late sixteenth century, around 1597–99, the tower was joined to
the gatehouse by a mansion block built by Sir Patrick Maxwell (one of those
involved in the feud between the Montgomeries and the Cunninghams). The
mansion block is 14.2m long by 8m wide and is joined at either end by wings
to the gatehouse and the tower and is noticeable for its ornamentation (Fig.
67). The ground floor contains cellars (for wine and food), a kitchen and
bakehouse. A scale-and-platt stair leads up to the hall, which has a large

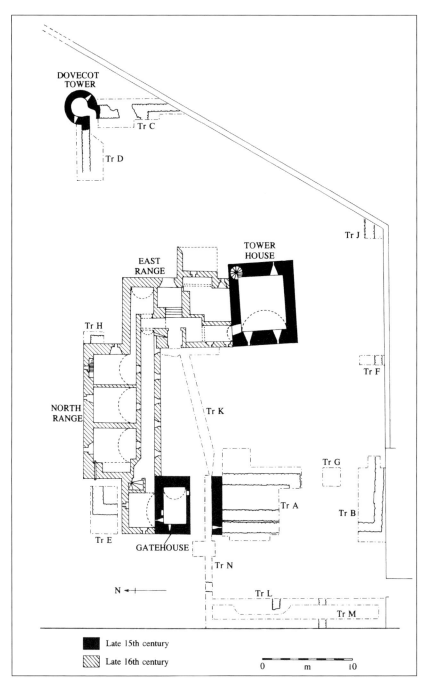

Figure 68   Plan of Newark castle showing two main phases and excavation trenches that located the outer barmkin wall that linked to the doocot tower (John Lewis & Society of Antiquaries of Scotland).

fireplace. The first floor also has a number of other rooms and service stairs down to the wine cellar and kitchen. The second floor contains a number of bedrooms in the roof space divided by timber walls. It is interesting to note that in order to be in keeping with the new mansion the windows on the tower were remodelled to give them pedimented heads.

Recent excavations revealed the full extent of the barmkin wall that surrounded the courtyard and would have been linked to the surviving north-east round tower (Fig. 68). The latter tower was converted into a doocot when the courtyard wall was demolished probably as part of Sir Patrick's late sixteenth-century conversion works. Evidence was found for buildings built up against the courtyard wall, and given the limited extent of the excavations there are likely to be others, especially as the courtyard is quite large.

In 1668 George Maxwell, who was an experienced merchant, sold some land to the burgesses of the city of Glasgow to allow the construction of harbour facilities, which were to become known as Port Glasgow. One of the few artefacts recovered from the excavations was a seventeenth-century Seville olive jar.

The restored late medieval hall-house at Blackhall, on the outskirts of Paisley, was built around 1600 by a Stewart descended from John of Ardgowan, who was an illegitimate son of Robert III. This is another excellent example of the changing fashions of domestic architecture in Scotland at the start of the seventeenth century. Instead of being a vertical construction (i.e. a tower-house) it is elongated, being 14m long by 6.7m wide. As a result of the reduction in the number of floor levels, the basement walls are noticeably thinner than those of towers and are only 1m thick. Although it probably provided more comfort than the traditional upright tower-house, it still demonstrated a need for security, as evidenced by the shot-hole which covers the entrance. The ground floor was divided into three barrel-vaulted cellars for storage, with narrow windows providing light and air. A spiral stair built within a slight projection to the north-east of the main door provided access up to the first-floor hall and chamber, and leading on upwards to the three bedchambers in the attic space with dormer windows in the sloping roof.

Located above the steep slope of the Neilston Gap, above the Levern Water, are the remains of the seventeenth-century hall-house of Cowden Hall. The remains are heavily overgrown and full of rubble into which a number of trees have taken root. The barony of Cowden was held by the Spreulls from at least the fourteenth century. In 1623, it was sold to Alexander Cochrane of Dundonald, and it may have been his son, William Cochrane of Cowden, who built the structure visible on the site today. This consists of a rectangular foundation 14.5m long, north-west to south-east, and 6m wide. The remains are divided into two halves; the southern half having slightly thinner walls may be a later addition. There are traces of an ingleneuk fireplace in the west wall of the northern room and a possible slot for a timber beam (or cruck) in the southern room. The walls are of faced uncoursed stone, roughly dressed, bound together by a strong mortar and are 0.8–1.0m thick. An engraving of 1831 suggests that the building was aligned parallel to the Neilston Gap and was more extensive. The present remains may be the western end of the hall-house with an outbuilding attached to its southern side. There are the remains of a possible lean-to structure abutted against the southern end of this outbuilding. The eastern half of the hall may have been demolished during the construction of the later Cowden Hall, a large mansion for the mill owner.

Other seventeenth-century houses include Auchenbothie Tower, at Rowbank Reservoir, variously called Auchenbothie (by the Ordnance Survey), Auchenbathie in the Poll Tax Roll, Auchinbathie (by Elizabeth Anderson, in her history of the parish) and Barcraigs (in Mike Salter's *Discovering Scottish Castles*). The B776 curves round a corner of the first floor of the old tower. Remains of the infield can be seen behind the ruins of the tower and three cottages (one occupied) line the road. There is also the more complete Killellan Manse, which was much altered in the seventeenth century. It is rubble built, with crow-stepped gables and a circular stair tower. The core of the Hall of Caldwell is also a gabled eighteenth-century structure with considerable later additions. This became the home of the Mures of Caldwell when they recovered their lands from forfeiture in 1698.

The design of tower-houses was also changing to reflect the changing times. Here are two examples from MacGibbon and Ross's great survey of more than 100 years ago (when more of the monuments survived). Dargavel House is a Z-plan tower near Bishopton. Z-plans were MacGibbon and Ross's Fourth Period – the final flourish of tower-house design, when defensive features such as gun loops were giving way to decorative stonework and large windows. The eastern gable has the Maxwell arms and the date 1584, and there is also a sundial dated 1670. In 1851, however, the Maxwell laird of Dargavel converted the house into a Victorian mansion, covering the interior in wood panelling and the exterior in roughcast. He also made considerable alterations to the tower.

Barr Castle, a substantial ruin near Lochwinnoch, is of a more traditional design, and here the earlier gun loops coexist with the later windows and lintels.

Tower-houses indicated peace by sprouting extensions and decorations or by being replaced by small laird's houses. It has been suggested that the architectural drawings on Pont's Map (especially the Place of Paisley) record these changes to previously fortified buildings.

A third peaceful development of the tower-house involves those which survived as part of a nucleated farm township, the tower surviving as a slightly grander farm.

The Poll Tax Roll of 1695 allows us to construct a picture of the Renfrewshire countryside towards the end of the period that we are considering. This is a sketch map of population distribution in the Cart basin based on the place names included in the Poll Tax Roll. The single range farms and unfortified lairds' houses were evenly distributed across the cultivable land. The land itself, though still unenclosed, was, from about the time of the Restoration (1660s), benefiting from the addition of (readily available) lime to the native clay of the lowlands. Although none of the many limeworkings in the county can be dated to this period, the effect would be to increase rural productivity and crop yield in those farms where lime was added to the soil.

Another unexcavated site near Long Loch in Neilston Parish is a single-range farmstead situated inside, presumably earlier, circular walling. The site has been reused as sheepfolds. The structure sits in a sheltered hollow at the end of Laggan Hill and is surrounded by an enclosed 'infield' area. This is potentially the best late medieval farm site in Renfrewshire and would merit archaeological examination.

The single-range farmstead was probably established during this period, and another early unexcavated example may be at Whittliemuir. This revealed surface indications of three structures roughly aligned with a series of enclosures and small fields nucleated around them.

Traces of medieval farming practices will have been, in many cases, ploughed away by subsequent agriculture. However, there are in the upland areas of Renfrewshire portions of rig and furrow which may date back to the medieval period, although they undoubtedly continued in use into the seventeenth and eighteenth centuries.

Rigs present the fieldworker with a problem. A pattern of parallel depressions up to approximately 5–6 metres apart in a field (often seen to best advantage in low light or in conditions of melting snow) could be drainage or rigs. When they follow the contours very closely, they are probably surface indications of the presence of drainage ditches, since old drainage systems tended to follow the line of rigs and/or the line of ploughing. Prior to 1830, the trenches were filled with stones, and after about 1830, tiles/clay drainage pipes were more common. If two patterns of ditches appear in a modern field without reference to the modern field divisions or contours and at an angle to one another then they are probably the remnants of an earlier ridge and furrow field system. The question then arises whether it is likely that traces of ridge and furrow would survive in this particular location since the enclosure of the land several centuries earlier. This is most likely in areas near the growing towns and villages where farming is more likely to have been given over to dairying at an early date.

One of the most extensive areas of wide rig and furrow to survive can be seen on the Oldbar hills, to the west of the road between Hurlet and Barrhead. The rigs here seem to be of the older 18-foot Scots rig, which may have been preserved by being under the (now removed) Rais Woods.

EARLY TEXTILE MANUFACTURE

The entry for Auchenbothie in the Poll Tax Roll introduces another main theme in the economic history of this period

Lands of Auchenbathie Blair

Robert Cochrane, in Tour of Auchenbathie, heritor, 100 lib val; weiver and mert, worth 10,000 merks is 10 lib 6 sh pole; Agnes Cochrane his spouse 6sh; Ro; Jo; Margt; and William Cochrane, childreine, each 6sh   11:16:0

William Wilson, cotter, weiver, and his wife   0:18:0

John Kerr, weiver, cotter, 12 sh trade and pole; Jen Dunsmuire, spouse, 6sh

John Young, prentice, 6sh   1:4:0

John Wilsoune, cotter, weiver, 12 sh trade and pole; Agnes Muire, spouse, 6sh   0:18:0

The tower was by this time a dwelling house for the landowner, his family and employees, and he is described as a weaver and merchant. He farmed the land around and the labourers, or cotters, were also weavers. What is interesting about Auchenbothie is that it is still possible to make out from the site as it is today, an idea of how it must have looked in 1695. The modern road passes very close to the remaining corner of the old tower, which consists of a section of the thick walls of the vaulted ground floor. The field walls of the old infield are clearly visible, as is the row of rebuilt cottages, one of which is still occupied. Built into the interior wall of the ruin of the middle cottage was a stone (visible until the 1970s), which probably referred to the Cochranes. It was inscribed '*16.98 IC. RC. NC*'.

Auchenbothie was not unusual. In the parish of Lochwinnoch 975 people were recorded in the Poll Tax Roll, of whom 37 were weavers, 4 were apprenticed to weavers and 2 were journeymen weavers. Unlike the later settlement pattern, these weavers were scattered widely over the parish, not centred in Lochwinnoch village.

Flax growing was often characteristic of the old multiple-tenancy, runrig, 'unimproved' agriculture. Initially, flax was grown generally only for domestic use. Although this changed throughout the eighteenth century, its contribution was to industrial rather than agricultural importance. Indeed, since the end of the seventeenth century, linen was the most exported Scottish commodity. Andrew Crawford, who wrote the multi-volumed manuscript 'Cairn of Lochwinnoch' held in Paisley Reference Library, states that 'at the Union or before that, some linen or muslin was made about Paisley. Of course, the farmers of Lochwinnoch were encouraged to sow flax seed or lint seed.'

Lochwinnoch itself was not unusual in terms of flax growing, weaving and spinning. The same picture of a distributed textile industry applies to other Renfrewshire parishes, as can be seen from the sketch map of the distribution of rural craftsmen listed in the Poll Tax Roll.

There is very little discussion in any of the standard histories about how Renfrewshire first became a centre for the textile industry, but it is safe to say that the industry was producing more than was needed locally by the late sixteenth and early seventeenth century. Excise and Burgh records tell us that there was a significant trade in wool and linen in the West of Scotland in the early years of the seventeenth century. The long period of relative peace which followed the Union of the Crowns (at which time there was already a sizeable export trade with Ireland and England), coupled with the growth of Glasgow and Paisley, stimulated the industry.

Renfrewshire, Angus, Perthshire, Fife and Lanarkshire were the principal centres for flax and linen production. In Renfrewshire, Paisley, as the lowest crossing point on the Cart (with a bridge from the 1490s), was the centre of this trade, which seems from this early date to have been geographically dispersed, but industrial and capitalist in organisation. The Paisley merchants who controlled the trade in the surrounding fermtouns and villages had access to, and connections with, English markets.

The development of tower-houses provides some archaeological evidence of peace. Is there any similar evidence for this very significant development of textile production? The answer has to be, very little – because it was domestic. The now missing lintel (described above) at Auchenbathie, may have been a pale imitation of the much grander inscriptions above doors and windows at Newark and elsewhere, but it is just possible that inscribed lintels on seventeenth- and early eighteenth-century farms and cottages, such as those at the Weaver's Cottage, Kilbarchan, Mid Linthills Farm, Lochwinnoch and Auchentiber in Neilston Parish, may represent the rising standards of living and increased prosperity resulting from the textile trade.

EARLY WATER-POWERED MILLS

There were also, according to documentary evidence, water-powered textile mills in the county at this time but, again, the problem is identifying early examples.

The technology of water-powered mills was well established for grain milling and, because of the legal obligation of multure, which required a farmer to use a particular mill, there are grain mill sites on rivers and burns all over Renfrewshire. The ruins of the Seedhill grain mill on the Cart at Paisley are a good example, as is Saucel Mill, Paisley, a corn mill powered by the White Cart, now the Watermill Hotel. Many of these early mills were later rebuilt as textile mills, since a good place to build a mill, like a good place to build a farm, does not change.

This adds to the difficulties of a fieldworker trying to find early sites. One early site may be the Mill of Syde for which there is a record of a bond taken by David Brown, Mill of Syde in 1669 and a testament of Robert Lochead, miller at Sydemyln, Neilston Parish in 1742. Traces of it, however, survive. The cart track to it from the road between Foreside and Mossneuk can be easily followed, and much of the lade and the dam is visible; there are also some foundations of the mill building. Further early meal mill sites survive relatively untouched, such as at Garnieland, Elderslie, Rouken, Glentyan and Ross Mill (Eaglesham). The latter site is a rare example of a mill of seventeenth-century date or earlier (shown on Pont's map) which was not reused in modern times.

Given the prevalence in documentary sources of water-powe[r]
mills and the domestic textile industry, it would be useful to identify an ea..,
water-powered textile mill, especially when we consider the later importance
of textile mills. Waulk mills are probably the most likely candidates. Fulling or
'waulking' mills were the only mechanised part of the production of woollen
cloth. The water wheel turned a camshaft, which moved wooden beams
up and down. Wooden blocks were suspended at the end of the beams and
they alternately pummelled the woollen material, which was submerged in a
tub. In the seventeenth century, these mills were an extra source of income
for landowners, and many were to be found on the banks of rural burns and
rivers. One such site which was not subsequently redeveloped was situated
on the Rowbank Burn, in Lochwinnoch Parish. The ruins of other waulk
mills survive in Busby Glen and at Dripps. At Busby the lade, mill walls and
tailrace are well preserved in plan. The mill had an internal wheel, and it is
documented from the seventeenth century.

THE BURGHS OF BARONY

The relative peace and modest increase in agriculture and mills led to the
growth of small hamlets and villages. Throughout Scotland 51 Burghs of
Barony were founded between 1660 and 1707. Renfrew was, of course, the
only Royal Burgh. Paisley was a Burgh of Barony. Its rights, as recorded in
the Register of the Great Seal, were that

> Inhabitants may buy and sell in the Burgh wines, woollen and linen cloth
> wholesale or retail and all other goods or wares coming to it; to have bakers,
> brewers, butchers etc. and workmen in various crafts; a market cross; a weekly
> market on Monday and two public fares yearly, one on St Mirin's Day, with
> tolls and other privileges enjoyed by the burghs of Dunfermline, Newburgh and
> Arbroath.

It is interesting to note that, as early as the end of the fifteenth century,
the wholesale woollen and linen trade was specifically mentioned. It was the
extensive privileges granted in the charter, the bridge and the river, which
contributed to Paisley Burgh's success. The bridge made it the focus of local
(and more long-distance) routes and, from at least 1600, the Sneddon, or
Common Quay, was another means by which the community was connected
to the wider world. By 1710, Paisley had one principal street, half a mile in

length with several other lanes, and it is probable that the population did not exceed 1,500. Paisley was not unusual in that throughout the United Kingdom at this period there was a measurable growth in small textile-producing communities that were close to larger settlements.

The Royal Burgh of Renfrew, as is well known, took exception to Paisley's success and unwittingly presented posterity with a record of Burghs of Barony in Renfrewshire when it petitioned the Convention of Royal Burghs in the 1690s:

> That they have in their presinct the particular burghs of barony or regality after specified viz. Paisley, Kilbarchan, Houston, Kilmacrom [sic], Newark, Cartsdyke, Greenock, Innerkip and Gourock. All of which are in a flourishing condition and have a considerable retail, and the worst of these have a much more considerable trade than themselves.

The Market Cross at Houston dated 1713, but believed by some to be earlier, may be one of the few surviving reminders of the prosperity of the early burghs (Fig. 69).

RENFREWSHIRE'S COASTAL TRADE

Apart from the textile burghs of Paisley and Kilbarchan, the main expansion was on the coast, which introduces one of the main themes of the economic history of the area in the seventeenth, eighteenth and nineteenth centuries: connections to the sea.

Most writers agree that the driving force in the development of the seventeenth-century economy was the large number of new industries established in the region at this time. These included woollen manufacture, soap making, printing and papermaking, sugar-houses and rope-works and coal mining. Glasgow has traditionally been given the credit for much of this, but the physical boundaries of the town were very limited at this early period, and much of what Glasgow has been given the credit for happened well outside the town.

Glasgow became a Royal Burgh in 1611, and the burgesses throughout the period had a very positive attitude to the development of trade. The principal problem they faced was the shallowness of the River Clyde, which meant that only small boats of very shallow draught could make a passage between Glasgow and the deep water of the Firth. The situation can be clearly seen on

Figure 69   Houston Merket Cross topped by
a later sundial (Derek Alexander).

Pont's map, which shows seven islands created by the river as it meandered across the flood plain. (Interestingly, Renfrewshire's only sizeable island and the only one even partially surviving from Pont's time is Newshot Island, which can be approached from near Inchinnan and is well worth a visit.)

Over the succeeding centuries, Glasgow adopted various strategies to solve this problem. The resulting roads, bridges, harbours, canals and, eventually, railways, all had an enormous affect on the establishment and development of Renfrewshire communities.

Attempts were made to dredge the river as early as the sixteenth century. In 1556, with a system of buckets and labour from Renfrew, Glasgow and Dumbarton, the burghs tried to remove the Dumbuck sandbank but by the seventeenth century Glasgow's problem had become acute. Relations between

Glasgow, Dumbarton, Renfrew, Irvine and Ayr were never easy, and there was continual bickering over trade on the river. When Glasgow applied to Dumbarton for land to build a harbour, it was refused. Further down the coast, Troon also rejected Glasgow's approaches.

THE FISHING VILLAGE OF GREENOCK

A similar attempt to purchase the lands of Easter Greenock and Cartsburn were frustrated by the purchase of the lands by Sir John Shaw to protect his own, recently founded, burgh and harbour of Greenock. The fishing village had become a burgh of barony in 1635, and the first feu was granted the following year. (The church had been completed in 1591, and a new parish had been founded in 1594 from part of Inverkip Parish.) The earliest settlement was around the kirk and the West Burn. By the time of the Poll Tax Roll of 1695, there was a population of 746 whose trades are, in the main, described as merchants, sailors, boatmen and seamen. Hamilton of Wishaw, writing in the early years of the eighteenth century states that 'The town of Greenock . . . hath ane good harbour for vessels and is become a place of considerable trade, and is like more and more to increase as specially if the herring fishing continue in the River Clyde . . .'

Sir John Shaw's attempt to frustrate the Burgesses of Glasgow may have had the result of holding back the development of Greenock for some time (although it did continue to flourish), since he inadvertently allowed a neighbouring landowner to benefit from Glasgow's ambition and economic power. It was Sir Patrick Maxwell of Newark who finally solved the problem by selling 'ane mark land of old extent' to the Royal Burgh of Glasgow. The sale was confirmed by a charter of Charles II of 20 January 1668 incorporating the lands into the 'port and harbour of Glasgow'. In 1693, Frances Stevenson was to 'draw ane draught of the hail ground and measure and divide plots for building'. The earliest buildings, which dated from this time and have been subsequently demolished, were situated along the shore and on Custom House Lane.

Greenock, however, continued to flourish. Its harbour had attracted the attention of the Cromwellian commissioner for revenues and customs, Thomas Tucker, and he described it being used by seamen or fishermen 'trading for Ireland or the Isles in open boats, at which place there is a mole or peere', and now attracted ever larger boats. The real impetus behind the development of

Greenock and Port Glasgow was the desire of Glasgow to trade initially with the Caribbean and later with the American colonies. After the Magistrates of Glasgow bought the land at Newark in 1668, John Barns (several times Provost and a prominent Glasgow merchant) bought the property of the Royal Fishery Company in Greenock when that company was dissolved in 1684. There followed the unfortunate episode of the Darien Scheme (whose ships left from Crawfurdsdyke).

Other small ports included Renfrew and the common quay at the Sneddon in Paisley, which had been in use since at least the seventeenth century but could only accommodate vessels of very shallow draught. Greenock began to grow well beyond the capability of natural increase. This relied on migrants coming south via the sea lochs of Argyll in a very early version of the 'Highland Clearances' of two centuries later.

PEOPLE

This chapter began by emphasising the relative peacefulness of Renfrewshire during this period. There were fewer instances when the lives of ordinary people were disrupted by the violent disagreements of the landowning classes which were catalogued in considerable detail by previous historians. Dr Metcalfe, in discussing this period is reduced for the most part to recounting a general history of Scotland, since the county did not figure as prominently as it had done in previous times in the political history of the land. However, Renfrewshire was not immune to the contemporary religious and dynastic disagreements. To paraphrase the history of one and a half centuries in a single sentence (an impossible task), Scotland, in these years, was generally divided into those who supported bishops and the Stewart kings and those who supported Presbyterianism and were opposed to bishops and, when provoked, the Stewart kings. Since the principal disruptions of the previous century had concerned church government and the Stewarts who were now the restored monarchs of the United Kingdom, there were many opportunities for those who wished to instigate civil war. It is, however, significant that Renfrewshire did not feature in the political history of the land as much as neighbouring counties (e.g. Lanarkshire in religious disputes; Stirling and Perthshire in dynastic wrangles). The overriding reason for this was the support for the Reformed church, but we should not totally discount the fact that, because of the increase in trade (demonstrated by the increase in the number of new burghs of barony) and the success of textile manufacturing described above, Renfrewshire was one of the most prosperous counties. As a consequence of this, more of its inhabitants had a vested interest in keeping the peace.

The population of Renfrewshire was strongly in favour of the National Covenant of 1638 and the Solemn League and Covenant of 1643 and may have modestly benefited from the union of Scotland and England under Oliver Cromwell. After the restoration of Charles II and his attempt to re-establish episcopacy, they resisted the provocation of having Highland soldiers billeted on them for two months. It did, however, make them more bitter in their opposition to bishops and patronage, so that there was considerable support for those ministers who stood by their principles and left their livings rather than abandon Presbyterianism. This is the background to the places and monuments in the county associated with Covenanters and their open-air conventicles.

It is noteworthy that, according to the records of Paisley Presbytery, conventicles were held in most of the parishes of the county although the surviving monuments associated with this time are mainly to be found in the upland parishes. The principal monument is the memorial in Eaglesham churchyard to Gabriel Thomas and Robert Lockhart who were killed in 1685. The Covenanters' Graves at the edge of the Moyne Moor in Neilston Parish are unlikely to be graves although the five stones and nearby mound have come to be associated with Covenanting times. They are similar sites to the Covenanter's (or White's) Well and the nearby Pulpit Rock, which are situated on the high ground behind Greenock. The Peden stone commemorates a Covenanting preacher and originally stood between Linthills and Dunconnel in Lochwinnoch Parish. The stone was blasted out of its original position and now stands next to a dyke at the gateway to a field in the farm of Mid Linthills. Also in Lochwinnoch, near Ladymuir Farm, is the Covenanters Hollow associated with the Covenanting preacher James Renwick, reputed to have preached here in 1684. Craigminnan on the Duchal Moor, on the boundary of Kilmacolm Parish, is also associated with Renwick who was the last Covenanting preacher to be executed, in 1688.

The downside of such devotion to Presbyterianism was to give considerable authority to the local presbytery. In the seventeenth century in the county, this authority was used to hunt down supposed witches and, under an Act of Parliament passed in 1563, put them to death. The most notorious case was the seven people burnt at the Gallow Green in the west end of Paisley in 1697 on the evidence of Christian Shaw, the daughter of the Laird of Bargarran. There were also witchcraft cases at this time in Inverkip Parish.

We have seen that Renfrewshire was a lot more peaceful in Covenanting times than the neighbouring counties of Ayrshire and Lanarkshire. It also managed to avoid the upheavals caused by the Stewarts' subsequent attempts to regain the throne which their own ineptness had led them to forfeit. The skirmish which took place at Muirdykes farm near Howwood was fought in 1685 between supporters of the Duke of Monmouth, led by the Duke of Argyll and supporters of Charles II's brother, James II. The Duke of Argyll was captured shortly afterwards near Renfrew and Argyll's Stone, the reputed site of the capture, can still be seen in the grounds of the Normandy Hotel.

Another possible Renfrewshire notable of this time was Captain William Kidd (c.1645–1701). He may have been born in Greenock (although Dundee is also mentioned as his birthplace) and he became a pirate in the late 1690s after a career as a merchantman based in New York. He was hanged in London in 1701. Mention should also be made of Habbie Simpson who was the village piper in Kilbarchan from 1550 to 1620. A statue of Habbie can be seen on the Steeple, in Kilbarchan. This two-storey square building with a tower was built in 1755 and rebuilt in 1782. It has been a school and a meal market and is now a public hall.

13

Agriculture to Industry

The Mid Eighteenth Century (1750–1800)

Economic historians have referred to the period immediately before the Industrial Revolution as 'proto-industrial'. This description is intended to indicate that much of what happened in the Industrial Revolution proper was already happening, and that the 'Revolution' was really a change in the scale of industrial activity and its consequences.

There is general agreement among economic historians that the Union with England did not produce immediate benefits for the Scottish economy. However, Renfrewshire was not typical of Scotland in general and benefited greatly from exploiting the quality English textile market from the start of the century. The years after 1740 marked a further quickening and widening of economic activity. Between the 1740s and the 1780s Renfrewshire was at the forefront of these developments, which were almost bewildering in their diversity, encompassing great changes in textile manufacture, foreign trade, mining, agriculture, transport and resulting in the growth of towns and villages (Fig. 70).

GEORGIAN MANSIONS AND CHURCHES

In the same way that earlier social and economic changes were reflected in the architecture of tower-houses, the increasing prosperity of eighteenth-century Renfrewshire is demonstrated by the large number of surviving Georgian churches and dwellings. The mansions generally consist of a Palladian façade surmounted by a triangular pediment; stairs leading up to a first-floor main entrance; alternate coigning; two to four storeys, with regular orders of

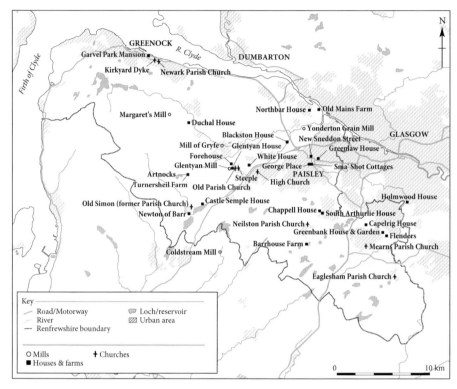

Figure 70   Map of early industry in rural Renfrewshire (Ingrid Shearer).

windows; the main block occasionally flanked by two symmetrical wings. Greenbank, Capelrig, Duchal, the remains of Castle Semple, Garvel Park, the mansions in Sneddon and Mansionhouse Road in Paisley, and Glentyan in Kilbarchan all date from this period and represent the proceeds of colonial trade, improved agriculture and textile and mining enterprises.

Greenbank House estate is located on the outskirts of Newton Mearns and is in the care of The National Trust for Scotland (Fig. 71). The house, built in 1765 by Robert Allason, is a magnificent example of a Georgian mansion with central block joined to two projecting wings by curving screen walls. The walled garden was constructed around the same time and originally consisted of six parts which are clearly shown on an estate plan of 1772 on display in the house. An archaeological evaluation of the area of garden closest to the house revealed traces of cinder paths and flower beds. Highlights of the site include the sundial, which is thought to date to around 1600, and the statue of Foam, a fountain designed by Pilkington-Jackson, which was first displayed at the Empire Exhibition at Bellahouston Park in 1938. Other features of note are the bee boles built into the north-west corner of the walled garden and the fine 'greenyman' sculpture on the pediment of the north-east façade of the main house. Beyond the garden and house, there is a designed landscape of fields surrounded by shelterbelts of trees and avenues. Traces of rig and furrow cultivation can be seen in many of the fields, especially in front of the house. These are remains of the agricultural improvements of the eighteenth century when much of the surrounding estate was enclosed with fences, dykes, ditches, hedges and shelterbelts of trees. Recent field-walking has recovered a large concentration of clay tobacco pipes in the field to the west of the house (Fig. 71 inset).

Only the pavilions (privately owned) and basement storey of the elegant three-storey Georgian mansion built by Colonel MacDowall in 1735 at Castle Semple House, Lochwinnoch, and demolished in 1970, still survive. The elaborate gateway from the village, the 'Warlock Gate' lodges, the walled garden and the 'Temple' (a folly on Kenmuir Hill), the boundary wall complete with horse trough and several features of the planned landscape are other prominent survivals of the estate. Similarly, only the west wing of the eighteenth-century mansion of Blackston House shown in Ramsay's Views survives as a barn. Blackston was once the grange of Paisley Abbey. Northbar House, Inchinnan, built around 1742 is three storeys, and has crow-stepped gables, a porch and armorial panel.

Elsewhere in the county, however, are other good examples of eighteenth-century houses, which reflect the increased prosperity that the rise of many of the early industrial processes brought. Greenbank House has already been discussed, but Capelrig House, in the grounds of Eastwood High School, is a nice example of a country house. It was built in 1769 by Glasgow lawyer Robert Barclay. Another Georgian house is the much altered two-storey gabled Chappell House in Barrhead constructed around 1770 with an associated stable block and pedimented entrance arch. The gabled part of the Hall of Caldwell is an example of a case where the old tower was abandoned early in this period and a new residence built.

This is also the case at Duchal House where the new three-storey, five windows wide, Georgian mansion with its central entrance stairs and a rectangular Palladian pediment was built in 1768 away from the old and no doubt dilapidated castle by the Portefield family, who had bought the estate from the Lyles in 1544. In nearby Kilbarchan, Forehouse is a two-storey, three-bay Georgian house built in 1773 by the Barbers, local bleachers; while just outside the village is Glentyan, a three-storey, five-bay Georgian mansion

Figure 71   Greenbank House built by Robert Allason in 1760s with inset of clay tobacco pipes found in field to west (Derek Alexander).

built between 1781 and 1795 by the Speirs. Garvel Park Mansion in Greenock is a three-storey Georgian mansion, five windows wide, dating from 1777. When local Baillie James Gemmell built it, it was surrounded by parkland.

Many of these houses would have been surrounded by designed landscapes of enclosed fields, gardens and stable blocks. The first Milliken House (1733) was demolished in 1801 and rebuilt in 1826, but again demolished in the 1920s. However, the White House was converted from the original home farm and although the house itself is obscured by trees, the eighteenth-century circular doocot in the grounds is visible from the A737.

The Georgian mansion of Greenlaw House is a two-storey, five-window house constructed by Paisley merchant Richard Corse in 1774 who also built the surviving Johnstone Old Mill in 1782. There is a 'Gothic coachhouse' in a nearby garden, which was originally part of the estate. While many of these wealthy merchants had country houses, they also liked to have ones in town as well. Number 38–40 New Sneddon Street, Paisley is a Georgian town house built for the Lounds brothers, silk manufacturers from London; with five-bay front and pediment it was built around 1775. Another can be seen at number 91–93: Adelphi House, which was built around 1800.

The churches have similar Georgian architectural features and are also expressions of the growing prosperity of Renfrewshire communities. They are generally square or octagonal, rubble or sandstone-built, coigned pavilions, the majority of which have square, tiered bell towers. They represent the prosperity of older Renfrewshire communities (the High Church, Paisley and the kirks at Neilston and Kilbarchan, which contain elements of earlier churches); newly feued, planned villages (Eaglesham, Mearns and Lochwinnoch); and booming coastal settlements (Newark). These substantial buildings, like the new mansions of the landowners, were the product of the increasing economic activity to which we must now turn.

A large number of churches in Renfrewshire date to the eighteenth century. Many are octagonal in form, such as the Calder U. F. (Burgher) Church in Lochwinnoch, 1792, and Eaglesham Parish Church with belfry tower, dating from 1790. The High Church in Johnstone is also an octagonal rubble-built church constructed 1792–94 with tower and spire at the front. All that survives of the former Parish Church of Lochwinnoch, built in 1729, is a crow-stepped gable known as Old Simon.

Constructed in 1773–74, Newark Parish Church is the oldest surviving church in Port Glasgow. It is a square, rubble-built pavilion with alternate coigning. The High Church in Paisley, built 1756–80s, is a square pavilion structure with four-storey bell tower and stepped steeple. Designed by John White, a local baillie who also designed the, now vanished, Paisley Tollbooth. One of the most elegant churches in Renfrewshire is Neilston Parish Church. This square pavilion church has a three-tiered belfry tower, and dates from 1762. The two circular gatehouses at the entrance to the churchyard are unique in Renfrewshire. The one on the left of the gate is the older of the two and is probably pre-1789 while the larger, on the right, probably dates from the early nineteenth century. They have conical slated roofs with unusual circular chimney-stacks. They were undoubtedly used for a wide variety of purposes including mort-house, watch house, offertory and session house.

A whole book could easily be devoted to the churches of Renfrewshire, and graveyards also have a lot to tell us about the county's past. Medieval gravestones bearing swords have already been mentioned at Inchinnan, Kilbarchan Old Parish Church (Fig. 72) and Killellan. Many graveyards provide an interesting visit for researchers pursuing family histories. At Kirkyard Dyke in Port Glasgow a number of gravestones of the earliest inhabitants of Port Glasgow are set into the churchyard wall which was constructed in the 1720s and 1730s, including that of Robert Allason, merchant, who built Greenbank House and died in 1785. The church dates from 1823 and replaced the original of 1717.

However, only in Kilbarchan has any archaeological work been undertaken within a graveyard. In September 2002, Renfrewshire Council rebuilt the wall along the southern side of the graveyard of Kilbarchan West Parish Church and unsurprisingly more than just one skull was found. The work would disturb not just the wall but the adjacent area within the cemetery. The Council therefore called in archaeologists Addyman Associates who undertook the excavation of a 2m wide, 25m long trench (Fig. 73). In total 64 burials were discovered, mostly within wooden coffins (Plate 11). Although the skeletal remains were often poorly preserved it still provided an unusual opportunity to analyse a set of post-medieval Scottish burials.

Excavation quickly revealed that the top metre of soil, which included large numbers of human bones (charnel), within the graveyard was all infill and explained why many of the table-tombs were sitting on the current ground surface. Removing the soil from around these flat tombstones revealed that their six stone legs were still in place below, standing on a former graveyard surface. The infill also contained a large amount of pottery including medieval wares of the fourteenth–fifteenth centuries, post-medieval wares of the seventeenth and eighteenth centuries, and industrial pottery of the eighteenth and nineteenth centuries. It is possible that this material came

Figure 72   Old Kilbarchan Church with medieval grave-slab
built into wall in foreground (Derek Alexander).

from a nearby domestic site, perhaps a backyard of a house. One remarkable
find from this area was a ceramic bird whistle possibly of fourteenth-century
date made in Saintonge, France.

The burials were found in pine coffins and often the lids had collapsed in.
The coffins were often closely spaced, sometimes intercutting, which could
suggest that there had been family plots. Certainly plot boundaries (*lairs*)
could be identified – laid in rows aligned east to west. It is fascinating that
high-status individuals in ornate coffins were placed in lairs adjacent to those
that contained the poorest, densely packed burials. The lowest level of burials
had been placed directly onto the underlying bedrock or indeed was cut into
it. Some of these burials had also been cut by the existing graveyard wall and
must pre-date its construction around 1790.

Of the 64 burials identified, only 56 individuals were preserved, most of
which could be assigned to one of three identified phases: Phase 1, 1724–91,
contained 15 burials; Phase 2, 1791–1850, included 35 burials; and Phase 3,

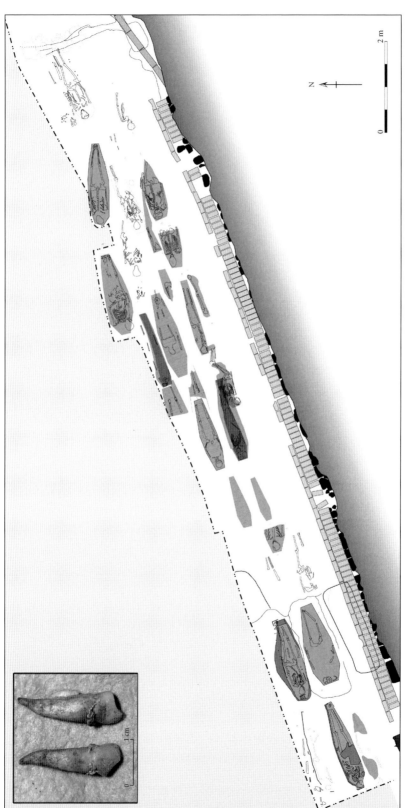

Figure 73   Kilbarchan graveyard plan of excavation of coffins. Inset shows teeth with notches possibly caused by biting thread (Addyman Associates).

1850–90s, contained 5 burials. The analysis of the bones was undertaken by Dr Julie Roberts of Glasgow University, who was able to determine the age and sex of many of the individuals. In addition, the bones provided an insight into the health of the population and how this changed over time.

One very unusual discovery was made when the teeth were examined. Five of the burials displayed a unique pattern of tooth wear. These individuals had a notch or groove worn into one side of the second incisor, canine or first premolar (Fig. 73 inset). In most cases, it was just on the top teeth and usually on the left-hand side. The notch was consistent with repeatedly drawing something through the teeth, perhaps wool or thread. The most likely explanation is that this was a practice carried out habitually by those involved in the weaving trade. In this respect, it is interesting to note that this wear pattern was not found on any of the burials from the earliest phase and was only associated with nineteenth-century burials: the period when weaving was at its most intense in Kilbarchan.

Apart from the teeth, the skeletal remains indicated that there was a general improvement in the health of the local population from the 1790s onwards, perhaps again due to the increased employment and wealth from the weaving industry, which must have led to improvements in the standards of living. It is notable but perhaps not unexpected that many of the remains identified as possibly those of weavers were to be found within the area of tightly packed poorer burials.

The cemetery excavation demonstrated that there were no pre-eighteenth-century burials in this part of the graveyard and that the medieval graveyard boundary must have lain a little further to the north. Of great interest was an area of gravel metalling found at the lowest level of the excavation and pre-dating any graveyard activity. Although badly truncated by the later graves, only medieval pottery was found within the feature, apparently confirming its early date. It is possible that the feature represents either an early road surface or a construction platform for a building, in either case the earliest in situ archaeological remains discovered in Kilbarchan to date. On completion of the project, the human remains were all re-interred in the graveyard.

THE DEVELOPMENT OF TRADE

The history of this period is again affected by the recurring themes of external markets. From a Glasgow base, this was colonial trade via the Renfrewshire

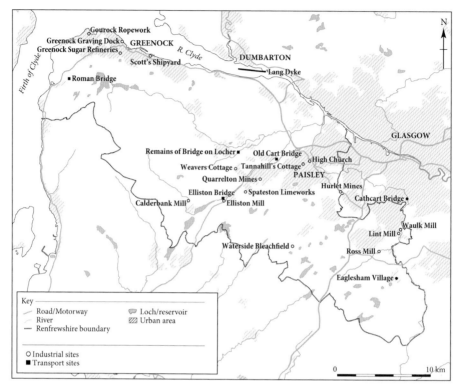

Figure 74   Map showing eighteenth-century industrial
and transport related sites (Ingrid Shearer).

ports, though largely bypassing the heart of the county; from Paisley and the
Cart Basin, it was the textile markets of southern England. These produced a
considerable influx of capital, which was reflected in the economic changes
that occurred throughout the county at this time.

It is, however, a mistake to think that trade was the principal engine of
economic growth. Of comparable importance in Renfrewshire was, for
example, coal mining at Quarrelton and the Hurlet; limeworking throughout
the lowland areas (still visible at Spateston); planned villages like Eaglesham
(Fig. 74); the growth of textile manufacture and bleaching throughout the
county; dramatically increasing agricultural productivity; the application of
water power and the building of turnpike roads. Trade was a part of this
sustained and diverse economic growth.

The disastrous Darien Scheme demonstrated Scottish determination to
participate in overseas trade. Its ill-fated ships left from the Renfrewshire
harbour of Crawfordsdyke in 1695. When the Act of Union of 1707 allowed

Scots merchants access to England's colonies, Glasgow's merchant class lost no time in opening up commerce with North America and the Caribbean (although the general effects of the success of this trade were not felt until the 1730s and 1740s). Glasgow had many advantages over other British ports. It was the starting point of a shorter Atlantic crossing, further from European interference, and Glasgow merchants developed the 'store system', which was an effective method of buying American produce by supplying European goods on credit against the forthcoming harvest. Among the local trades that benefited from exporting to America were pottery and textile manufacture. It should also be remembered that west of Scotland ports traded with England, Ireland, Europe and the Caribbean as well as North America. Foreign trade also provided a model for speculative commercial partnerships in the landowner/merchant class and a stimulus to banking, both of which were important in the later development of the textile industry.

In Renfrewshire, the newly established township at Port Glasgow was the first to feel the effects of increased trade. In the period from 1700 to 1780, the population doubled every 10 years. There were three main phases of development at Port Glasgow. From its founding in 1668 right on the shore, houses gradually spread up Custom House Lane, and a breastwork was built along the sea to the west in 1675 and warehouses and cellars established to serve shipping.

The second phase of growth was the general development inland up narrow lanes and closes from the Breast towards King Street. The original expansion around Custom House Lane had been haphazard, but from 1718 a planned layout was established, with the building of the first church. Kirk Street, leading from the shore to the church, together with King Street at right angles, formed the basis of Glasgow Council's grid plan of the town. Some idea of the speed of development and probably the prosperity of the new settlement can be deduced from the discovery that in 1677 several unauthorised buildings were taken down to allow those who had feued to build.

Given its importance, it is unfortunate that so little remains from the earliest phase of Port Glasgow's history. Much of the oldest part of the town was redeveloped in the early twentieth century by the Lights to provide housing for their workers. One of the few remaining relics of the early town is the Churchyard Dyke. First thought of in 1721 to improve the drainage in the churchyard, it did not reach completion until 1734. Then the dyke was built '3 ells high with divisions by pillars at eight foots distance with a bosom stone in the middle betwixt each pillar for distinguishing the burial places which are to consist of eight foot bridth and twelve foot length'. The burial plots, or lairs, were sold off to the most prominent merchants and shipmasters in the 1730s for £18 Scots.

The old story was that the first Glasgow-owned vessel did not cross the Atlantic until after the Union of 1707. In fact, the Clyde ports were trading sugar with the Caribbean Leeward Islands from the 1640s. It was in 1716 that a vessel of 60 tons burden was launched at Crawfurdsdyke, the first built in the Clyde for the American trade. By 1735 there were 47 square-rigged vessels belonging to Glasgow, 15 of which were engaged in trade with Virginia. This trade was controlled mostly by Glasgow merchants, and the people of Port Glasgow and Greenock supported this work by often acting as storekeepers and forwarding agents.

Almost nothing survives of these seventeenth- and eighteenth-century stores and docks, which were obliterated by the exponential expansion of nineteenth-century Greenock. Three remnants of seventeenth- and eighteenth-century Greenock and Port Glasgow which survive are the well and the gate posts of the mansion house (or factor's house) dating from the 1630s in Greenock; Garvel Park Mansion (1777) in the dock area and Newark Parish Church (1773–74) in Port Glasgow. The original Graving Dock in Port Glasgow (1762); the Gourock Rope Work (in Port Glasgow – the surviving building is more recent); the West harbour (the original Greenock harbour, now filled in); Scott's shipyard (1711) and the Greenock Rope Work were all, until recently, survivors from this period.

The increasing trade passing through Greenock and Port Glasgow brought great wealth to the wider region. In the year 1770, for example, half of all the tobacco brought into Britain belonged to Glasgow merchants. This exponential growth made the problem of onward transport of goods from the Renfrewshire ports to Glasgow all the more pressing. In 1768, Glasgow Town Council asked John Golborne of Chester to report on means of improving the depth of the Clyde between Greenock and the city. He suggested assisting nature by dredging the shallows, and forcing the current, by the construction of jetties and dykes. He claimed that this would allow vessels of up to seven-foot draft to pass up river, at neap tides. A detailed survey of the Clyde by the young James Watt in 1769, and an Act of Parliament in 1770, allowed work to commence on the improvements the following year, with John Golborne as the contractor.

One of the main obstacles was the 'Dumbuck Shoal', caused by the river dividing into two channels and depositing mud. Here Golborne built a dyke which forced the river into one channel and scoured away the obstruction. This structure, built in the summer of 1763 (and added to in later years) is known as the Lang Dyke. It can be seen to this day between Longhaugh Point and just east of Langbank. Quarries which produced the stone for Golborne's jetties and dykes can be seen just south of the shoreline at Erskine, where the remains of a gravity railway survived until recent landscaping removed them.

COLONIAL MONEY; THE MACDOWALLS OF LOCHWINNOCH

If the expansion of trade had a dramatic effect on the coastal areas, the wealth it created had an equal effect on some parts of the Renfrewshire countryside.

At this time, it was quite a common career pattern throughout Britain for the younger sons of the landed gentry to make money in the colonies and return home to purchase property. Land, in the days before the banking system was fully developed, represented wealth and, more particularly, power. The law of entail secured the land, which in turn provided the landowner with social control (through the church and the workings of the poor law, etc.); the possibility of exploiting the mineral rights (for coal, limestone, clay) and water rights (to power mills); and the ability to feu the land for housing or lease it for farming. Many of these new landowners also continued their merchant activities, which were centred in Glasgow as well as in Renfrewshire.

The MacDowalls of Castle Semple in Lochwinnoch Parish are a Renfrewshire example of such a family. William MacDowall, whose family originally came from Dumfriesshire, was sent to the Leeward island of Nevis around 1695 as an apprentice slave overseer. Until recently, much of his background was hidden, and a supposed military career concealed deep involvement as a sugar planter and slave owner. On retiring from the Leeward Islands, MacDowall and his friend James Milliken formed Alexander Houston & Co., which became Glasgow's largest merchant house. The traditional retirement destination of British sugar merchants was the south of England, but MacDowall and Milliken both chose Renfrewshire. Their company specialised in shipping sugar, rum and molasses from their plantations back to Port Glasgow. The principal source of their profits was from the use of hundreds of enslaved Africans whom they personally owned. A 1750 inventory of one of MacDowall's estates lists 192 slaves, worth £4211. Another Renfrewshire landowner, William Cunningham of Craigends, had a plantation on Jamaica, which in July had 296 slaves, collectively worth £15,170.

Figure 75   MacDowall's Georgian mansion house at Castle Semple was one
of the earliest of its type built in Scotland (Ramsay 1839).

There was therefore a group of wealthy Glasgow merchants in the slave,
tobacco and sugar trades, which included MacDowall, Speirs, Milliken and
Cunningham, who were partners in various local enterprises and had large
estates in Renfrewshire. Their significance in this story is that they spent
some of their wealth on agricultural and industrial improvements within
the county

MacDowall bought the estate of Castle Semple in 1727. By 1735, he had
demolished the old Castle Semple and built a new mansion house on the site
(Fig. 75)

Apart from the landed gentry, the eighteenth century was the period
when it first became possible to rise from a humble background to the
peak of achievement. A Renfrewshire example of such an individual was
Robert Allason, grandson of a Mearns farmer, born in 1720. He served an
apprenticeship as a baker in Gorbals, which gave him the key to success in Port
Glasgow – a Glasgow burgess-ship. Moving down to the Port, he cornered
the market in ships' biscuits and soon had shares in several vessels. He built his

own tanyard and weaving factory, and a partnership in the Paisley Stocking Factory provided further goods for export. From the 1760s, he developed a country estate in Mearns, and built Greenbank House and Garden.

Like other improving landlords in Renfrewshire and elsewhere, MacDowall and Allason made changes which increased the productivity and rental value of their lands. From our point of view, one of the most significant projects in which they took part – and which brings together the two strands in our account of this period – is the investment of money derived from colonial trade in the mechanisation of the already expanding textile industry and the promotion of the use of water power.

THE EARLY DEVELOPMENT OF THE TEXTILE INDUSTRY: THE EARLY LINT MILLS

MacDowall was the principal backer of the earliest textile factories in Lochwinnoch Parish. In the great collection of manuscripts entitled *The Cairn of Lochwinnoch*, Andrew Crawfurd reports the formation of a company which 'built a small factory in which they wove linen' about 1740. This is known in Crawfurd's papers and was known in the village as *The Factory Company*. The enterprise was a success. In 1750, the company opened a bleach-field and in 1752, according to Crawfurd, they built 'a large factory in which they made lawns; sprigged; spotted; flowered and purled, gauzes and cravats all of linen'. By 1773 Crawfurd's *History of Lochwinnoch* also records 'two lint mills which go by water'.

MacDowall was not alone in seeking to promote the manufacture of textiles. Allason of Greenbank also developed a lint mill on his lands, at Roadside on the White Cart. As we shall see when we come to discuss the introduction of cotton mills, there were many local landowners (and established merchants) who provided venture capital. There was a willingness in Renfrewshire to speculate on textile developments. The magistrates of Paisley, for example, had put up money for the earliest lint mill in Scotland in the 1730s. Other lint mills were established on the Levern, the White Cart and other smaller rivers. These mills marked an early realisation that economic growth would rely on the application of power to manufacturing processes. Apart from the MacDowalls, other prominent Renfrewshire textile families included the Speirs and Barbours of Kilbarchan and the Carlisles, Polloks, Kerrs and Orrs of Paisley. From the 1750s textile 'manufactories' developed in

Paisley. Initially these were not powered but used centralised production to control quality.

Most of the early partnerships consisted of combinations of three types of people – the person (usually a landowner/merchant) who put up the capital; a skilled, usually small-scale, manufacturer who had practical knowledge of the trade; and a merchant who could deal with the distribution. Part of the explanation of Renfrewshire's enormous success in textile manufacturing in the next century was due to the existence of the sort of social networks within the county, in the early years, which could produce such partnerships. The distribution was from a very early period based on Renfrewshire merchants who controlled all stages of textile production through weaving and spinning to bleaching and finishing, and ready-for-sale. In general, as we have noted, the industry was from the start capitalist in nature, but dispersed in operation. After the advent of water power, the dispersed nature of the textile trade was due to the development of water resources in rural areas.

The establishment of the textile industry was as significant as the development of Port Glasgow for the future prosperity of the county. The linen trade was the principal trade of Scotland at the time of the Union of the Parliaments in 1707. In 1727, this parliament passed two Acts that were to have a profound effect on the development of the industry. (This was in the wake of the 1715 Jacobite rebellion, so part of the motive may have been to encourage the Scots to work in peace rather than revolt.) The first was *An Act for the better regulation of the linen and hempen manufacture in Scotland*, and the second was *An Act for encouraging and promoting fisheries and other manufactures in Scotland*. These resulted in the formation of The Board of Trustees for Manufactures – 21 public-spirited landowners, lawyers and merchants, together with a small staff, who set out, by means of grants, examples and regulation, to improve the quality and quantity of Scottish production. This far-sighted example of government intervention involved, among other things, the payment of a bounty of 15 shillings per acre to farmers to grow hemp, setting up spinning schools for girls and stamping all Scottish linen to guarantee quality. Its success can be judged by the fact that by 1782 there were 371 lint mills in Scotland. Angus, Fife and Perthshire were the principal centres, but they were closely followed by the counties of Lanark and Renfrew, which could command a higher price because of the finer quality of their linen.

We should bear in mind that, because the linen industry is so well-documented with Board of Trustees and other records, it obscures the importance of other textile manufactures, such as silk and muslin, which from the 1750s became much bigger industries in Renfrewshire. Renfrewshire's independent success overtook the Government-controlled Board of Trustees for linen manufacture.

Where can we see the physical remains of the mid eighteenth-century textile boom? In Lochwinnoch, according to Andrew Crawfurd, 'many houses of two stories in a better style of masonry than before were built with freestone from the quarry about 1720'. They must be in the main street of the village since they were described as the first significant addition to the 'Auld Kirktoun'. The proceeds of flax dressing, spinning and the weaving of linen cloth can be seen in other Renfrewshire villages, although many of the cottages built at this time have undergone several subsequent changes, and many surviving weavers' cottages date from the late eighteenth and early nineteenth centuries. The weaving areas of Maxwellton, in Paisley, and Kilbarchan expanded from the 1740s onwards. Firstly, the weavers produced fine linen cloth (a significant amount of which was bound for the London market), then from about 1759, silk weaving increased, with the help of Spittalfield capital.

Where are the sites of the earliest textile mills? This is a more complicated problem. Industrial concerns tend to rebuild on the same sites and we are faced once again with the problem we have with settlement sites in a small county like Renfrewshire – a large number of significant early sites must be under or part of buildings that are currently occupied. Elliston Mill, at Howwood, was advertised for sale as a flax mill in the mid nineteenth century; this building has had many subsequent uses, which have removed all traces of textile manufacture, although the mill dam and lades can still be traced on the hillside behind.

The difficulties encountered trying to discover the position of eighteenth-century lint mills is a good introduction to the general problems encountered by fieldworkers trying to identify early industrial sites. Apart from the question of rebuilding, there is the problem that these early mills changed use and ownership quite frequently. The same buildings are therefore described differently, even in the same documents. From the references to the Lochwinnoch example already quoted, we know that the mill was set up in 1740 and may have been one of the two still in existence in 1773. In another reference, Crawfurd mentions a plash mill which was started by Mr Cameron of Mittown bleach-field at Calderbank in 1828. He states that it was formerly a flax mill. It is a likely business for a bleacher since plash mills were small-scale yarn washing operations. This gives us the hint that one of the two original lint mills was at Calderbank. The site has gone through several phases, including a cotton mill, and is currently a private residence.

One other mill is described in the sources as a flax mill, but the reference is in a newspaper advertisement for the sale of the building in the 1830s – 100 years after the period in which we are interested. This building, like Calderbank, has been through many phases and uses and, apart from the reservoirs at the back, it is difficult to relate it to textile processing. There are many other remains of early textile mills. For example, the ruins of a former waulk mill can be seen on the eastern bank of River White Cart, below the railway viaduct at Busby.

The importance of the two early Lochwinnoch flax mills and the others in the county (e.g. on the Levern at Neilston – Brimstone Bridge and the first phase of Crofthead Mill) were that they represented the application of water power to textile manufacture. This was a significant stage in the transformation of textile manufacture from being a predominantly domestic industry. There are the remains of a lade and the outline of a lint mill

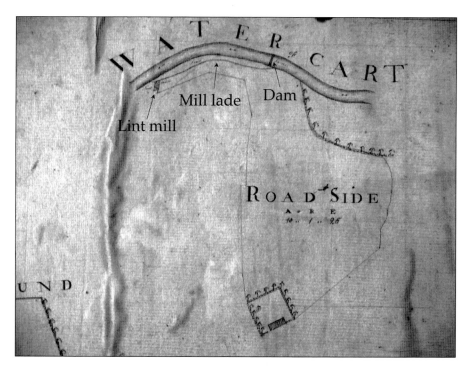

Figure 76   Extract of Greenbank House estate plan showing lint mill beside the White Cart (courtesy of the National Trust for Scotland).

at Greenbank, on the bank of the White Cart (Fig. 76). It was built on a detached part of the Greenbank estate and was funded by the Board of Trustees in the year 1750.

BLEACH-FIELDS

The early linen manufacturing in the county, along with the less well-documented but much greater success in the silk and muslin trades from the mid eighteenth century, in effect established the commercial and industrial infrastructure which made the establishment of cotton mills merely an extension of existing partnerships and processes. (It should be noted, in passing, that the development of coal mining and limeworking also contributed to these processes.)

Weaving, bleaching and textile finishing trades were an important part of the infrastructure that flourished in the mid eighteenth century. Like linen manufacture, the bleaching trade received state encouragement from the Board of Trustees, but Renfrewshire became so successful on its own that the Board refused to fund fields there. However, as Shaw notes in his book on water power, 'despite the radical changes in the chemistry of bleaching the industry's mechanical technology, once introduced, changed very little, and the heavy cumbersome machinery which typified the bleach-field in the eighteenth century continued to be used into the nineteenth century and even the twentieth'. The main requirement was a sizeable, floodable, level area, with boiling and drying houses, which, in Renfrewshire, benefited from readily available supplies of coal.

There was a considerable growth in the number of bleach-fields between 1765 and 1790, aided by the introduction of the quicker process of chlorine bleaching in the 1780s. Most bleach-fields had water-powered wash mills, and where the capital and the head of water allowed, after the 1790s, some installed water-driven textile printing machinery (as at Crofthead and Fereneze Bleachfields on the Levern), providing another example of technical advances leading to the extension of existing partnerships and sites.

Renfrewshire had many bleach-fields, but few traces survive. An example, where the water supply arrangements survive, although the watercourse has been diverted, is at Waterside where the remains of the lade from the Commore Dam and tanks are visible to the south of the buildings, which are now a private residence. It was in use much later than this period but is one of the few bleach-field sites with recognisable features not subsequently redeveloped. Further remains survive at Broom in Mearns and in Kilbarchan village.

THE RENFREWSHIRE COUNTRYSIDE IN THE MID EIGHTEENTH CENTURY

This study has so far identified the growth of textiles and trade as engines of economic and social change. Another factor, of equal importance, left its mark on buildings that survive to this day. In Renfrewshire, as in the rest of Britain, the early to mid eighteenth century marked the beginning of the phenomenon known as the 'Agricultural Revolution'. Like the 'Industrial Revolution', it was gradual in its progress but revolutionary in its effects. As with industrial sites, it is difficult to identify early examples of agricultural improvement. The success of improvements can be inferred from the aggrandisement of laird's houses and the fact that the growing population could always be fed even during the leanest years.

Most landowners were keen on improving their holdings, and the founding of the Honourable Society of Improvers in 1723 can be seen as an important indication of intent. The use of leases and the introduction of single tenancies and cash rents, from the middle of the eighteenth century onwards, dramatically reduced the number of farms, replacing the old nucleated fermtouns with the typical single-storey buildings that incorporate the byre and the living quarters in one long structure.

What this meant, on the ground, was that many of the Renfrewshire farms listed in the Poll Tax Roll of 1695 disappeared. It was the start of a process that accelerated through the eighteenth and early nineteenth centuries. John Wilson, in his 'General View of the Agriculture of the County of Renfrew', compares the population as represented in the Poll Tax Roll with 'lists of the occupiers of land in 1795' and concludes 'it appears that the number of farmers is diminished'.

The holdings that survived were no longer nucleated settlements (such as those which can still be recognised at Whittliemuir and Threepwood) but single-range buildings which sometimes survive intact (at Mid Linthills, Lochwinnoch), as one wing of a later 'courtyard' (Brownside near Paisley) or as a deserted farm on more marginal land, farms like Turnershiel (Lochwinnoch Parish), Long Loch or Barrhouse near Neilston.

In some cases, whole villages were remodelled. The best Renfrewshire example of an eighteenth-century planned village is undoubtedly Eaglesham, built between 1769 and 1797 on the site of an earlier settlement which was cleared away. Planned by the tenth Earl of Eglinton, it was completed by the eleventh and was laid out like a letter A. Many of the original buildings survive on Polnoon Street and Montgomerie Street, which run either side of a large public green (Plate 12). Whereas eighteenth-century planning in Lochwinnoch, Greenock and Johnstone has been largely obscured by later developments, it has survived almost intact in Eaglesham, which went into relative economic decline in the nineteenth century due to the closure of the cotton mill and its failure to attract a railway.

Other Renfrewshire villages retain their eighteenth-century feel. In Houston there are numerous eighteenth–nineteenth century buildings. Houston Inn, built in 1784, forms the focus of the conservation area of the village, which also contains one of the few surviving mercat crosses in Renfrewshire, with the shaft now topped by a sundial and sphere.

In the surrounding fields there were changes too. The old arrangement of infield, outfield and rigs was disappearing. There are few remains of infield and outfield left in the county (possibly at Auchenbathie) and very few remains of rigs (apart from the remarkable area of wide rigs surviving at Oldbarr between Barrhead and Paisley).

This, in turn, raises the problem of when exactly this fundamental change to the whole Renfrewshire countryside took place. It seems likely that the work of enclosing more substantial fields with stone dykes must have mainly taken place from the mid eighteenth to the start of the nineteenth century. This is confirmed by Wilson's statement, written in 1812, that 'The county is, in general well enclosed'. He compares rents in the 1760s with rents in his own time, attributing the dramatic rises in areas both near to and far from towns, in part to enclosure. He notes 'the enclosures in the arable parts of the county are generally from 5 to 12 acres. In the higher parts they are considerably larger. The mode of enclosing in the middle and low divisions, is generally by hedges and ditches. In the highest ground it is generally by stone dikes'.

Enclosure changed the face of the Renfrewshire countryside, removing the rigs and decreasing the number of farms. At the same time it increased productivity and contributed to increased rents and increased efficiency in supplying food for the growing industrial population. The other significant change was that in the crops grown. This is noted by Wilson. He remarks on the preponderance of dairy farming in the arable areas and 'In the vicinity of Paisley, Greenock and Port Glasgow, there are considerable portions of land set apart for the culture of all sorts of vegetables'.

There are some examples in the county of larger-scale improvements. One of the more spectacular of these was initiated in ongoing schemes by the various owners of Castle Semple who gradually deepened the channel of the Black Cart for 2 miles. This had the effect of lowering the water level on Castle Semple Loch and also reclaiming 250 acres known as Barr and Peel Meadows. Drainage was carried out in phases from the 1690s, by cutting a channel down the centre of the loch and gradually deepening and canalising the Black Cart. It was resumed in the 1720s and 1770s. In 1814, a canal and tunnel (which survive) were constructed along the south side of the loch to bypass Castle Semple and drain Barr Loch independently.

Other evidence of agricultural expansion and improvement at this time can be found in outbuildings and additions to individual farms, which, though difficult to date, may have been introduced from the mid eighteenth century onwards.

Water-powered grain mills were an important part of the eighteenth-century landscape, although many early corn mill sites were later reused by textile mills, making the remains harder to locate. A still-operational corn mill is to be found just over the county boundary at Coldstream Mill, in Beith Parish. Another substantial early modern example is Margaret's Mill, also known as Maul's Mill, in Kilmacolm Parish, close to Duchal Castle. Extensive remains of corn mill buildings, which had an internal wheel, and traces of header dam and lade can still be seen (Fig. 77). Millbank Mill, near Lochwinnoch, is probably the best surviving example of a corn mill with the wheel and grindstones still in position. It has to be emphasised that a visit to this site is not advised since the whole structure is in a very delicate condition. The present range of buildings probably dates from the late nineteenth century, incorporating several earlier phases which may predate the first mention of the place name in the early seventeenth century. The site includes the mill dam, lade, two-storey main building, wheelhouse, overshot wheel and a corn-drying kiln. At Old Mains Farm, Inchinnan, there is a well-preserved, stone-lined corn-drying kiln set into a bank in a private garden. Remains of one of the few remaining circular, horse-drawn grain mills in Renfrewshire can be seen at Yonderton. Other sites include upstanding remains of a grain mill and lade of eighteenth-century date or earlier at Glentyan Mill, Kilbarchan, and the lade and walls of an early grain mill at Mill of Gryffe which continued to

Figure 77   Remains of the eighteenth-century Margaret's Mill
just upstream from Duchal Castle with date of 1760
on re-used lintel (Derek Alexander).

operate into the cotton mill era by a complex series of lades. Finally the lade
and walls of Rouken Mill, a sixteenth-century grain mill, survive below the
waterfalls in a steep-sided glen within Rouken Glen Park. This site is shown
on Ainslie's farm plan of 1789.

The growing townships created an increasing market for vegetables and
dairy produce, and this increase in demand led to the cultivation of marginal
land. The deserted farm at Barrhouse near Snypes Dam in Neilston Parish
may be an example of this. It is not represented in the Poll Tax Roll of
1695 but appears on Roy's and Ainslie's maps of the 1750s and 1790s. Recent
excavation of this single-range byre and dwelling house farm on marginal
land in Neilston Parish has revealed potential occupation of the site from a

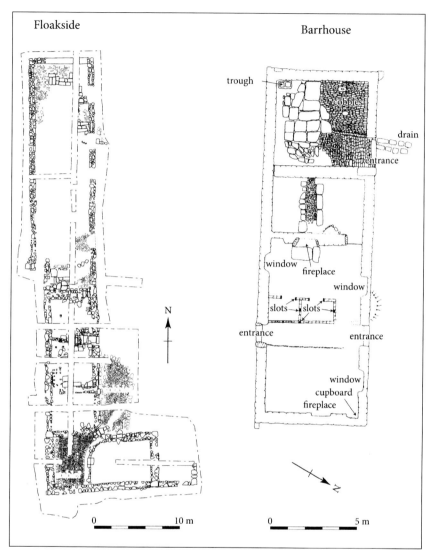

Figure 78   Plan of the excavated farmsteads of Floakside and
Barrhouse (AOC Archaeology Group and Bruce Henry,
Renfrewshire Local History Forum).

much earlier date. Initial research in estate papers has established that the final
farmhouse was occupied from 1730 to no later than 1840. It appears on the
first edition OS map as a ruin, but alternate inclusion and omission in Blaeu,
Poll Tax Roll and Ainslie might suggest early occupation intermittently,
depending on agricultural demand.

Excavation revealed a basic two-room house with lime mortared walls 0.5m thick built of rough stone (Fig. 78). Floors were of lime mortar and internal walls had been lime plastered. The building was likely to have been thatch- or turf-roofed but there was no evidence of the structure of the roof, nor of roof timbers. The two substantial rooms were separated by a corridor with a door at each end to the outside. The room to the east had a fireplace, a recess or cupboard and one window facing north. The other room was almost a mirror image with a fireplace, a recess or cupboard but two windows, one in the north wall and another in the south. Additional features uncovered in this west room were two possible bed recesses and a doorway leading to a possible workshop or dairy. The byre to the west of the living quarters was entered from the north, and there was no evidence of any entrance directly from the house. The floor of the byre was partly of flagstones and partly cobbles with evidence of supports for partitions to make two stalls in the northwest corner.

Artefactual evidence found in the west room was largely pieces of rural pottery and household metal wares dating to the eighteenth to mid nineteenth centuries, including one prestigious piece, the remains of a Spode bowl dating to the beginning of the nineteenth century. In the byre, pieces of glass milk and soft drinks bottles were found, indicating that the structure was used as a field shelter up to the mid twentieth century.

Continuing the line of the building to the west, a substantial foundation layer 1.0m thick was revealed abutting the byre wall at its south-west corner. Only the south and west foundation layers remained, with the east incorporated into the west wall of the byre and the north wall completely robbed out. Finds of green glazed medieval pottery from the area outside the south of the house and within the area enclosed by this substantial foundation tend to confirm that this appeared to be the location of an earlier structure. Post-excavation work continues on this project.

Other examples of eighteenth-century farms survive across the county. Turnersheils farm, Lochwinnoch is a deserted farmhouse noted on Ainslie's map of 1796. The ruin is a typical eighteenth-century farm with byre and dwelling part of one long rectangular structure. It is one of a group of deserted farmhouses in Lochwinnoch Parish, which may be the result of rationalisation of land holdings. Another deserted farm site is Artnocks, near the junction of Barnaigh and Kilmacolm Road. It is a good example of a mid eighteenth-century improvement farm with coigning on windows and doors. The byre is part of a separate range from the dwelling. A rare survival can be found near Greenbank House, at Flenders Farm, where there is a seventeenth-century B-listed farm dwelling, now used as a barn with carved detailing around windows.

A word of caution is possibly appropriate, in case this general survey gives the impression of uninterrupted agricultural improvement. In the late eighteenth century, for example, a group of farmers, many of whom came from Inchinnan Parish, formed a society to buy land in America, so unhappy were they with their prospects in Renfrewshire.

RURAL DEPOPULATION AND EMIGRATION

The agricultural improvements of the eighteenth century in Renfrewshire, as elsewhere in Scotland, led to the abolition of the old runrig, infield/outfield, system of agriculture and the amalgamation of former joint tenancy leases for small farms in favour of single tenancy leases for improved, larger agricultural units. Many tenants were forced off the land either as a direct result of this process or later, when they were unable to pay the higher rents asked by the landowners or unable to afford the improvements. Many of these people either worked as seasonal farm hands or took up new craft industries such as handloom weaving, as in Kilbarchan, or were attracted to the growing urban centres such as Paisley, Greenock and, of course, Glasgow.

In the second half of the eighteenth century, many emigration societies were formed in lowland Scotland such as the Scots American Company of Farmers, which was set up at Inchinnan in 1773. This group of 138 farmers bought an area of land in Vermont. Some managed to buy land for the same price as a year's rent in Renfrewshire.

In the early part of the nineteenth century, many Renfrewshire families took the decision to leave and emigrate. For example, one letter from a Margaret Stevenson of Kilmacolm describes how one of her sons left with 105 others from the surrounding area in 1820 and took a ship to Prince Edward Island, Canada.

Unlike the large numbers of abandoned farms and settlement remains that characterise many Scottish highland landscapes, relatively few houses have been abandoned in Renfrewshire. It is likely that many ruins were swept away by the agricultural improvements. The history and archaeology of the agricultural improvements and rural depopulation in Renfrewshire requires further research.

MINING

Agricultural improvement leads us on to a consideration of the other principal change taking place in the Renfrewshire landscape: the exploitation of minerals. Its prominent role in the economic growth of the county has been largely forgotten since many of the operations were small scale (although, cumulatively, very significant) and many of the larger mining communities (like Quarrelton, Inkerman and The Hurlet) have disappeared, while textile enterprises survived into living memory.

In the lowlands of the Cart basin, beds of coal and limestone exist side by side, often very close to the surface. Little capital was needed to set up a small-scale working. Transport was relatively easy and, close by, there was a growing market for limestone for soil improvement and building, and coal for fuel. There were a large number of small 'coal heuchs' throughout the area. An example is the Black Dyke Coal Heuch described by Andrew Crawfurd in the 'Cairn of Lochwinnoch' as being sunk, by George White, to a depth of 35 fathoms *c.*1810. The pit produced limestone and coal. Earlier examples also survive, such as in the Cart valley at Cathcart, and on the Gryffe at Kaimhill.

It is generally difficult to find these small workings, although their presence is often revealed by the waste tip or by small uncultivated rough woodland areas in fields. The important point to note in this example is the proximity of the seams of coal and limestone.

This facilitated the spread of the most widespread surviving monuments relating to this stage of mineral exploitation in the county, which have been largely overlooked until recent survey work by Stuart Nisbet. He has identified a large number of horseshoe-shaped earth mounds in limestone areas. These are remains of 'clamp kilns', simple hollowed-out earthen mounds, within which burning coal was overlain with lime, which was in turn covered with another layer of earth to make a simple kiln which would be left to burn for days. The kiln was easily constructed to work a small local deposit and could be abandoned or reused. Spreading the lime produced in these makeshift kilns on Renfrewshire's clayey fields was an important factor in the dramatic eighteenth-century increase in agricultural productivity. The early exploitation of lime suggests that agricultural improvement pre-dates the increase in demand for food created by the growth of the cotton mill villages, suggesting that agricultural improvements may have come before or, at least, at the same time as industrial changes. Lime was also a readily available building material and, for both these purposes, represented a very exploitable resource for large and small landowners.

The growth of mining in the eighteenth century had many factors in common with the establishment of the textile industry. For example, the partnerships which set up the larger-scale operations such as the limeworks at Spateston and Craigends involved the same people who were setting up textile mills (in this case Houstons, MacDowalls and Cunninghams) and, like the mills, water power was used – to operate pumps to drain the workings.

The Spateston limework was a sizeable operation which survives relatively intact. The wooded site at Meikle Corseford, Spateston, conceals an extensive lime quarry surrounded by more than 20 clamp kilns (Fig. 79). Care should be taken if visiting this site as it is quite dangerous. A lade on the adjacent Swinetrees Burn is all that remains of the water-powered water pump which kept the workings dry. Documentary evidence identifies MacDowall and Houston as partners in this venture, which, by the scale of the workings and the water-powered drainage system, testifies to the growing market for lime for building and agriculture. It is further evidence of the variety of activities undertaken by the local network of entrepreneurs and the scale of their enterprises.

Though there are few physical remains which are identifiably early eighteenth century, documentary sources confirm that the Quarrelton coal mines (remains of numerous sealed mineshafts still to be seen in the Bluebell woods, Johnstone) and the mineral enterprises (and copperas or iron sulphate works established in 1753) at the Hurlet were well established by this time. This area, like Quarrelton, has been landscaped, built over or allowed to return to untended woodland. In the winter months it is possible to make out various features including disused shafts, buildings and lades. Shafts are particularly noticeable in the field to the west of the A736 near West Hurlet House

There is a description of Quarrelton in 1782 in Semple's continuation of Crawford's history of the county:

In his lands at Quarrelton, there is one of the most uncommon coal works in Scotland, perhaps, in Britain, from the thickness of the seem. In most of the pits, from the roof of the coal to the pavement, is fifteen fathom, or ninety feet. But this extraordinary thickness proceeds, in a great measure, from the coal lying a great deal upon edge, deepening about one in three: But supposing the coal to lie horizontally, it is between fifty and sixty feet thick. I remember of seeing smoke coming out of one of the old waste pits, the coal having taken fire below, which

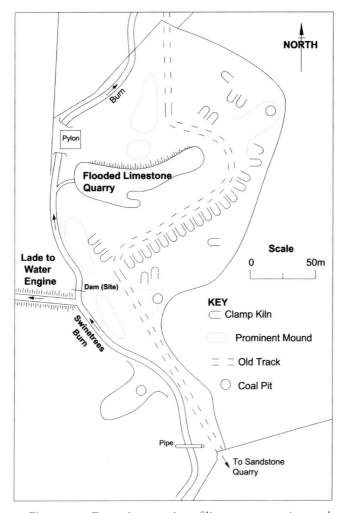

Figure 79   Extensive remains of limestone quarries, coal
pits and over 28 clamp kilns at Meikle Corseford, Spateston
(© Stuart Nisbet).

burned for several years, but is now, many years since, happily extinguished. In
the year 1770, the above gentleman built a fire-engine for drawing the water from
his coal; which goes by the steam or vapour, arising from the boiling water.

About the year 1776, great part of the roof of the old wastages gave way, and
sunk the ground, for near an acre, about two feet lower. There is from twenty
to thirty coaliers employed, at an average, at this work by him; and horses draw
the coals, below ground, from the coalliers to the pit bottom; from thence they
are taken up by a horse gin above ground. As this coal is inferior to none in this

country in quality, the greatest part of the town of Paisley, with most part of the village of Kilbarchan, and the country adjacent, are supplied by it, which is not above three miles south-west from the town of Paisley. At Quarrelton coal-work are thirty-six houses, containing sixty-seven families . . .

The steam engine which operated a pump described above replaced an earlier water-powered pump. At Spateston and Quarrelton, from the 1730s or earlier, water was carried a considerable distance in lades and turned wheels which operated pumps in both workings.

Hurlet was similarly well developed by the mid to late eighteenth century. Coal had been mined here since late medieval times, ironstone and lime also being worked. The earliest alum and copperas works, providing chemicals for dyeing, were also situated at Hurlet from the 1750s.

TRANSPORT

Throughout Scotland, the years between 1770 and 1800 were the peak years for the construction of turnpike roads. These roads were the result of economic development and, at the same time, a spur to further advances. Many local landowners were the principal supporters of the trusts who built the roads, the completion of which made a considerable impact on the economic development of the county. By 1812, £100,000 had been spent on building a great number of bridges, and in making and repairing above 140 miles of turnpike roads.

Glasgow Town Council was the other principal promoter of Renfrewshire roads. An Act of Parliament of 1753 (followed by two other Acts) provided for the turnpike roads to Greenock and Beith and the bridges at Inchinnan.

The Greenock road was enthusiastically supported by the Glasgow Town Council. The principal barriers were the rivers Black and White Cart. A new bridge was built over both rivers and was opened at Inchinnan in 1759. This was a toll bridge (paid for by 1787) the foundations of which can still be seen at low water. In 1788, Glasgow Town Council obtained permission to build a new road between Glasgow and Greenock skirting the high ground. This was completed by 1792 and is known to the west of Bishopton as 'The old Greenock road'.

Several narrow single-arch bridges can be dated to the expansion of the road system in the eighteenth century. The packhorse bridge, known erroneously as the Roman Bridge, between Cornalees and Inverkip may date from this or an earlier period. Remains of another similar bridge can be seen at a ford on the Locher to the east of Bridge of Weir. The old Cart Bridge over the Black Cart at Linwood dates from 1776. Below Cathcart Castle, Cathcart Bridge over the White Cart is of eighteenth-century date on the former main route from Glasgow to Kilmarnock and incorporates an earlier datestone of 1624.

GROWTH OF TOWNS AND VILLAGES

The result of this further increase in trade, agriculture, mining and textiles led, as in earlier times, to an expansion of small Renfrewshire towns and villages. The prime example was Paisley which, as Stuart Nisbet has shown, had trade links with London, Liverpool, Nottingham and the American colonies by the mid eighteenth century. The large number of substantial dwellings constructed in the town and surrounding villages reflect this. As Sylvia Clark points out in her book *Paisley – A History*, by this time the trade was controlled by the 'Corks' (a local name for the capitalists who controlled the supply of raw materials to, and bought the finished products from, the weavers). She continues 'Corks, like other prosperous men, tended to invest in house property in the eighteenth century (banks were still not universally trusted)'. Some idea of what Paisley looked like can be gained from an engraving dating from 1767. It shows a view of the town seen from the Glasgow road with prominent buildings such as the nave of the Abbey; the Cross Steeple and Tollbooth (erected in 1757); the Grammar School (the second building to house the school, now converted into flats) and its near neighbour, the High Church (1750–56; steeple completed 1770). The High Church is the most notable survivor of this time, although what is currently the Arts Centre began life as a church built between 1736 and 1738. Beauchamp House in New Sneddon Street (38–40) is an example of a grander style of domestic architecture from this time, and there are several humbler dwellings still upstanding, for example, Tannahill's Cottage in Queen Street, which dates from 1774. This is a typical weaver's cottage of the period and was one of many built in the Broomlands area of the town after the Corporation laid out several streets in the area in 1764 to accommodate the expanding textile industry. It is a single-storey, rubble-built weaver's cottage which has survived because of its association with the poet, Robert Tannahill. Constructed in 1774 for £20 with a narrow central hall with living accommodation to the left and a workroom for the looms on the right, this building used to be thatched until around 2003 when it was destroyed by fire and reconstructed with a slate roof.

In 1767, the population was approximately 4,600. Although Paisley looks like a small tree-lined rural town, the reality was less idyllic. William Kelso in his book *Sanitation in Paisley*, quoting from council records, writes about the first regular effort at cleaning the streets:

> On 24th July, 1771, the Council entered into a contract with Francis Douglas, Abbotsinch, for carrying this into effect. The agreement with him was that he was, at his own expense, to have the exclusive privilege to 'clat the whole streets and lanes in the town, and to carry of the dung, ashes, straw, and other garbage that shall be laid down without the front or street doors, for the space of three years'.

The phenomenal increase in the textile industry in the period immediately before powered manufacture relied on a similar increase in population. The overall effect was an early example of the migration from the Highlands which would occur much more widely in the following century. In the 1750–90 period, Renfrewshire had the highest population increase in Scotland. Much of this was from southern Argyll, as we have already seen in Greenock.

The effect of the textile money on Renfrewshire villages can still be seen. Kilbarchan is a good example: the Steeple and the Weaver's Cottage both date from this period. Although the charter of the land at Barngreen, where the weaver's cottage stands, dates from 1650, and the current building incorporates an earlier marriage lintel, on which is carved the names of Robert King and Grizel Marshall who were married in 1656, the lintel above the front door records the fact that it was built in 1723 by Andrew, John and Jenet Bryden. The weaving shop was originally in the basement floor of the cottage, and the northern half of the building has a cruck roof similar to Cowden Hall in Neilston. The cottage is well worth a visit, since it is now the property of The National Trust for Scotland and its exhibits cover the history of weaving in the village.

The Weaver's Cottage is a split-level structure built on a slope and was probably originally two separate houses (Fig. 80). The upslope part is interesting because its roof is of cruck construction. The building like so many others in the village originally functioned as part dwelling and part workshop for weaving

Recent excavation work in the garden behind the cottage recorded the

Figure 80   The Weaver's Cottage in Kilbarchan is typical of early
eighteenth-century houses combining both workshop and
house (courtesy the National Trust for Scotland).

remains of a weaver's shed. This excavation located a large pit which contained thousands of sherds of mid nineteenth-century pottery. In addition, there were large quantities of bottle and window glass, some of which had names scratched into the surface. A human skull was also found in the pit. It proved to be that of an adult male between 30 and 40 years old, and a radiocarbon date placed it sometime between 1480 and 1670. It is likely that the skull had been disturbed during construction work of the nearby churches (either in 1724 or 1900) and had been kept for a while as a curiosity along with a Neolithic stone axe which was also recovered during the dig.

Although there were between 30 and 40 weavers in Kilbarchan at the time of the Poll Tax in 1695, all but one were scattered throughout the parish, and it was not until the mid eighteenth century that the industry in the village started to expand with the establishment of one linen factory in 1739 by the Barbours and another in 1742 by the Speirs. Also in Lochwinnoch, local landowners involved in colonial trade put some of their capital into textile manufacture. The main part of the Old Parish Church was built in 1724 and the original Steeple building was constructed in 1755 as a school and meal market, public buildings which reflected the growth of the village.

Other examples of weavers' cottages survive throughout Renfrewshire. For example, Sma' Shot Cottages in Shuttle Street, Paisley, built in 1733–38, are a good example of one- and two-storey structures. At Newton of Barr, Lochwinnoch, there is a row of eighteenth-century weavers' cottages, one of which was a tollhouse. At South Arthurlie House, Grampian Way, Barrhead, the right-hand side of the building has a marriage lintel with the date 1735 set into the (original?) single-storey house with crow-stepped gables.

Some Renfrewshire communities underwent changes that were more fundamental than the addition of new buildings. The tenth Earl of Eglinton demolished the Kirkton of Eaglesham in 1769 and built an A-plan village of two streets (Montgomerie Street and Polnoon Street with a green of 15 acres between). It is now a conservation village, and many of the original buildings still survive. One of the reasons he built the new village was to keep the population numbers who no longer leased their own farms thus forming a pool of seasonal labour.

From this brief summary of the effects of the expansion of trade and textile manufacture, the improvement of agricultural land and roads, the increasing exploitation of minerals, and the resultant growth in the population and size of villages and towns, it can be seen that although the Industrial Revolution is thought to have started with the coming of the cotton mills in eighteenth-century Renfrewshire, much of the technology, enterprise and infrastructure needed to make it happen was already in place. For example, Stuart Nisbet has identified 90 bleach-field sites which were in existence before 1800 and documents which show the use of cotton in the West of Scotland as early as 1701.

When the Jacobite Rebellions of 1715 and 1745 took place they were actively opposed by the majority of Renfrewshire people. Paisley sent and supported 140 men, while Greenock sent two companies, against the Earl of Mar. The Burgh of Paisley raised, equipped and supported 210 men to fight against Charles Edward Stewart. One minor Renfrewshire landowner who supported the Stewarts – William Cochrane of Ferguslie – appears to have forfeited his estate after the 1745 rebellion.

There are other indications, however, of Renfrewshire inhabitants rebelling in their own small way against the establishment. A small stone-built foundation 7m long by 5–6m wide adjacent to Coplie Burn, high on Duchal Moor within Muirshiel Park, was once interpreted as a possible mill site but on comparison with other similar isolated structures, such as those at Mar Lodge, may in fact be the remains of an illicit still site. The fall of water does not appear to have been sufficient for a mill site, and water would have been required for distilling whisky. A turf-built hut on stone foundations in the dip beside the burn would have blended in against the background of the extensive moor and avoided the eyes of the Excise Officers. Illicit distilling was rife throughout Scotland in both the Highlands and the Lowlands in the seventeenth and eighteenth centuries. It really only disappeared following the Distillation Act of 1823. One of the best-preserved examples of a copper still worm was recovered during the archaeological excavation of a pit inside the basement of Carrick Castle on Loch Goil, Argyll, and is now on display in the National Museum in Edinburgh.

Renfrewshire by the mid eighteenth century had made significant economic advances and its population proved, equally significantly, to be firmly on the side of the Hanoverians.

14

Renfrewshire in the Industrial Revolution (1)

WATER POWER AND CANALS

—◆—◆—

WATER-POWERED TEXTILE MILLS

It is difficult now to realise that the county of Renfrew was, for a time, in the forefront of European, and indeed world, industrial development. What 'Silicon Valley' in California is to the twenty-first century, Renfrewshire and a small number of other areas in Britain were for a time to the end of the eighteenth and the early part of the nineteenth centuries. This was largely due to the developments in textiles and trade described in the previous chapter, and the network of individuals who were not afraid of experiment and change. The introduction of water-powered cotton mills, the concentration of labour they required and the changes in land use and settlement they brought about ushered in a period of dramatic change. Although Glasgow is often given the credit for such changes, in fact they originated in the countryside (Fig. 81).

The best summary of the reasons why cotton was so successful in Renfrewshire can be found in John Shaw's *Water Power in Scotland*. He points to four factors that confirm the arguments presented above – viz. the already established spinning, weaving and bleaching industry; the nearness of Glasgow as a market and the existing transport links; the established use of water power; and the fact that 'Landowners were well disposed towards industrial growth'.

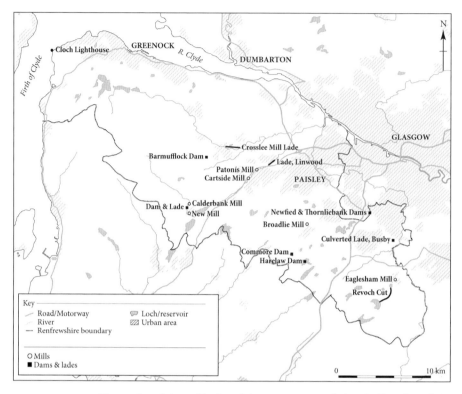

Figure 81   Map of industrial water-powered sites in Renfrewshire
including mills, lades and dams (Ingrid Shearer).

The demand by planters during the American War of Independence that
Scottish vessels should include cotton as part of their return cargo led to a
halving of the price of raw cotton between 1776 and 1780. This was one of
the factors that persuaded existing textile manufacturers to change to cotton,
but it is important to emphasise that tobacco traders did not simply switch
investment to cotton. In fact, recent studies of the names of those involved
in partnerships in insured cotton mills show that only about 17% of those
named came from family groupings associated with the tobacco trade. In fact,
there was no significant link between colonial trade and the new powered
textile industry, which took off thanks to the pre-existing infrastructure and
expertise within Renfrewshire.

The 'trigger' of the cotton boom was the adoption of several remarkable
English inventions. It was these inventions and the accompanying improvements in production methods that allowed the cotton revolution to happen.

Factories existed in this area from early in the eighteenth century, but the principal technical advance which, given the right conditions, caused dramatic changes to take place was Richard Arkwright's spinning frame, patented in 1769 (and first powered by water at Cromford Mill on the Derwent in 1771). Three of the first six mills constructed in Scotland were built in Renfrewshire – Busby (1778), Dovecothall, Barrhead (1780) and the Old Mill, Johnstone (1782) – and, as Stuart Nisbet has pointed out, all of them had some connection with Arkwright's developments, or people who had worked with him. In the early 1790s, many more cotton mills were constructed in Renfrewshire. By this time, the adoption of Compton's 'mule' allowed the spinning of much finer yarn and transformed the supply position for the high quality weavers.

In Renfrewshire as elsewhere, the people who made change possible were the surveyors and millwrights who dealt with the practical problems involved in erecting the new water-powered factories and machinery: practical men like John Ainslie, the Watt family from Greenock and John Robertson, the millwright from Neilston.

Written evidence of the changes that took place in Renfrewshire in those years is not hard to find. One of the best sources is *The Statistical Account*, a collection of essays written at the behest of Sir John Sinclair, describing the agricultural and social changes taking place in the parishes of Scotland as depicted by the local ministers. The Renfrewshire contributions, when considered in conjunction with the map of the county drawn by John Ainslie published in 1796, give a unique insight into the period. Contemporaries were aware that they were living through a period of dramatic change. The same picture is replicated in all the parishes of Renfrewshire that could produce a fall of water adequate to support a mill. The size of the mills and the scale of their operations brought irreversible changes to the essentially rural communities where they were built. The following table, which is not intended to be exhaustive, gives some indication of the number of mills built in the Cart basin within this relatively short period.

Water-powered Renfrewshire cotton mills constructed 1780–96	
River	Mill (with date)
Black Cart	1782, Old (in use until recently, meal mill site and used lint mill dam); 1783, Laigh; 1791, Elderslie (meal mill adjacent); 1792, Linwood (used dam of meal mill); 1794, Cartside (below two meal mills); 1794, Hag (used waulk mill dam)
Calder	1788, Calderpark; 1789, Calderhaugh (now flats); 1790, Boghead.

Cart	1781, Busby Upper (lint and meal mills on site); 1790, Busby Lower; 1790, Eaglesham Old (remains visible); 1792 Eaglesham Orry; (remains visible) 1792, Pollokshaws; 1785, Thornliebank; 1796 Newfield.
Gryffe	1792, Bridge of Weir Old (lint mill site); 1792, Burngill (beside existing tannery); 1793, Bridge of Weir Gryffe (meal mill adjacent); 1793, Crosslee (extensive lade survives); 1793, Houston;
Levern	1780, Dovecothall (beside existing meal mill, remains visible); 1790, Broadlie (now a leather works); 1795, West Arthurlie; 1792, Crofthead (lint mill site, later mill now on site); 1789, Gateside; 1798, Levern (beside Dovecothall)

Source: Ainslie's Map

By the mid 1790s Renfrewshire had half the cotton mills in Scotland. Water-powered cotton spinning mills continued to be built in Renfrewshire until the 1830s (e.g. Fereneze on the Levern in 1803, Gryffe Grove in 1822, and Cross Arthurlie in 1825) but the 27 mills noted above, all built within the space of 16 years, give some idea of the size and speed of the revolution which came to Renfrewshire.

It is worth noting the sheer number of Renfrewshire water-powered textile mills (even a minor upland, rural, burn, the Rowbank in Lochwinnoch Parish, had four water mills on it). Furthermore, water-powered textile manufacture survived longer in Renfrewshire than in other comparable areas. This is for the very reason that they first appeared in such profusion – the clever management of water resources which were otherwise unspectacular.

The documentary evidence is overwhelming, but how many of the sites survive? Of the 1780s' Arkwright mills, the lower courses of Dovecotehall now lie under an old folks' home and the Upper and Lower Busby Mills have gone, although the tunnel and culvert of the Lower Mill have survived (Fig. 82). The 'Old End' of Paton's Mill in Johnstone is one of the few early mills occupied until recently. It was constructed in 1782 for Robert Corse, whose mansion house at Greenlaw also survives. The 'Old End' is an A-listed building, and now the oldest surviving cotton mill in Scotland.

A considerable number of sites survive in the Calder valley. The New Mill, Calder Bank and extensive remains of Calder Glen still stand in a garden. The New Mill, Lochwinnoch, is a four-storey cotton mill dating from 1789. Known as the 'New' or Calderhaugh Mill, it survives much reduced in scale as a block of flats. Calderbank Mill, also in Lochwinnoch, is an extensively

Figure 82   Interior of the brick-built Busby mill tunnel (© Stuart Nisbet).

remodelled and reused water-powered textile mill and bleaching enterprise, now converted to residential housing. Remains of the wheelhouse and lade can still be distinguished. It may have begun life as an eighteenth-century flax mill.

Similarly, there are traces of a number of sites on the upper reaches of the White Cart, the Gryffe and the Levern valley. On the Levern, Broadlie Mill at Neilston is now a leather works, but began life in 1790 as a cotton spinning mill, then a weaving factory (Fig. 83). The lower storeys of the original cotton mill, a round stair well and the course of the lade are still visible from the hill behind the mill.

On the Black Cart, the A-listed Cartside Mill, built in 1794, was demolished in the 1990s, though some of the lower walling can still be seen from the opposite bank. The lade, which started at the low dam on the Black Cart, continued for 2.5km serving Hagg, Johnstone Old and the Laigh Mill (Fig. 84). On the White Cart only the foundations and retaining wall survive from the original (1778) upper cotton mill at Busby (Plate 13) but the dams, sluices and culverted lade to Busby Lower mill (1790) still exist. The walls of the New or 'Orry' cotton mill in Eaglesham can be seen by the burnside. The lower gable

Figure 83   Broadlie Mill, on the Levern Water, with Neilston village
and parish church on the hill behind (C. Taylor 1831).

of the Old Mill also survives at Townhead and the mill was partly converted
into the adjacent dwelling. The Revoch Cut, a 2.5km-long aqueduct which
carried water from Dunwan Dam to Picketlaw Dam to power the Eaglesham
cotton mills, can still be seen in places and is part of a group of lades which
are earlier, and on a par with, Robert Thom's works at Greenock.

The largest surviving monuments of the cotton boom are, of course, the
dams and lades which fed the water to the mills. They are mainly situated on
the river valleys and moorland headwaters of often quite small Renfrewshire
rivers and burns, and have thus avoided the development which has destroyed
many urban monuments. Here is a selection of the principal surviving dams
and lades. The semi-circular dam and lade at Lochwinnoch were constructed
in 1787 to power the original cotton mill constructed in 1788 (the 'Old Mill').
According to Ainslie's map, the water from the mill fed into the lade for
The Calderhaugh Mill (the 'New Mill', see above). For the Levern mills,

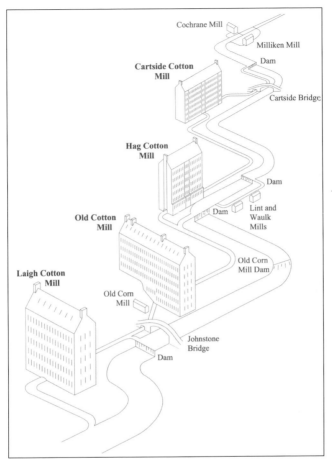

Figure 84   Mills on the Black Cart in the new
planned town of Johnstone (© Stuart Nisbet).

there is a series of dams including Commore Dam built in 1804 and Harelaw
Dam built in 1822. The Long Loch, a natural loch, drained to provide extra
grazing during the eighteenth-century was dammed in the 1780s to increase
and control the flow of the Levern. Likewise, there are massive stone-lined
dams, sluices and reservoirs hidden in a corner of Rouken Glen Park, which
provided water supply and power for Thornliebank and Newfield cotton
mills and printworks from 1770s.

In the Gryffe valley, although there is now no trace of the Crosslee Mill
(Fig. 85) constructed in 1793, Stuart Nisbet has demonstrated that a walk
down the lade from the centre of Bridge of Weir to Crosslee reveals a complex
arrangement of weirs, branch lades and tunnelling, which allowed the river

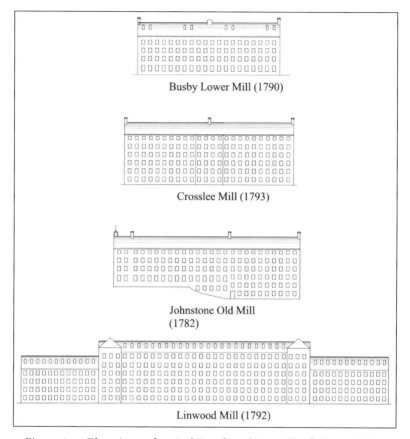

Busby Lower Mill (1790)

Crosslee Mill (1793)

Johnstone Old Mill
(1782)

Linwood Mill (1792)

Figure 85   Elevations of typical Renfrewshire mills (© Stuart Nisbet).

to power three early cotton mills (which led to the growth of both villages) and still provide water for the pre-existing grain mill. The remains of one of the Bridge of Weir mills can be seen as can two lime-working sites and a coal pit. At Barmufflock there is also a large masonry dam (now drained) as back-up to the Bridge of Weir mills.

The Linwood Mill (1792 onwards) was the largest in Scotland (Fig. 85) and had two water wheels, one of them raised above tidal water. The mill has gone, but the lade can still be seen amid landscaped parkland at Linwood, commencing from Mill of Cart (grain mill) dam on the Black Cart.

Many mill dams are now under threat since their original use is long gone and their owners no longer wish to continue with their high maintenance costs. Some of the dams have been drained although the earthworks and masonry still remain (e.g. Kirktonfield Dam near Neilston and Barmufflock above Bridge of Weir) but many survive in East Renfrewshire.

One industry which has not left much evidence in Renfrewshire is whisky distilling. A number of whisky distilleries were built in lowland Scotland after 1779 (and after the Wash Act of 1784). What is possibly a remaining wall of the Elderslie distillery can be seen from the opposite bank of the Alt Patrick Water (Fig 86).

POPULATION GROWTH AND SETTLEMENTS

It is estimated that, by 1800, 60% of textile workers were employed in cotton spinning. This rapid development of large water-powered cotton mills was the origin of many Renfrewshire communities. It is instructive to compare Ainslie's map of 1796 with the map contained in Wilson's *General View of the Agriculture of Renfrewshire*, published in 1812. Wilson's book is another key source for information about the county as it was written in the early stages of the Industrial Revolution. The map clearly shows the influence of the cotton mills on the growth of Renfrewshire communities.

All of these villages had to deal with a population explosion (similar, as we shall see, to the population growth in the coastal towns). It was at this time that the shape of many Renfrewshire towns was established. By 1831 Neilston had developed from being a 'kirk toun' into a dispersed village with houses nucleated around the mills and bleach-fields.

Other communities were feued by the landowners in a more systematic manner, with workers' housing situated adjacent to industrial sites or existing communities. These areas can often still be detected today because the street plan still follows a grid. George Houston feued Bridge of Johnstone in 1781–82, for example, according to a plan by Paisley surveyor, Charles Ross, into eight blocks set on either side of the axis of the main street running from the Thorn to the Bridge, and incorporating Houston and Ludovic squares (named after the proprietors). In Greenock likewise, on the land to the south and west of the houses adjoining the eighteenth-century harbours and shipbuilding yards, the four early nineteenth-century feuing grids are evident from the street map (based, according to Frank Arneil Walker on the axes of Lynedoch Street: south of Roxburgh Street; West Blackhall street and the West End). The plans for these grids seem to have been initiated in two surveys produced by Richardson c.1780 and later by Edinburgh surveyor William Sibbald. The final version of the plans appears in 1818 in *Plan of the town of Greenock and its environs, with intended improvements* by David Reid.

More modest surveyed and feued development in Renfrewshire at this time included Houston, feued by Sir John Houstoun (by 1782, all 38 feus were taken) and Lochwinnoch, where the laird, William MacDowall, feued the Calderhall (haugh?) estate between 1788 and 1795. Fifty-three new houses were built and further feus were granted. These areas joined Port Glasgow, Eaglesham and the Maxwellton area of Paisley, which had been surveyed and feued earlier in the eighteenth century.

The speculative builders moved in after the land was surveyed and feued. The houses they built for the middle classes (for example, in the West End of Greenock) or for better-off workers (like the weavers of Kilbarchan) are still standing, but the houses they built for the Lowland and Highland Scottish and Irish immigrant workers in the early years of the nineteenth century only came to public notice after the cholera outbreaks of the 1830s and 1840s. Many were very poorly built and lacked any provision for proper ventilation or sanitation. It is not surprising that no example of early nineteenth-century slum housing still exists, although some two-storey tenement properties in Greenock, Port Glasgow, Lochwinnoch, Bridge of Weir, Linwood and Paisley probably date from this time. The principal surviving monuments to the large number of immigrant workers who flooded into Renfrewshire at this time are the Gaelic churches in Paisley and Greenock and the later chapels which served the Roman Catholic Irish population

At the Western end of the county, Greenock and Port Glasgow continued to flourish, although many of the sites associated with the eighteenth-century growth of the towns were demolished in the succeeding century. In Barrhead, Neilston, Houston, Crosslee, Bridge of Weir, Thornliebank, Pollokshields, Eaglesham, Busby, Lochwinnoch, Elderslie, Linwood and Johnstone, the remains of the mills, dams and lades, the mill-owners' houses, the workers' houses, and some early public buildings can still be seen. The mill-owners' houses seem to have survived the years better than the other structures of the time.

TRANSPORT AND TRADE

The increased pace of economic development, and successful English examples (such as the Bridgewater Canal of 1769), encouraged local promoters of canal schemes. The earliest Renfrewshire canal was the Renfrew Canal, which followed the bed of the old watercourse that lay between Sand Inch and the

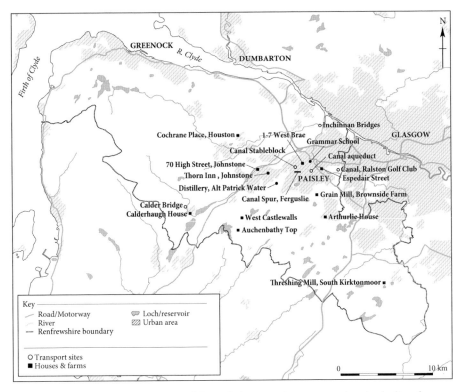

Figure 86   Map of nineteenth-century sites including houses,
farms and transport features (Ingrid Shearer).

King's Inch, known as the Pudzeoch, running from the river to the present
Canal Street. It was opened in 1786. The digging of a channel to improve
the navigation of the River Cart in the 1790s, while not strictly a canal, was
another attempt to improve waterborne transport, to accommodate increasing
trade. An Act of Parliament had been obtained in 1787, and the dried-up bed
of the original channel can be seen under a span of the eastern of the two
bridges at Inchinnan, while the end of the channel is visible near Porterfield
Road, Renfrew.

After the 'canal mania' of the 1790s, the Earl of Eglinton proposed a
Glasgow to Ardrossan Canal, which was another solution to the long-standing
problem of linking the city to the coast. The original plan was to connect
a deep-water port at Ardrossan (and the Earl's Ayrshire coalfields) with
Glasgow. By 1810 the canal, following a design by Thomas Telford (another
of the real heroes of the Industrial Revolution), had reached Johnstone. It

Figure 87   View of the chimneys and spires of Paisley from south-east
with the canal aqueduct crossing the White Cart (Ramsay 1839).

never did reach Ardrossan (Glasgow solved its port problems in other ways)
but for over 30 years, until the establishment of the railways – and after – it
was instrumental in the development of the Hurlet and Quarrelton mines
and the growing industrial town of Paisley. Remains of the canal can be
seen in three places: a heavily overgrown, but quite extensive stretch on the
other side of the Canal railway line at Ralston Golf Course; the Canal line
railway viaduct, the original canal viaduct near Canal station in Paisley (Fig.
87); a spur of the canal extending into the former Coats Thread works at
Ferguslie, terminating in a basin and incorporating a building which may be
a small stable block contemporary with the construction of the spur. There is
an ingenious arrangement whereby the Candren Burn runs under the canal.
This gained notoriety as 'Tannahill's Hole', which was the spot where the
noted Paisley poet committed suicide shortly after the opening of the canal
in 1810. This area has recently been extensively redeveloped for housing and
the spur of the canal and the basin have been altered but retained. The course
of the canal is clearly marked on a map from Taylor's *The Levern Delineated*
of 1831.

Figure 88   Timber ponds at Port Glasgow (Ingrid Shearer).

There was continued expansion at the other end of the county. John Wilson, in his account written in 1812, provides an easy-to-read summary of the increasing trade in the harbours of Greenock and Port Glasgow. He mentions four sugarhouses (the last refinery closed in 1999) and the shipbuilding and shipyards (and their growth after the American War of Independence). Most of the Greenock sugar sites have been redeveloped, and the buildings date from the nineteenth century. The earliest dates from 1765 and is located in Sugarhouse Lane.

The coastal areas of Port Glasgow and Greenock have since been extensively redeveloped. One of the few remnants of the period of wooden shipbuilding are the timber stakes which can be seen sticking out of the Clyde near Port Glasgow – relics of the timber 'ponds' where wood was stored, in the water, until needed for shipbuilding (Fig. 88).

The City of Glasgow bought 13 acres of land from the Newark Maxwells in 1667 upon which the town of Newport was founded to act as a harbour for the city. Prior to about 1790 most wood used for shipbuilding was imported from the Baltic but around this time logs from America and Canada started to be imported. These were brought as logs in ships fitted with special bow doors and were stored in the timber ponds until ready for use. By leaving the logs tied together in rafts the potential storage problem was solved and the water preserved the wood for years. The use of the timber ponds continued for over 100 years but eventually came to an end with the gradual introduction of iron ships. The last wooden ship built on the lower reaches of the Clyde was in 1859. The other factor that led to their eventual demise was the gradual improvement, by dredging, of the Clyde channel, which meant that most of the industry transferred upstream to Glasgow.

There are, however, two very substantial monuments to the growing seaborne trade of Greenock and Port Glasgow at this time. An enabling Act of Parliament in 1784 led to the construction of the Cloch Lighthouse in Inverkip Parish, which, with the Gantocks off Dunoon, marked the channel for the increasing number of ships bound for Greenock and Port Glasgow. Built between 1795 and 1797, the dome containing the light is about 24m above the ground. The coastal road (A78) was constructed after the light. Robert Stevenson was involved in the design of the lighthouse, which was manned until 1973. The other surviving monument is the Greenock Customs House. Its size and architectural grandeur is a silent witness to the port's prosperity and importance in the early years of the nineteenth century.

Since most of Greenock and Port Glasgow's imports and exports were bound to, or from, Glasgow, the old problem of transhipment to the city became more urgent. It had been greatly eased by Golborne's improvements to the river mentioned in the last chapter. There was, however, considerable road traffic passing over the rivers Black and White Cart between Glasgow and the coast. The destruction of the 1759 Inchinnan Bridge by floods in 1809 led to its replacement by the current bridges in the years 1809 to 1812. The Calder Bridge in Lochwinnoch dates to the seventeenth century but was altered in 1814.

THE EFFECT OF INDUSTRIAL CHANGE ON THE COUNTRYSIDE

Because of their need for water power, the new mills were, of course, situated in the countryside. Their advent, and the growth of the villages, had a considerable effect on rural Renfrewshire.

There is evidence from documentary sources of rural depopulation in the non-industrialised parishes of Kilmacolm, Inchinnan and Eaglesham. The physical evidence for this is to be found in deserted farm sites.

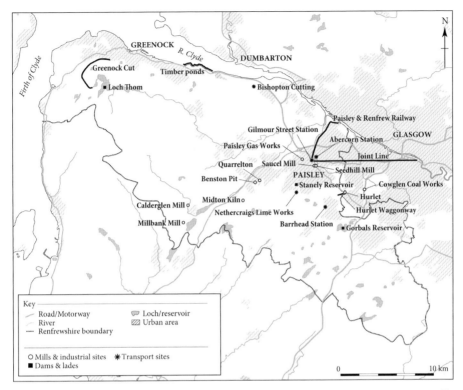

Figure 89   Map of nineteenth-century mills,
industrial sites and railways (Ingrid Shearer).

The reasons why individual farms were abandoned are obviously complex. As well as the attractions of industry, they include agricultural prices, marginal soil conditions, rationalisation of holdings and flooding of land for mill dams. There are, however, three areas of Renfrewshire where there are concentrations of deserted farms (in the upland areas to the north and south of Lochwinnoch Parish and in Eaglesham Parish). It is likely that workers for the new cotton mills came from the surrounding countryside and that some of the deserted farms (like the Gaelic churches, new chapels and square street-grids) are the physical reminders of the population changes caused by increasing industrialisation.

John Wilson's *General View of the Agriculture of Renfrewshire* gives a detailed description of contemporary farm steadings. He writes

> The stable and byre or cow house were commonly in the same range of building with the dwelling house, and a barn detached, many of the farmers still preferring

this arrangement of the buildings to any other. The neatest and best farm steadings are now generally in the form of a square or court; on one side the dwelling house is situated; the opposite side being commonly left open. The houses are mostly one story high, built with stone and lime and covered with thatch . . .

The deserted farm at South Castlewalls (and Brownside Farm in the Gleniffer Braes Country Park between Barrhead and Paisley) fit this description of 'courtyard' steadings. At Castlewalls the T-plan deserted farm site is noted on Ainslie's map. A recent survey of Brownside identified the western wing of the farm as housing a small water mill, probably a grain mill, powered by the burn which runs by this side of the building. Another small water-powered farm mill is at South Kirktonmoor, Eaglesham, dating to the 1830s, and is one of thirteen water-powered threshing mills identified in Eaglesham Parish. It was dismantled during house conversion around 2000.

In general, by 1800, the effects of the accelerating pace of change – when compared to the county as described in the Poll Tax Roll of 1695 – could truly be described as 'revolutionary'.

15

Renfrewshire in the Industrial Revolution (2)

STEAM AND RAILWAYS

———◆———

It would be wrong if this account gave the impression that economic progress was unbroken. In the years 1800–15 (due to the French Wars), 1830–40, and particularly 1841 and 1842 in Paisley, there were periods of severe depression. Despite this (and the fact that all artificial divisions are arbitrary), it could be said that expansion continued with the second stage of the Industrial Revolution, which involved the widespread adoption of steam engines, and the resultant growth of engineering, mining for raw materials, and the railways.

The real heroes were the engineers – the people who made it happen. And principal among them was Renfrewshire's most famous son.

JAMES WATT (1736–1819)

Watt grew up in the boom town of Greenock. His family were part of the vigorous changes to eighteenth-century Renfrewshire which we have been describing. His grandfather was a mathematician, a teacher of surveying and navigation. His father was a ship chandler who became involved with the improvement of docks. His uncle was a surveyor and mapmaker. Watt's principal characteristic was the compelling logic with which he analysed engineering problems. He was a practical man but his forte was logic and analysis. He was influenced by the rational methods of enquiry taught in the Scottish universities at this time.

He had difficulty in his early career because of the grip still exerted by Glasgow guilds. When he was 17 he went to London to learn his trade. He tried to set up shop on his return but was prevented by the Glasgow Guild of Hammermen. John Anderson, the Professor of Natural Philosophy at Glasgow University (and founder of what is now Strathclyde University), employed him as an instrument maker at the university.

It was here, in 1764, that he came into contact with the Newcomen steam engine which can still be seen in the Hunterian Museum. It had never worked very satisfactorily. Watt decided this was because of a design fault. Following the logic of his discoveries about the lack of efficiency of the engine, he successively modified it by adding a separate condenser, an air pump, a closed cylinder, a double acting parallel motion and governors to keep it parallel. Each development followed on logically from the previous one. The key was the separate condenser, the effect of which was to increase the main cylinder's efficiency because it did not have to be reheated at each stroke. Watt himself said later about his discovery, 'the invention will not appear so great as it seems to be'. He patented the steam engine in 1769.

His attempt to build the engine in partnership with Roebuck at the Carron Works ended with Roebuck's financial failure in 1772. Watt went south again in 1774 and in the following year went into partnership with Boulton to manufacture steam engines at his Soho Works in Birmingham. Watt's patent was extended by Act of Parliament in 1775 for 25 years.

The partnership was very successful, and in 1781 Watt developed and marketed a rotary engine that made steam-powered factories a realistic possibility. Many others saw the potential of this invention. By 1785, a rotary engine had been installed in a spinning mill and in the same year the power loom was invented.

Watt's contribution to the Industrial Revolution cannot be overestimated, and, while he was a product of the enormous changes which were taking place in eighteenth-century Renfrewshire (and in the booming port of Greenock in particular), it has to be said that he met reversals and opposition (and some encouragement) during his early years in Scotland. He supported himself at various times during these early years carrying out surveys and reports on various engineering schemes. Despite his association with steam power, Watt was also an expert on water and designed many water-powered engines and canals in Scotland. In Renfrewshire he prepared a scheme for a canal and waggonway from Hurlet to Paisley in 1773. George Houston of Johnstone consulted him in 1788 regarding a water dispute between Johnstone Old and Laigh cotton mills.

Watt was concerned at various times in two significant problems confronting his home town. The first was that, discussed above, of the shallowness of the Clyde and the need to trans-ship goods onto the small craft which plied between Greenock/Port Glasgow and Glasgow. In 1769 he reported to Glasgow Town Council on the depth of the river at various points – as part of Golborne's improvements discussed in an earlier chapter.

The second problem Watt tackled was a product of the remarkable eighteenth-century growth of Greenock. He designed and constructed Greenock's first freshwater supply between 1772 and 1774 .Two small dams were constructed at the top of what is now Lynedoch Street, storing water from two burns running down from the Whin Hill. A header tank in Wellpark was served from these dams by wooden pipes. The problem of supply of water to Greenock (as a source of power) was soon to be solved in a spectacular fashion.

Watt was also involved in drawing up plans for the improvement of Greenock and Port Glasgow harbours and a scheme, which was never completed, for a short canal to join the Clyde in Renfrew.

STEAM POWER AND THE SURVIVAL OF WATER POWER

Steam power defined the second stage of industrialisation and, as far as archaeological remains are concerned, marked a move from rural to urban industry. Steam power did not immediately replace water with the invention of the rotary drive steam engine. Steam-driven Newcomen engines, powering pumps, had been in use in Renfrewshire for decades (for example, to help drain the Quarrelton mines). Steam pumps were also used to power water-driven textile machinery where the flow was inadequate. Where it had been adopted, it allowed industry to be located where there was no source of water power (in Paisley it replaced horse power and man power in textile mills). But the engines employed in these early applications were expensive, difficult to maintain and not as powerful, or as cheap, as water.

Water power had defined the location of industry (e.g. sites on almost every minor Renfrewshire stream like the Espedair, Rowbank Burn, Kirkton Burn). Water power survived longer in Renfrewshire than in many other counties, probably because it was established, cheap and already well managed.

The Shaws water scheme, which brought water for power to Greenock at a time when steam power was available, is probably the most remarkable extension of the use of water in the county. At the second time of asking in 1824, Robert Thom produced a plan to supply water to Greenock from a nearly 300-acre reservoir (and a compensation reservoir) situated on moorland behind the town. From these dams, a five-and-a-half-mile aqueduct would carry the water by a circuitous route round Shaws and Dunrod Hills (to preserve the maximum height/fall at Greenock) to the Long Dam at the back of the town. The Shaws Water Company, with capital of £31,000 and an enabling Act of Parliament, was constituted in 1825 to carry out Thom's scheme. It was completed in 1827. By the mid century there were at least a dozen sizeable water-powered factories in Greenock using Shaws water. The cut and the dams can be seen today and they are the most dramatic water-powered industrial monument in Renfrewshire and a testament to the work of its creator, Robert Thom.

The need for improving the water supply to Greenock was first investigated in the late eighteenth century when increased population growth led to an increased demand on the water supply. In 1790 James Watt and George Robinson surveyed the hills behind Greenock to look for ways to increase the water supply; this resulted in the construction of two dams but proved inadequate to meet demands. Robert Thom had built a water system to supply his factory on Bute and was persuaded to construct a similar system above Greenock. This involved the construction of a large reservoir, now called Loch Thom, which dammed the upper end of the Shaws Water. In order to allow the Shaws Water to continue to flow down to Inverkip a smaller compensation reservoir was also built. The water from the reservoir was transported around the west and north side of the hills to behind Greenock by means of an aqueduct or water cut c.7 miles long. This consists of a stone-lined cut 3–4m wide and up to 1.5m deep. The scheme was accepted and construction started in 1825 taking two and a half years to complete, finally being opened on 16 April 1827. At the eastern end, the water was collected into the Overton Reservoir where a series of 19 falls was used in a range of different industrial processes including powering flour mills, a flax mill, a woollen mill, sugar refineries, an iron foundry, a paper works and a chemical works. Drinking water was piped through a number of filtering tanks down to the town. The water works continued in use until 1971 when it was replaced by a tunnel, one and a quarter miles long, under the hills, which transported water from Loch Thom to a new filter station at Overton.

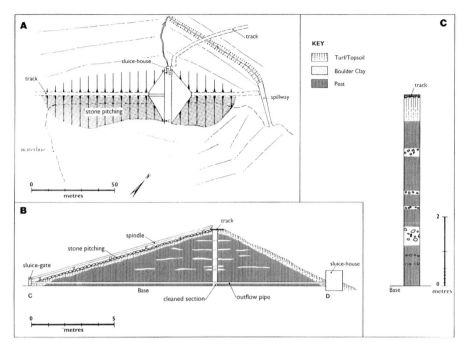

Figure 90   Plan and section of cutting through Greenock Reservoir No. 1
(Centre for Field Archaeology & Derek Alexander).

A series of eight other reservoirs were constructed around 1829 on the hills above Greenock in order to capture more water and feed it into the aqueduct system. The south-western two of this series of dams are Greenock Reservoirs 1 and 2 which were dismantled in the 1990s by cutting a breach through them. In both cases, this allowed the make-up of the dams to be confirmed as largely peat-based (Fig. 90). The whole system of reservoirs and associated aqueducts are protected as Scheduled Ancient Monuments, under the Ancient Monuments and Archaeological Areas Act 1979.

Robert Thom, like Watt, was one of the other heroes of the Industrial Revolution in Renfrewshire. He was born in Tarbolton in 1775. He studied at the Andersonian Institute in Glasgow, managed a cotton mill in Blackburn and, in 1813, with a partner, purchased Rothesay cotton mill. In 1821 although steam power could have been used, he increased the capacity of the water-powered machinery by constructing an aqueduct to Loch Fad. Robert Shaw said that Thom was '. . . one of the great proponents of water power . . . [who] . . . helped continue its continued viability into the steam age'. The Shaws water scheme was his greatest achievement.

STEAM POWER AND THE TEXTILE INDUSTRY

As noted earlier, recent unpublished research has established that there were various centralised textile factories in Renfrewshire towns and villages in the early eighteenth century. From the mid century, work was increasingly centralised and motive power was provided from whatever source was available. Thread mills in Paisley in the 1780s, for example, were worked by hand. The gradual introduction of steam power was therefore particularly important for the Paisley textile industry, although it must be remembered that a large part of Paisley's prosperity rested on handloom weaving. Another development is described by Sylvia Clark. Silk had been largely ousted by cotton and '. . . silk reached prohibitive prices during the Napoleonic War. Either Peter Kerr or Patrick Clark was the first to make a satisfactory heddle twine from six-chord machine spun cotton; it was the Clarks who realised that this product could be put on sale as sewing-thread'. Thus by 1812 or earlier, Renfrewshire's well-established linen thread industry was being replaced by cotton, and steam power had been applied to the process.

Although water power persisted in rural areas, the availability of local supplies of coal led to the introduction of steam power in urban areas as engines became more reliable and the workforce more skilled in their operation. A rare surviving example of a steam house added to a water-powered cotton mill can be found at Calderglen Mill at the junction of the Cloak Burn and the Calder in Lochwinnoch. The ruins of this small mill can be seen in the garden of the present dwelling house. The mill was originally powered by the Cloak Burn and later by steam. The (separate) engine house and brick chimney still survive. The Calder Haugh Mill also had an engine house until recently. It was added in 1825 and, according to Crawfurd, 'marred the appearance of the building'.

MINING

Any geological map of Renfrewshire shows clearly the carboniferous deposits of coal and limestone which had been worked from late medieval times and during the earliest years of industrialisation. The economic developments we have described created a greatly increased demand for coal, limestone and clay. The building of the Glasgow–Ardrossan canal meant that the existing eighteenth-century mining centres at Quarrelton and the Hurlet had a new outlet to the expanding markets in Glasgow and beyond.

Figure 91   Coal workings exposed during the digging of foundations for the
Fever Hospital site at Cowglen, Thornliebank in 1937. The unexcavated
pillars would have supported the roof of this shallow mine (courtesy of
the British Geological Survey IPR/117-7OCT).

Coal became more significant with the more widespread adoption of steam
power and the growth of heavy industry after the 1830s. The exploitation
of ironstone also grew after the introduction of Neilson's hot-blast furnace
in 1828. The Quarrelton Mines were reckoned to produce at this time more
than 20,000 tons of coal in a single year. To the casual observer there is now
little evidence of this great coalfield. A walk in the woods in the winter
months, when there is less undergrowth, reveals the remains of pits, worked
faces, covered shafts, spoil tips and diverted water courses. A recently erected
memorial in the nearby park and an opening to the Benston Pit are the most
visible remains. An air shaft or entrance to a mine is visible in the centre of a
field near St Vincent's Hospice. Substantial sandstone mountings for winding
gear can be seen. The pit itself is blocked with rubbish. This is a dangerous
site and should only be approached with care. In the winter months, however,
mineshafts and spoil tips can be seen in the Rannoch and Bluebell woods.
The stoop-and-room coal workings of Cowglen were exposed in 1937 during
the digging of foundations for the building of a hospital (Fig. 91).

Figure 92   Engraving of Caldwell House (centre) and tower (left) with a working
draw-kiln for lime production in the foreground (Ramsay 1839).

Limeworking continued to be an important industry in the area (Fig. 92).
Ainslie's map of 1796 shows several coal pits and limeworks. He notes four
limeworks in the area of Howwood. These are Low Howwood, Whitefaulds,
Laigh Corsford and, towards Lochwinnoch, Netherhouses. Extensive
remains of limeworking which probably can be dated to the late eighteenth
century are to be found at Skiff Wood, Midton, Howwood. These workings
include extensive spoil tips, mine openings, a complete draw kiln and various
clamps kilns. The Midtown draw kiln is the best example of a limekiln so
far discovered in the county of Renfrewshire and is well worth a visit (Fig.
93). The kiln may be tentatively dated to the early nineteenth century. The
stonework of the main chamber is in good condition with three blocked off
smaller chambers branching off it. The area to the south of the kiln shows
considerable evidence of quarrying and spoil tips. The lime was used for
agricultural, industrial and construction purposes and was an important
industry in the area for some time.

Moving to the mines and workings nearer to the western edge of Paisley,
clay and ironstone were exploited as well as coal and limestone. The principal
limeworks were at Nethercraigs, where spoil tips and the mine opening

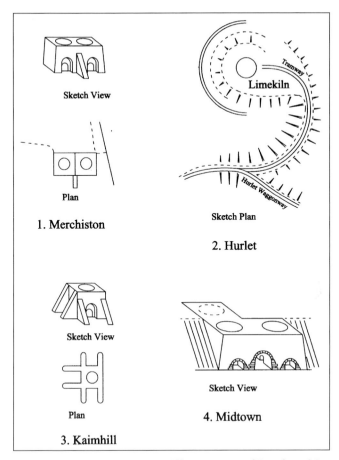

Figure 93   Different types of Renfrewshire
lime draw-kilns (© Stuart Nisbet).

can still be seen. There was a significant pit at Newton in Elderslie and a short-lived pit in Castlehead (is the mound a motte or a spoil tip?). Clay was mined extensively in the area to the east of the Linwood road where there were several brick kilns. There are still remains of Walkinshaw and Ferguslie brick works which survived well into the present century. In the early nineteenth century Brown's brick works provided many bricks for the Greenock railway. Ironstone was mined at Blackhall and in the area to the east of the Linwood Road.

A second large area of mineral exploitation was around the Hurlet. Here coal, lime and ironstone were extracted. Hurlet was at this time expanding as a small mining village. There was also, from 1753 to 1820, a copperas work (the only one in Scotland up to 1807). In 1797 the earliest alum work was established. There is now little trace of the extensive workings in the Barrhead and Nitshill area. Indeed, the Levern valley at this point is an area of woodland and a public park. The manse now survives as kennels, and the long vanished main street was parallel to the Nitshill Road. Further east, limeworking was an even bigger industry at Darnley, Arden and Waulkmill Glen, persisting from the eighteenth to the twentieth centuries. The embankments of the Hurlet waggonway (Fig. 93), identified by Stuart Nisbet on an estate map of the 1820s, can still be seen on either side of the Hurlet–Barrhead road near to the Waterside Inn. It runs from a pit to the Levern, where the remains of a bridge can be seen. The embankment then turns northward along the opposite bank of the river.

There were also a large number of small quarries for road-metal and building stone, traces of which can be seen in the Renfrewshire countryside (e.g. Stewarton Road south of Neilston). Traces of more sizeable quarries are to be found at Giffnock (see below) and at Stonecraigs in Paisley.

GROWTH OF ENGINEERING AND SHIPBUILDING

One of the most significant developments took place at Port Glasgow. Although it was not the first steamboat in the world, the voyage of Henry Bell's *Comet* in April 1811, from Helensburgh and Greenock upriver to Glasgow, inaugurated the first regular steamboat service in Europe. The boat was built at John Wood's yard in Port Glasgow, and a full-size replica is currently on display next to the Port Glasgow Town Hall (Fig. 94). There was another Renfrewshire connection. The engine of the *Comet* was designed and built by Neilston-born Glasgow millwright John Robertson (1782–1868). The engine is in the collection of the Science Museum, South Kensington, and there are memorials to him in the Southern Necropolis, Glasgow and in the square in Neilston.

The docks and shipyards of Greenock and Port Glasgow were well established by the early nineteenth century, although traces of most have been obliterated by later developments A walk along the shore side of Coronation Park in Port Glasgow reveals the remains of the retaining walls of earlier marine activity. Greenock's first dry dock was constructed in the 1780s near the West Harbour. One of the earliest recorded shipyards was Scott's Shipyard, opened in 1711, which lasted into 1960s.

Figure 94   This replica of the 1811 steamboat Comet
can be seen at Port Glasgow (Derek Alexander).

Until about 1850, all ships were constructed of wood. Although some timber in the early years of the nineteenth century came from the Baltic, Grangemouth was more prominent in this trade, and from about 1800 to about 1870, most imported Clyde timber for construction and shipbuilding came from Canada. Greenock had a great capacity to store this timber in 'ponds' or tidal stretches of water divided by upright wooden posts. Remains of the ponds can still be seen between the high and low water marks on the southern shore of the Clyde between Port Glasgow and Langbank.

The career of John Robertson, mentioned above, was not untypical of the early engineers. He was by trade a millwright and may have been responsible for two patents and other inventions. One of the reasons for the success of industrial innovation in this and other areas was the fact that millwrights, who gained a new importance in the local economy after the establishment of textile factories in the 1780s, could adapt and advance the application of technology. Engineering blossomed in the wake of the establishment of textile factories. This happened particularly near the River Cart in Paisley, in the Abercorn and Sneddon areas, though almost all traces of the former works have now disappeared.

COMING OF THE RAILWAYS

If the period *c.*1780–1830 was characterised by the coming of the cotton mills and their effect on Renfrewshire communities, the period *c.*1830 to the mid nineteenth century is defined by the advent of steam railways. The 1830s railway boom also reintroduces two of the recurring themes of this book. The first is the importance of certain stages in the economic development of Renfrewshire in the establishment of present-day towns and villages. Just as the seventeenth-century boom had created a group of small Burghs of Barony with limited market functions and the cotton boom had turned small villages beside rivers into small manufacturing towns, the third identifiable cause of the growth of communities in the post-medieval period was the coming of the railways. The second theme is Glasgow's desire to link with the coast. The railways were another chapter in this saga (Fig. 95).

The earliest British railways were often gravity- or horse-drawn, and were, like canals, generally associated with minerals – mainly coal. A few traces of an early gravity railway connecting a quarry at Erskine with the Clyde have survived recent landscaping. The quarry, and the gravity railway, may have been associated with improvements to the banks and channel of the river.

Probably the earliest Renfrewshire railway which can still be identified on the ground is the 3.5-mile waggonway that connected the mineral and chemical workings at the Hurlet with the Johnstone-to-Glasgow canal. First planned by James Watt in the 1770s, this was in existence in the 1820s, if not before, and a stretch of the waggonway can be seen on either side of the Hurlet-to-Barrhead road at the Waterside Inn. The section from the side of the pub car park to the site of an old mine is quite distinct, and the section of the line from the road to the river can be easily traced in winter when it is not obscured by undergrowth.

The earliest steam railways were also connected with mineral workings. This was the case with the Stockton and Darlington Railway of 1825 (although it also carried passengers). The first mainline passenger railway was between Liverpool and Manchester, and opened in 1830. The railway mania soon

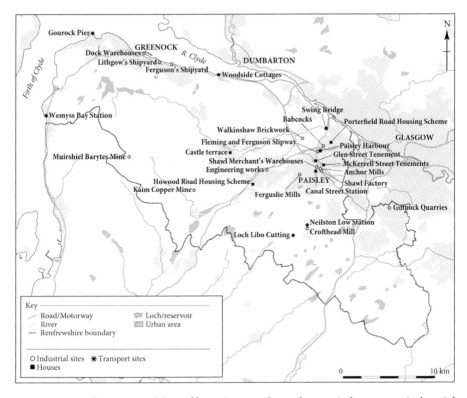

Figure 95   Map of late nineteenth- and twentieth-century industrial
sites and houses in Renfrewshire (Ingrid Shearer).

spread to Scotland. In 1831, the Glasgow to Garnkirk line opened, though it
is interesting to note that a short-lived steam-powered railway had been in
operation bringing coals to Troon harbour as early as 1808. The first railway
projects in Renfrewshire were all connected in some way with the desire to
connect Glasgow to the coast.

Pride of place goes to the Paisley and Renfrew Railway Company – founded
in 1834. The enabling Act of Parliament was passed in 1835, it opened in 1837
and was completed by 1841. The company had a goods yard at Greenlaw, a
station at Abercorn, a spur to the harbour, Fulbar Street and Wharf Station
in Renfrew. The plan to divert the Glasgow–coast traffic through Renfrew
was not a success, and the railway reverted to horse power in 1842 and was
sold in 1847. The line was re-laid as a standard gauge track in 1866, during
the next railway boom, and linked to the main line at Greenlaw. The track
can be clearly seen behind Reid Kerr College in Paisley and at various points

towards Renfrew. The platforms of Abercorn Station, which Professor John Butt claimed to be the earliest railway station in Scotland, can be clearly seen from the supermarket car park next to the college.

The next two local companies were the Glasgow, Paisley and Greenock and the Glasgow, Paisley, Kilmarnock and Ayr Railway Companies, both authorised by Act of Parliament in 1837. The government encouraged competition, but one of the rare examples of co-operation was the line between Paisley and Glasgow, built by both companies in direct competition to (and with opposition from) the operators of the canal. The engineer for the line was Joseph Locke, who, along with Stephenson and Brunel, was one of the three giants of early British railway development. He took considerable care over the construction of the stone bridge over the White Cart in Paisley, which his biographer describes as 'an early masterpiece which became the model for his later work'. It consists of 2,200 tons of light-coloured sandstone with a span of 85 feet, 54 feet above the river. The light-coloured sandstone marks the original viaduct and the earliest parts of what was then called Paisley Station. It was renamed Gilmour Street Station when St James Station was opened. The accesses and arches to the west of the station are also part of the 1840s construction. The magnificent sweep of the red sandstone façade of the station and its approaches dates from the 1880s when the line was quadrupled. The Glasgow and Paisley Joint Line opened in 1841 and was an immediate success. The coach companies gave up. It is still the current main line between Paisley and Glasgow.

At Paisley, the two lines parted company, heading for the coast at Ayr and Greenock. The Greenock line was difficult to construct. The main problems were opposition from the Canal Company (on the Glasgow–Paisley stretch) and the Blantyre Estate at Erskine, who were very uncooperative. The company was also faced with the physical problem of making the cut through the high ground at Bishopton. At one stage 3,500 navvies were employed. Although enthusiastically supported in Greenock and Port Glasgow, the line was not an immediate success, due to the increase in steamboat connections to Glasgow (themselves another result of the application of steam power to the dredging of the river in the 1820s).

The increased trade between Glasgow and Greenock and Port Glasgow eventually justified the expenditure on the line, which cost £35,624 per mile – considerably higher than the estimated cost. (The estimate was £393,000 for 22 miles. By 1843, £666,666 had been spent.) The opening of the line in 1841 also created the conditions for Bishopton and Langbank to become railway suburbs. Late Victorian stone villas near Bishopton Station, and the row of stone villas stretched out parallel to the shore (including the possibly 'Greek' Thomson Woodside Cottages) in Langbank, are possibly the first of many suburban dwellings built in Renfrewshire soon after the advent of the railway. It is a credit to the original surveyors that the line still follows the same route, and the cutting which caused so many problems at Bishopton can still be admired.

The Ayr line from Paisley is also the current main line, passing through Elderslie, Johnstone, Milliken Park and the present Lochwinnoch Station (at some distance from the village). This created the possibility of suburban development in these communities. The line was built in a shorter time, at less cost, than the much longer Greenock line. The main opposition was from Kilmarnock Council, which wanted the Ayr line to pass through the town.

In the eastern part of the county, another line which would eventually stretch to Ayrshire was under construction. In 1848, the Glasgow, Barrhead and Neilston Direct Railway opened from the South Side Station in Glasgow to Barrhead and Speirsbridge. Although much altered, the Italianate coigning of Barrhead Station is a good example of 1840s railway architecture. In 1853 the line extended to the mills at Crofthead.

As elsewhere in Britain, the railway boom of the 1830s and 1840s established the backbone of Renfrewshire's railway network. Many lines which opened later have since closed while the earliest lines are still in use. They established suburban communities in many Renfrewshire villages and transferred the movement of some goods from the (much slower) roads and canals. However it should be noted that the Glasgow–Johnstone Canal and the connecting waggonways (e.g. from the Hurlet and Nitshill mines) remained the main artery for the transport of coal to Glasgow well into the second half of the nineteenth century. Like the survival of water-powered mills after the introduction of steam-powered manufacture, the canal survived long after the widespread introduction of railways.

A range of narrow gauge railways can be found across Renfrewshire. These include a surviving example of a mineral railway embankment, which can be seen at Linwood associated with clay, coal and ironstone extraction. There are many miles of narrow gauge track within the Bishopton Ordnance Factory, and there were smaller systems at, for example, Greenock and Paisley Docks, the Coats factory at Ferguslie and the barytes mine at Muirsheil. The track, platform and engine shed of a moorland narrow gauge railway, for sporting purposes, exists on Duchal Moor.

HOUSING

The growth in the population of Renfrewshire became exponential in the early years of the nineteenth century. The evidence of the Old and New Statistical Accounts show the total population of the county rising from 26,645 in 1755, to 78,501 in 1801 and 112,175 in 1821. The numbers were swollen by people from Ireland (especially after the start of steam-powered ferries in the 1820s). The poorest lived in slum conditions in Paisley, Greenock and Port Glasgow, in houses which have long since disappeared. Only the better-built two-storey stone tenements from this period in the early to mid nineteenth century survive (e.g West Blackhall Street, Greenock; Napier Street, Linwood; West Brae, Paisley).

WATER SUPPLY

Overcrowded, sub-standard housing, inadequate water supply from wells, and almost complete lack of sanitation could only have one result. To modern eyes, the 1832 cholera outbreak in Paisley and Greenock was inevitable. It was followed in both towns by further outbreaks in 1834, 1848 and 1854. At the time, however, the medical connection was not established in the popular mind and there were mill-owners, and in Greenock sugar refiners, who wanted to use the available water supply in their factories.

There had been schemes for a water supply since the early 1820s (in fact, a paper had been presented to the Paisley Philosophical Institution before this), but it was the cholera epidemic which produced action. Robert Thom and Dr Kerr were the main supporters of a scheme which was authorised by the 1835 Act setting up the Paisley Waterworks Company. This established the reservoir at Stanely in 1838 (receiving the headwaters of the Espedair Burn) for drinking water, and the Harelaw Dam on the Glen Burn for the textile interests. In Greenock, the Shaws Water Company provided 21,000 cubic feet per day for the supply of houses and ships. By the end of the 1830s, Renfrewshire had one of the best water supplies in the country. Water from the Brock Burn in the east of the county was used to supply the then separate Burgh of Gorbals. The grandly named Gorbals Gravitation Water Company, under the terms of an act passed in 1846, constructed the four reservoirs (Balgray, Ryat Lin, Waulkmill Glen and Littleton), which are still such a feature of the landscape on the road between Barrhead and Newton Mearns (Fig. 96).

Figure 96   The Balgray dam, part of the Gorbals Reservoir
complex built at Barrhead (Derek Alexander).

GAS

The earliest application of small-scale gasworks gas was in the abundant cotton mills and bleach-fields, for heating and lighting. Paisley was one of the first towns in Scotland to build a gasworks and institute a public supply. Greenock took a little longer because the citizens could not agree where to site the works. The Paisley works are now gone, but the walls of the 1827 plant can still be seen in McKenzie Street in the town.

THE 1857 ORDNANCE SURVEY MAP

The developments described above shaped early Victorian Renfrewshire in the same way that cotton spinning had created communities and designated industrial areas. The best description of these areas at this time is to be found in the first edition of the Ordnance Survey map published in 1857. The growth of the textile and shipping and the attendant growth in engineering industries and mining, along with the coming of the railways, the increase in population and resultant demand for housing and services (and the continued increase in agricultural productivity, despite the crop failures of the 1840s) were the most significant developments.

16

Early Modern Renfrewshire

1850–

Even at the height of Renfrewshire's Victorian prosperity, there were indications that the world was changing. An economic downturn, known to some contemporaries as 'the Great Depression' led many to doubt Britain's continued ability to hold its position as the foremost industrial power. Although the products of Renfrewshire's textile, engineering and shipbuilding industries were sold throughout the world, people became aware of foreign competitors and new, emerging, technologies with which the country would have to contend in the coming twentieth century.

There are significant surviving industrial monuments representing these two groups, i.e. those which were derived from the well-established and still-expanding industries like cotton spinning, shipbuilding, railways and engineering, and those which developed as a response to the emergence of new technologies like electricity, aviation and motor cars.

THREAD

By the mid nineteenth century, the two principal thread manufacturers in Paisley were Clarks (Anchor Mills) and Coats (Ferguslie Mills). These two companies for a time dominated the world thread trade and the town of Paisley itself. Coats' mills at Ferguslie have largely disappeared apart from a gatehouse and the counting house, and the site has been given over to speculative house builders, but there are more substantial remains of Clarks'

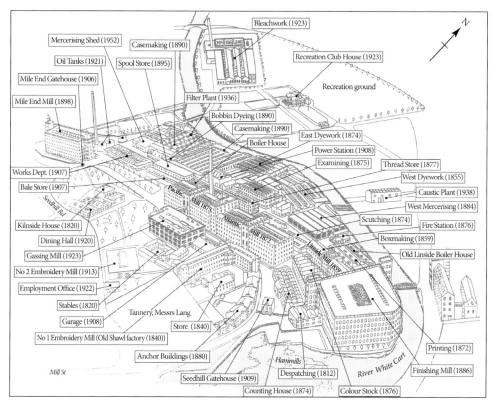

Figure 97   Anchor Mills, Paisley, showing the different building phases (re-drawn by Ingrid Shearer from drawing provided by Paisley Museum).

mill, particularly the East building or Mile End Mill, and gatehouses and other structures at Seedhill.

The Anchor Mills are located on the northern side of the White Cart in the centre of Paisley (Fig. 97). The main five-storey red-brick block of the spinning mill (1872) and twisting mill (1878) were demolished in 1973. The five-storey Mile End Mill, with its two towers, still survives, dominating the view of the weir from the modern road bridge. This red-brick structure with its arched topped windows on the upper floor and balustrading around the edge of the flat roof was built in 1899–1908. Other structures survive within the complex, including two large chimneys. The old grey stone building that is now the 'Abbey Mills Business Centre' at the Seedhill Gate was originally a shawl factory.

Travelling along the main road from Barrhead to Lugton, via the Barrhead Gap, the immense white painted structure of Crofthead Mill seems to appear suddenly as you round the bend (Plate 14). The group of buildings is dominated by the eastern structure: a six-storied flat-roofed building with numerous large round-headed windows. The cotton mill here was founded in 1792 but the original structure was burnt to the ground in 1883. What are left are No. 2 and No. 3 mills, built in 1880 and 1881 respectively. In addition to the mill buildings themselves, there is a series of related features such as the settling ponds and the dams further upstream on the Levern Water at Holehouse. Rows of millworkers' cottages can be seen at Crofthead Cottages and at the western end of Neilston village looking down to the mill itself. The remains of the mill owners' landscaped gardens around their house at Cowden Hall lie to the west of the mill. Traces of many features can still be seen, such as trackways lined with mature trees, tennis court and boating pond. The works were originally owned by the English Sewing Company, but were taken over by Tootal, who were in turn taken over by Coats Viyella. The mill was closed down in 1993, and its long-term future must now be in doubt.

SHIPBUILDING

Wooden ships sailed to Clyde harbours well into the twentieth century, but iron ships heralded the start of the great era of shipbuilding. The first iron ships built by Greenock owners were constructed around 1853. The predominance of the Clyde in nineteenth-century world shipbuilding is now difficult to comprehend. Renfrewshire contributed a considerable amount of the gross annual tonnage. Unfortunately little now remains of the early nineteenth-century yards in Paisley, Renfrew, Port Glasgow and Greenock where the ships were built.

The last few years have witnessed the regeneration of the shoreline of Greenock and Port Glasgow. One inevitable by-product has been the destruction of many Victorian docks and shipyards. Coming downriver, passing Port Glasgow, it was possible to see (listing only the most prominent) a ship breakers; Lamont's yard; Ferguson's yard (still there beside Newark Castle); Lithgow's; Hamilton's; Lithgow's Kingston Yard (ship repair still continues on the Lithgow sites); 700 yards of brick warehouses at Cartsburn; behind them, Garvel Graving dock (1871); James Watt Dock (1878); a number of smaller shipyards; Victoria Harbour; East Harbour; Custom House (still there); West Harbour; Scott's Yard; Albert Dock; and Princess Pier with the railway terminus.

Figure 98   Industrial archaeology – the Inchinnan
swing bridge built in 1923 (Derek Alexander).

There were other shipbuilding centres at Renfrew and Paisley. The magnificent swing bridge built in 1923 and canalised stretch of the river at Renfrew are testimony to the long struggle to keep the Cart navigable (Fig. 98). There are extensive remains of the silted-up harbour, which was heavily used during and after the Second World War. On the opposite bank of the river just before the entrance to the airport, there was a concentration of shipbuilding and marine engineers (Fullarton, Hodgart and Barclay, Bow Maclachlan and Fleming and Fergusson) but only the end of Fergusson's slipway can be seen opposite the harbour. Shipbuilding was also carried on in Renfrew. William Simon moved to the town in the 1860s, and the firm of Simon and Lobnitz was famous for building dredgers.

MINING

Although Renfrewshire's mining past has almost disappeared from living memory, there are many sites, in several areas of the county, which still bear witness to this once-flourishing industry. The mid nineteenth century was the boom time for Renfrewshire coal, clay, sandstone and ironstone. The growth of heavy engineering in West Central Scotland (in particular, Lanarkshire) led to greatly increased demand for Renfrewshire coal and a new demand for ironstone. Deposits of this mineral were extensively worked in a series of relatively short-lived pits at the Hurlet and between the west of Paisley, Linwood and the outskirts of Johnstone. The 1863 OS map records the position of many of these pits (e.g. at Darluith, Clippens and East Fulton). Shale from the spoil tips was exploited after the discovery of James 'Paraffin' Young that shale oil could be distilled from the mineral, and the Clippens Shale Oil Company flourished in late Victorian times. Coalmining continued and some of the adits and shafts of deeper workings at Quarrelton and Hurlet possibly date from this period.

The expansion of industry and housing led to the development of Renfrewshire quarries and brickworks – mining the clays to be found in the same area around Linwood. Brown's Brickworks at Ferguslie in Paisley and Walkinshaw Brickworks near Inkerman provided millions of bricks. There are still extensive remains of the Walkinshaw Brickworks. Building sandstone came from quarries at Giffnock which commenced about 1835. By the 1890s there were six quarries in action in the area, including those at Braidbar, Orchard, Patterton and Whitecraigs, and the stone was extensively used in Glasgow. Traces of these quarries (most of which were later infilled and their spoil tips removed) could be seen in the 1960s at NS 561595 and 571589 and can still be seen in the Giffnock–Thornliebank railway cutting. In 1908 over 150,000 tons of sandstone were produced. Coal and limestone were also worked. Wood for construction, as has been noted, came from Canada via Greenock and Port Glasgow.

Mining, clay, lime and ironstone working and quarrying in turn led to an expansion of the railway network and the continuation of the use of the canal as the central artery of a whole system of mineral railways until its closure and the reopening as a railway in 1881. The remains of the embankments of the network of mineral railways which connected clay and ironstone workings at Walkinshaw, Inkerman and Ferguslie can still be seen. In the east of the county, stone was transported by rail after the completion of the East Kilbride line in 1864. A siding was laid for this purpose from Giffnock Station to the Orchard Quarry.

One of the more unusual metals mined in Renfrewshire was copper. This took place at Kaim and at Calder Glen in Lochwinnoch Parish. The remains of sandstone buildings associated with the copper mine can still be seen at Kaim.

They include a powder store, remains of a crushing mill, another structure and spoil tip. Judging from the rise in copper prices in the 1850s, the venture probably dates from the mid nineteenth century. According to a local history, it was 'short-lived'. There were several copper mines in Scotland at this time, but by the 1870s they had all ceased production.

Vestiges of another unusual mining enterprise can also be seen in the Calder Valley and Eaglesham moors. Barytes mines are a very evident scar on Muirsheil Moor with the pink barytes seam and track of the mineral railway evident. About a mile away is the ruin of the water-powered crushing mill. The working was reopened in 1941, but closed in 1969.

RAILWAYS

In 1847, the Glasgow, Paisley, Kilmarnock and Ayr Railway became part of the Glasgow and South Western Company, and in 1851 the Glasgow, Paisley and Greenock amalgamated with the Caledonian Railway Company. The 1860s and 1890s booms in railway construction in Renfrewshire can largely be understood in terms of the rivalry between these two concerns.

During the 1860s boom the Glasgow and South Western's allies made clear their intention to compete with the Caledonian for the Greenock trade. In 1861, a group of Renfrewshire landowners (supported by Ayrshire collieries, Greenock merchants and Glasgow and South Western capital) promoted the Bridge of Weir Railway Act, which was passed in 1862. The line from Johnstone was opened in 1864 as far as the cotton mills. In 1865, the Bridge of Weir Railway Company sold out to the G and SW.

Bridge of Weir was never the same again. The railway was, for evermore, the dividing line between the existing mill village (1790s) and the mid nineteenth-century commuter belt, on the recently feued Ranfurly estate. Frank Arneil Walker quotes an advertisement from the Greenock and Ayrshire Railway Company offering a half-price annual season ticket to those building a house in the village '. . . for the convenience of house builders a copy of the Ranfurly feu charter could be seen a Bridge of Weir railway station'. The present Castle Terrace was built in 1882 as the Ranfurly Hotel.

The G and SW pushed on towards the coast. James Murray, in his history, reports a similar effect on Kilmacolm. He writes 'On that summer day in 1869, when the first railway train steamed into the newly erected station, modern Kilmacolm was born . . . For centuries the population of the village had not exceeded 300, in 1871 it had risen to 395, in 1889 it was 1,170, in 1891 it was 1,647, in 1900 it was close on 2,000, and it is now [1907] probably above 2,500'. The railway had created another Renfrewshire commuter village. Later in the century the Ranfurly Hotel was joined by the (now demolished) Kilmacolm Hydropathic, and railway passengers were encouraged to visit Renfrewshire's own spa.

The line reached its terminus at Princess Pier station in Greenock, opened in 1875, and proceeded to take the trade of the Caledonian Railway, whose station was in the centre of the town.

Determined to re-establish its premier position (and a steamer pier), the Caledonian had two plans. The first was the construction of a branch line from Port Glasgow to Wemyss Bay and Inverkip, which was completed in 1865. The steamer connection from Wemyss Bay to Rothesay commenced in 1870. This was another Renfrewshire community which owed its development to the railway. Many of the distinctive red sandstone buildings date from this time, and the red sandstone was quarried locally.

The Caledonian Railway's other plan was less successful. They owned the pier at Gourock and intended to construct a three-mile branch line from their existing track, under Greenock in a tunnel longer than any other, to the pier. This plan had to wait another 20 or so years before it came to pass.

The rivalry continued in other parts of the county. In 1865, the Caledonian bought the Busby Railway (a branch of the 1840s Barrhead line), constructed the previous year, serving the Giffnock Quarries and terminating at Busby Printfield. This led to the spread of more Victorian villas (in Giffnock and Busby – another 1790s cotton village) and was extended in 1868 to East Kilbride. The following year, the G and SW bought the Renfrew railway, doubled it and connected it to the rest of the network at Greenlaw junction. The 'Caley' unsuccessfully opposed the purchase of the canal by the G and SW when the canal finally closed. There was some co-operation on the Neilston and Barrhead Direct line. Like the Bridge of Weir and Busby Railways, this was first built to a textile works (Crofthead) and subsequently extended past Neilston Low station (now a scrapyard) into Ayrshire, although the cut at the Loch Libo Gap caused difficulties. A stone wall and remains of the platform are all that remains of the earliest Neilston station, which was the terminus of the Glasgow line in 1840s. Stuart Nisbet has pointed out that many of the earliest lines ended at industrial sites.

Modern Bridge of Weir, Kilmacolm, Busby and Giffnock were largely the products of the 1860s railway boom. In the 1880s, two pieces of unfinished business were completed. The Caledonian finally opened Gourock Pier Station, and the G and SW opened the line laid along the canal in 1885.

The last period of railway construction took place between 1890 and the First World War and mainly included goods and passenger lines which were closed in the mid twentieth century. From the archaeologist's point of view, these are more interesting since, being abandoned, they can be visited. The rivalry between the two companies continued unabated but expansion was less successful. Competition had been supported by the growth of trade in the mid nineteenth century, but by the 1890s the most viable railways had been constructed; the tramcar was taking passenger trade and, from the 1920s onwards, more goods went by road.

The G and SW built two new Ayrshire lines. One extended the Canal line in the first decade of the twentieth century and involved the construction of stations in Kilbarchan and Lochwinnoch for a line passing down the western side of Castle Semple Loch. The other Ayrshire line served the south side Glasgow suburbs and provided Neilston and Uplawmoor with second stations (the much later, surviving wooden signal box at Lugton Junction is worthy of note). Meanwhile, at the coast, the 'Caley' rebuilt Wemyss Bay. This station, described by Frank Arneil Walker as 'a miracle of intersecting curves: the finest railway architecture in Scotland', was completed in 1904.

There was some co-operation on the Glasgow and Renfrew Joint Railway, which had stations at Renfrew, Ibrox and Deanside (still an operational goods siding) and connecting back to the Glasgow to Paisley joint line. The line no longer exists but it can be traced in surviving land boundaries from Paisley to Renfrew (e.g. behind Reid Kerr College, where the track can be clearly seen).

The most remarkable example of rivalry, however, must be the so-called 'Battle of The Braes'. Travellers between Paisley and Barrhead cannot fail to notice the railway embankments and cuttings which criss-cross the fields between the two towns. These were also the result of competition between the Glasgow and South Western and the Caledonian. The G and SW built a branch from Meikleriggs junction to Potterhill on the south side of Paisley. They later extended this line to Glenfield then Barrhead and finally connected to the new line via Neilston High to Ardrossan. Not to be outdone, the 'Caley' built a line from Paisley St James via Ferguslie, Stanely, Glenfield, Blackbyres West Junction and Barrhead. At the junction, there was a connection to a line which headed north via Dykebar, Hawkhead and the east end of Paisley to rejoin the Paisley and Glasgow Joint Line at Greenlaw. Both companies had thus constructed circular routes (G and SW from St Enoch's to Paisley to Barrhead and back via Pollokshaws, and the 'Caley', a circular route from Barrhead to Paisley). The existing lines and the tramcars had got there before them; both lines closed for passenger traffic well before the First World War.

We have already noted the extensive network of mineral lines (e.g. the north–south running embankment at NS 460 645, which served the pits and brickworks at Inkerman and Walkinshaw). There were other mineral lines at Greenock Docks and Muirsheil Barytes Mine. The most unusual line was the one built for grouse shooting on Duchal Moor. The track, engine shed and grouse butts are still extant.

ENGINEERING

In Paisley, the area north of Gilmour Street station on the east bank of the Cart was formerly occupied by several engineering works but little trace of them now remains – but there was another significant centre nearby. Several Johnstone firms specialised in the manufacture of machine tools, and some of their machines can be seen in operation at the Summerlee industrial museum in Coatbridge. The site of an iron and brass foundry and several early nineteenth-century stone-built workshops still survive. The last firm closed recently.

HOUSING

From the 1870s onwards, substantial sandstone-fronted tenements took the place of the two-storey buildings and 'jerry-built' slum properties of the early nineteenth century as the predominant form of working-class housing in the Glasgow area. In Greenock, for example, the Burgh was extended in 1801, 1832 and 1866, and much of the new housing was tenement property. Paisley, Port Glasgow and the industrial areas of Renfrewshire's villages were no exception. Indeed, many late nineteenth-century tenements survive to the present day surrounded by countryside or later suburban sprawl when the industrial site for which they provided accommodation has long since been obliterated (e.g. Foxbar House, Paisley and nearby vanished bleach-field, NS 483 613). It was principally in the towns that the late Victorian redevelopment took place. For example, what is now Dunn Square and the Abbey grounds in

Paisley were cleared, and construction commenced on the tenements in the area at the rear of the present Grammar School. (The earliest surviving are probably the streets off Seedhill Road and Argyle Street in the West end. The Brisbane Street tenements in the west end of Greenock and Bouverie Street (*c*.1870) in Port Glasgow date from the same period.)

Tenements were not exclusively working-class housing, and many very grand tenements were constructed (e.g. Carriagehill, near Brodie Park in Paisley). Other tenement frontages reflected current architectural trends, such as the Co-operative Buildings in Lady Lane, Paisley designed by Peter Caldwell (1891–92) and (another Co-operative commission) the tenement in Glen Street, Paisley, designed by noted local architect W.D. McLennan in Art Nouveau style.

Following the earlier example of Ranfurly in Bridge of Weir, several areas were feued for large detached villas for the urban middle class. McLennan was involved in several commissions in Potterhill, in Paisley. Kilmacolm and the West End of Greenock developed similar enclaves. The part of Renfrewshire nearest the south side of Glasgow had long been a favoured area for successful city businessmen to settle. This is still the case, but over the last century and a half the average size of property has dramatically declined in size. A good eighteenth-century example is Greenbank House (Newton Mearns), the Georgian mansion house of Glasgow (and Port Glasgow) Merchant, Robert Allason. Holmwood House (just over the county boundary in Cathcart) is a mid nineteenth-century, southside, suburban villa. It was designed by Alexander 'Greek' Thomson for James Couper and was built in 1857–58. James Couper and his brother Robert owned the Millholm paper mill on the river below Holmwood House. The mill was founded in 1730 and continued in use until the 1930s (Fig. 99). The house is situated on a gentle hillside above the steep bank of the White Cart. This classically inspired villa, with its columns and pediments, is considered to be Thomson's finest domestic work. The property was acquired by The National Trust for Scotland in 1994 and has been wonderfully restored following its use in the early twentieth century as a convent school. Painstaking conservation work continues in the interior to reveal the original stencilled wall decoration. During the restoration work, an archaeological excavation took place in the small walled garden to the north-west of the house. Comparing map evidence with the excavated remains allowed at least five phases of garden development to be identified. This work removed a large twentieth-century concrete pond, and it is now displayed as a Victorian kitchen garden. Robert Couper also

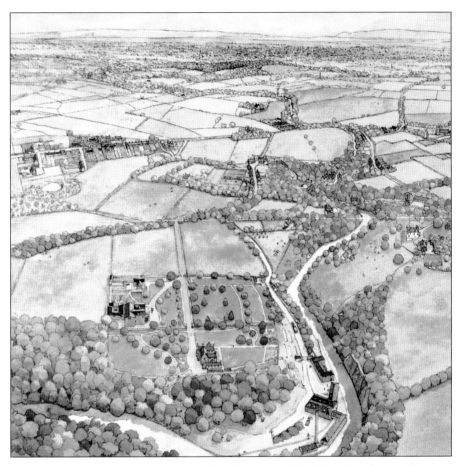

Figure 99 Millholm paper mill with Sunnyside villa and Holmwood House above (courtesy Jim Proudfoot and the National Trust for Scotland).

had a villa called 'Sunnyside' that sat to the east of Holmwood House but was demolished.

It was, however, the railway which turned the north-eastern part of the county into commuter-land and led to the breaking up and disposal of earlier estates and farms to speculative builders. This process accelerated as more lines were opened after the 1860s. The Busby and Giffnock Railway led to the development of Busby as a suburb (the East Kilbride line was made double track from Busby in 1881 to accommodate this). Clarkston dates from speculative building at the end of the nineteenth century on the hill between Sheddens and Clarkston station. On the other hand, Giffnock did not really flourish as a suburb until the quarries passed their peak of production.

Railways also led to the expansion of settlements at the other end of the county. One of the results of the Glasgow and South Western/Caledonian rivalry was that areas to the south of the coastal strip were opened up for housing, and Greenock was able to expand when the railway line was built. In particular, the Caledonian line extension to Gourock allowed people to conveniently live or work close to stations throughout the built-up area since it established a line linking Port Glasgow to Gourock via Bogston, Cartsdyke and Fort Matilda. Further (negative) proof of the importance of the railway in the development of Renfrewshire communities is shown (although there were other factors at work) by the decline of Eaglesham after the fire and closure of the cotton mill in 1876. Although population was in decline before then, numbers went from over 2,000 in the mid nineteenth century to fewer than 800 in 1900. There was no Eaglesham railway to tempt other industries or commuters.

The 1905 Neilston/Ayrshire line, mentioned above, led to further expansion (for example some early twentieth-century villas in Neilston). Other communities on the line were established later. Newton Mearns' suburban housing dates more from the development of the Broom Estate in the 1920s, by which time, the motor car was beginning to become a factor, and Patterton Station was not opened until 1929.

WATER SUPPLY

The increasing populations centred on Paisley and Greenock led to a continuous expansion of the public water supply for industrial and domestic use throughout the later nineteenth and early twentieth centuries (Fig. 100). Harelaw (1841) Reservoir was linked with a filter station to the earlier dam at Stanely, but continued water scarcity in the 1860s led to the construction of Rowbank Reservoir (1870) with filter stations at Howwood (NS394594) and Craigenfeoch (NS433608) to supply the Johnstone and Elderslie areas. A drought in 1879, and continued scarcity thereafter, was in part remedied by the addition of the Glenburn Dam (1881) and the Camphill Reservoir between Largs and Dalry (1886), which was linked by trunk piping via Kilbirnie to Rowbank. The system was further augmented in 1916 by adding Barcraigs to Rowbank, and, due to increased demand (particularly from the Ordnance Factory at Bishopton), adding Muirhead Reservoir to Camphill (1943).

Water supply to Greenock had been provided early in the nineteenth century

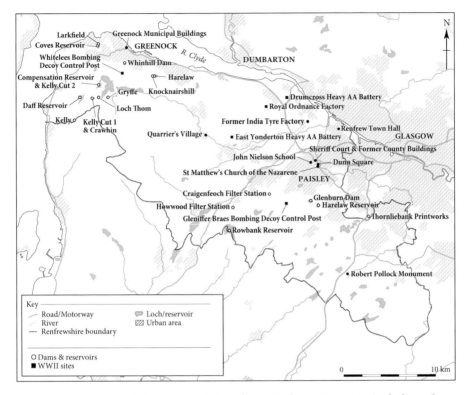

Figure 100   Map of twentieth-century sites including, dams, reservoirs and Second World War sites (Ingrid Shearer).

by the Shaws water scheme involving Loch Thom and the Compensation Reservoir, which were joined by the Cut to the Whinhill Dam above Greenock. This was supplemented in 1846 by reconstructing the Whinhill Reservoir (following a disastrous dam burst in 1838) and linking two new dams (Kelly and Crawhin) by the Kelly Cut to the original Compensation Reservoir. By an Act of 1866, the supply was further increased by constructing two further dams below Loch Thom on the Gryffe and linking the lower dam by a direct tunnel to Whinhill Reservoir. The embankment of Loch Thom was also raised, considerably increasing its capacity. Gourock's supply came from the Coves Reservoir (1862), supplemented in 1889 by Larkfield and, in 1919, by the Daff Reservoir. Port Glasgow was served by the Glenhuntly Burn and then the Gryffe Reservoir, via dams at Harelaw and Knocknairshill. Further east the cotton mill reservoirs at Eaglesham were adapted for public drinking water use from the twentieth century.

PUBLIC BUILDINGS AND BENEFACTIONS

Many of the monuments and public buildings of modern-day Renfrewshire are products of the county's late-Victorian prosperity and confidence. They are part of the area's rich and varied architectural history – rather than its archaeology – and are comprehensively described in Frank Walker's excellent guide *The South Clyde Estuary* (1986), which covers the present Renfrew and Inverclyde districts.

The public buildings of this era were built for many purposes. Some, like the Quarrier's Homes between Kilmacolm and Bridge of Weir, the John Neilson School and Dunn Square in Paisley, were the products of philanthropy. Quarrier's Homes was a Victorian model village built from the 1870s onward as the Orphan Homes of Scotland by Glasgow philanthropist William Quarrier. The prominent domed building at the west end of the Oakshaw ridge, in Paisley, was originally a school, built in 1852 as the benefaction of Paisley grocer, John Neilson, and is now private dwellings. Dunn Garden and Square was gifted to the town by former MP and South Africa merchant Sir William Dunn. Other buildings were the product of the more complicated relationship which existed between wealthy citizens (mill owners etc.) and their fellow townspeople (workers) and which might be more accurately described as paternalism. There are many Paisley examples: The George A. Clark Town Hall (1879–82), The Museum and Art Gallery (1868–81), Coats Observatory (1883) and the Coats Memorial Church (1894). On a slightly smaller scale are the Glen Hall, Neilston and the Crum Memorial Library in Thornliebank. Very little survives of the enormous printworks that the Crum family ran throughout the nineteenth century at Thorliebank until its closure in 1929 (Fig. 101). Landowners in rural areas also undertook these sort of benefactions (e.g. the Mure Hall in Uplawmoor).

The prosperity of the times was also evident in the construction of elaborate churches and public buildings. The town halls of Paisley and Greenock were and are particularly ornate expressions of civic pride. Renfrew Town Hall was built in the 1870s with a prominent, elaborately decorated clock tower, designed by Paisley architect James Lamb. The Sheriff Court in Paisley, built in 1885, and the adjacent former County Buildings of 1890, and Greenock Sheriff Court are suitably grand and even in Police Burghs like Barrhead the council buildings are noticeably grander than their neighbours. Frank Walker in his book lists many of the notable nineteenth-century churches in the county. Designed in the early twentieth century, in the Glasgow Style

Figure 101   The huge Thornliebank printworks run by the Crum family
from 1789 until it closed in 1929 (East Renfrewshire Council).

by architect W.D. McLennan, St Matthew's Church of the Nazarene was
formerly St George's United Free Church. Frank Walker designates it as
'perhaps Scotland's most Art Nouveau church', both inside and out. Walker
describes it as beginning 'as neo-Perpendicular Gothic' and ending 'in a
Glasgow Style idiom'. The original plans included a massive spire, which
would have stood out boldly over the surrounding area.

   Another group of buildings whose origins are distinct, but less immediately
identifiable, are the Co-operative buildings which stand in every
Renfrewshire community. They range from shops, to tenements, to factories
and indicate the influence and wealth of the Co-operative movement at this
time. They are often decorated by wheatsheafs or the initials of the society
and were sometimes very grand (PCMS Tenement, Lady Lane, Paisley or
the adventurous Co-operative tenement designed in Art Nouveau style by
William McLennan in Glen Street, Paisley).

NEW INDUSTRIES

There are a few surviving buildings which came into existence as a result of
the 'new' industries of the period 1880 to 1914. Probably the most complete is

Paisley's first electric power station built around 1900. Although now reduced in status to a sub-station, it still stands in Blackhall Street in Paisley from where it powered the local tram system and the first electric lighting. Almost all evidence of the extensive tram network has now disappeared, apart from some brackets to secure the overhead cables to the walls of tenement buildings in Paisley (e.g. at the Gordon Street and Causeyside Street junction), and the remains of one wall of the Elderslie Depot. The India Tyre factory at Inchinnan is a reminder of the early motor industry, and nearby is the site of early airship and aircraft construction and the area's first airport.

Early airstrips (like trams), which were formerly part of the Renfrewshire landscape, have disappeared almost without trace. There was an airstrip associated with the Scottish Aviation Company flying school 1911–12 at Barrhead. Whiteforeland Point, Battery Park, Gourock was used in the 1930s by various civil flying-boat operations including West of Scotland Air Services. There was also a civil flying-boat terminal at Greenock in the 1930s. During the Second World War the former Caird's shipyard was used by the RAF for flying-boat maintenance. Civil flying-boats, including Aquila Airways of Hythe, operated again from Greenock between 1950 and 1955. William Beardmore and Company manufactured and tested airships and aircraft at Inchinnan between 1916 and 1921. There was a flying club strip at Windhill, Newton Mearns, between 1934 and 1936, and Barns Farm, Whitecraigs, was home to the Glasgow Gliding Club in the 1930s. The best remembered former airport was at Renfrew.

WARTIME REMAINS

The two World Wars of the twentieth century left their mark on the Renfrewshire landscape. Look-out and anti-aircraft emplacements have survived best, since they were generally situated on high ground, though some still survive in lowland farms. There are some air raid shelters which survive as garden huts and more substantial remains, for example, the enormous Bishopton Ordnance factory (Fig. 100). The Royal Ordnance factory at Bishopton grew out of the First World War facility at Georgetown with the acquisition of Dargarvel House and the surrounding farmland. In the Second World War, the workforce expanded to 22,000 operatives and the area was enclosed by patrolled security fencing. After the war, under the Ministry of Defence several thousand were employed in the manufacture

Figure 102   A concrete shelter and ammunition store of the East Yonderton anti-
aircraft battery with another gun emplacement behind (Derek Alexander).

of explosives, rocket fuel, etc., but it is currently being decommissioned. A
solitary wartime hanger survives at Abbotsinch, and the remains of a coastal
battery can be found at Cloch Point.

The heavy anti-aircraft battery at East Yonderton consists of a command
post, four octagonal gun pits (Plate 15), electrical board structure, two
rectangular buildings and Nissen hut in the woods just off the approach road.
The command post is built below ground with its roof at ground level. It
consists of one large room and three smaller ones plus two emplacements
above ground. Its walls are constructed from brick and its roof from concrete.
The gun pits are constructed from concrete and brick (Fig. 102) and the gun
holdfasts are still in situ. The main electrical distribution board housed in a
small open-fronted brick building in the centre of the site still has some of
the electrical ducts in situ.

More overgrown remains of a heavy anti-aircraft battery can be found at
Drumcross and includes a command post, four octagonal gun pits, two five-
bay magazines, a single ten-bay magazine and a gun store. The gun pits are

constructed from concrete and brick with earth piled up against the outer walls. The gun holdfasts are still in situ. There are still some remains of the paths running from the magazines to the gun emplacements and the original road to the site is now a farm track. Other good anti-aircraft batteries can be found at Larkfield, west of Coves Reservoir, south of Gourock, and at High Mathernock. These were all part of the 12th Anti-Aircraft Division, which was responsible for the defence of the Clyde Basin during the Second World War.

There are also a number of good bombing decoy control posts in Renfrewshire, as at Whitelees and on the Gleniffer Braes. The Whitelees site consists of a rectangular building 4.3m × 3.6m with an internal height of 2m. It has an entrance in the south-west corner with a small porch projecting over it. This is flanked on either side by brick 'cheeks' for blast protection. The structure is built of bricks with a reinforced concrete roof 0.3m thick. In the roof is an observation hole 0.6m square, which has a protecting concrete rim 0.6m high around it. On top of the rim are the remains of a hinged cast-iron drain cover. This observation hole is reached by an internal ladder constructed from seven iron rungs set into the north-east wall. Close to the entrance at ground level is a circular opening, possibly a cable duct. The structure is situated on a rocky knoll and shows evidence of an earth mound surrounding. There is still earth on the roof of the structure.

Gleniffer Braes bombing decoy control post lies in farmland at the junction of two field boundaries and consists of a rectangular building 3.9m by 3.3m with an internal height of 2.2m. It has an entrance in the south-east wall with a small porch projecting over it. This is flanked on either side by concrete 'cheeks' for blast protection. The structure is constructed from bricks, three bricks thick with a concrete roof 0.3m thick. In the roof is an observation hole 0.6m square, which has a protecting concrete rim 0.6m high around it. This observation hole is reached by an internal ladder constructed from seven iron rungs set into the north-west wall. Also in the roof is a circular hole 120mm in diameter. The structure is surrounded and partially buried in an earthen mound 14m in diameter and at a maximum of 1.5m high.

One of the most famous Second World War incidents of the county happened at Floors, near Eaglesham. On fields near this farm, Rudolf Hess, Hitler's deputy, crash landed a Messerschmidt 110 on the evening of 10 May 1941 and was arrested by members of the Busby Home Guard. He had flown 1,000 miles from Augsburg near Munich in an attempt to contact the Duke of Hamilton as part of an abortive peace mission.

MOTOR CARS AND PLANNERS

The tramcar may have come and gone, leaving little trace on the landscape, but the motor car is a different story, in Renfrewshire, as elsewhere. The Arrol-Johnston car factory in Underwood Road, Paisley has been built over by houses and only the office block of the giant car plant at Linwood now remains, but the effect of the motor car is everywhere to be seen.

The increasing volume of vehicles has been demonstrated by both the construction of the M8 motorway (the latest chapter in the long history of the links between Glasgow and Greenock) and the Erskine Bridge, which replaced the chain car ferry (the slipway of which can still be seen). The most striking effect of the motor car is the suburban sprawl, which has swamped the Renfrewshire villages of Houston, Crosslee, Erskine and Inchinnan, doubled the size of Neilston, Newton Mearns, Renfrew and Wemyss Bay and added to the extent of most other communities. Coupled with the effect of the earlier, planned estates built on the fringes of Paisley, Greenock and Port Glasgow, the result has been to produce a very different Renfrewshire from the county as it was 200 years ago. Probably only the main streets of Eaglesham, Lochwinnoch and Kilbarchan would be recognisable to an inhabitant from those days.

Another effect of the motor car has been to alter people's view of the landscape. You don't see much from an air-conditioned car travelling at 60 miles per hour. Many of the sites mentioned in this book are not accessible by car. To find them you have to read former descriptions of the county; follow the river valleys; look at old buildings; walk down country lanes and turn into side streets; climb small hills and hike out onto the moors. If you do, you will be rewarded by finding traces of other Renfrewshires, left behind by 8,000 years of our common history.

Conclusion

The Future of Renfrewshire's Past

Renfrewshire's past is often missing from present national syntheses of archaeology and history, but the previous chapters have undoubtedly shown that upon closer examination there is a wealth of material surviving across the county. Prehistoric evidence abounds: from the struck flints of Mesolithic hunter-gatherers and buried pots of Neolithic farmers to Bronze Age burials with jet necklaces and the hill forts of the Iron Age. Likewise Renfrewshire's Roman sites have been examined and the early Christian crosses drawn and recorded. Medieval castles of timber, earth and stone have been excavated and planned, while the ecclesiastical centre of the county, Paisley Abbey, has been the subject of wide-ranging research, especially the artefact-rich fills of the wonderful drain. Some of the other church sites have also been recently investigated. Finally, Renfrewshire's important remains from the agricultural and industrial revolutions have also started to attract the attention they deserve.

People often ask archaeologists 'hasn't it all been found?' and 'is there anything left to discover?' The answer is there is plenty of research to be undertaken. Field-walking will continue to find artefacts in ploughed fields, and the recent discovery of the Bronze Age burnt mounds in East Renfrewshire and the ditched and palisaded enclosure at Mar Hall clearly show that there are major new discoveries still to be made. Developer-funded archaeological work, such as that at Mar Hall, carried out by professional archaeology companies, will continue to play an important role in increasing our knowledge, but there has always been a strong amateur input into research in the county and local individuals and groups will have a major role to play. The Renfrewshire Local History Forum and its Archaeology Section will continue to be at the core of this work.

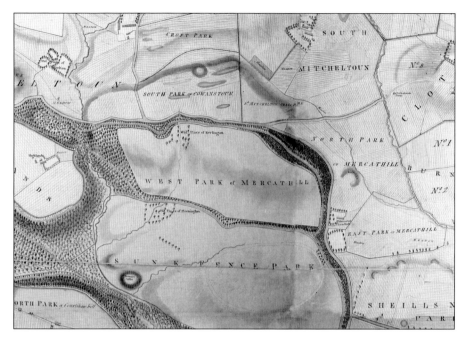

Figure 103   Extract of 1780 Castle Semple Estate map showing abandoned
farm/village sites at Fleemingston, Hersington and Chapelton.

Survey and targeted excavation of prehistoric sites would certainly help in the understanding of the development of settlements in the area. Few of the hut circles and hill forts, for example, have been subject to radiocarbon dating. Well-resourced research projects could easily tackle these issues. For the later periods, as Stuart Nisbet has demonstrated, there needs to be detailed analysis of the historical records in conjunction with fieldwork, if the right sorts of questions are to be asked and answered. Topics such as the urban archaeology of towns such as Greenock, Paisley and Renfrew, or the industrial development of rural Renfrewshire would easily fill books in their own right. Church archaeology is crying out for attention.

The use of old county or estate maps, such as the wonderful colourful example of Erskine Estate by Charles Ross in 1774 (Plate 16), would merit further investigation. The Royal Commission surveyors produced some interesting results in East Renfrewshire by comparing the farms on Ainslie's eighteenth-century farm plans to those shown on nineteenth-century Ordnance Survey maps and checking them against what survives on the ground today (Alex Hale, pers. comm.). Understanding how the landscape we see today was created, especially over the last 300 years, is key to understanding the evidence of Renfrewshire's past.

As a final example, the Castle Semple Estate map (Fig. 103) is worth considering close up. The map, drawn around 1780, is a fantastic record of part of Renfrewshire during the agricultural improvements. These changes were often instigated by new wealthy landowners such as the MacDowalls who had made their money from slave-run sugar plantations in the Caribbean. The map shows changes made but also shows older sites that have been abandoned prior to the date of the survey. Of particular interest are the abandoned farm/village sites that are marked as 'old place of Hersington' and 'old place of Fleemingston', which may be medieval sites as the place names appear to possibly be Anglo-Norman (twelfth century). Further to the north, there is another site marked as 'old yards of Chapelton'. These sites, and others marked on the map, can be located accurately on the ground and would surely merit investigation.

This book has highlighted some of the major sites of Renfrewshire's past and it is hoped that future work will ensure that they do not remain 'hidden'.

Appendix

LIST OF MAJOR ARCHAEOLOGICAL INVESTIGATIONS

———◆–◆–◆———

Site	Site type	Date exc.	Date pub.	Excavators
Cuff Hill, Lugton	Chambered cairn	1874	1876	Love
Milton Bridge, Kilmacolm	Motte	1894	1907	Murray
Langbank East, Langbank	Crannog	1901–02	1908	Bruce
Capelrig, Newton Mearns	Cross (site of)	1926	1927	Lacaille
Whitemoss, Bishopton	Roman fort	1950–54	1997, 1998	Newall
Camphill, Queen's Park	Earthwork	1951	1953	Fairhurst & Scott
Walls Hill, Houston	Fort	1956	1960	Newall
East Green, Kimacolm	Cairn?	1956, 1967	1973	Newall
Knockmade, Lochwinnoch	Homestead	1959–60, 1967	1996	Livens
North Wood, Pollok Park	Earthwork	1959–60, 2007	DES	Johnson, Driscoll & Mitchell
Knapps, Kilmacolm	Homestead	1961–62	1965	Newall
Craigmarloch, Port Glasgow	Vitrified fort	1963–65	1996	Nisbet
Levan Castle, Gourock	Castle	1966, 1970–72	1993	Denholm
Mearns Castle, Mearns	Castle	1970	DES	Talbot
Barochan Hill, Houston	Roman fort	1972, 1984–86	1998	Keppie & Newall
Old Barr Castle, Erskine	Castle	1973	DES	Hunter
Sheils, Renfrew	Ditched enclosure	1973–74	1996	Scott
Crookston castle, Crookston	Ring-work and tower	1973–75	2003	Lewis (Talbot)
South Mound, Houston	Round cairn	1974	1996	Stables

South Mound, Houston	Cists	1976	1979	Morrison
Cathcart Castle, Cathcart	Castle	1980	DES	Kerr
Newark Castle, Port Glasgow	Castle	1984, 1997	1998	Lewis
Paisley Abbey, Paisley	Monastery drain	1990	2000	Malden
Greenbank House	Garden	1994	DES	Turner
Picketlaw, Neilston	Hut circle	1995–97	1996	Alexander & Henry
Barrhouse, Neilston	Farmstead	1995–2003	DES	Henry
Holmwood House	Garden	1997–98	DES	Glendinning & Neighbour
Renfrew Castle, Renfrew	Castle (site of)	1997	DES	Alexander
Elderslie	Moated manor	1998	2000	Alexander
Braehead, Renfrew	Ditched enclosure	2001	2008	Ellis
Floakside	Farmstead	2002	DES	Stentoft
M77, Loganswell	Roundhouses	2002	DES	Cook
Titwood, Mearnskirk	Palisaded enclosure	2002	2003	Johnston & Rees
West Acres, Newton Mearns	Round house	2002	2005	Toolis
Old Kilbarchan Church	Graveyard	2002	2004	Addyman
Weaver's Cottage, Kilbarchan	Weaving shed	2002, 2007	2004 & DES	Alexander
Neilston Parish Church	Church	2003	DES	Sneddon & Swan
Mar House, Erskine	Ditched and palisaded enclosure	2007	DES	Lynchehaum

DES = summary entry published in *Discovery and Excavation in Scotland*

Select Bibliography and Further Reading

GENERAL HISTORIES AND GUIDES

Crawfurd, G. A *General Description of the Shire of Renfrew*. 1710. *Continuation* William Semple (Paisley, 1782). *Revised* George Robertson (Paisley, 1818).

Hector, W. *Archaeological and Historical Collections referring to the County of Renfrew*, 2 vols (1890).

Marwick, J.D. *The River Clyde and the Clyde Burghs* (Glasgow: Scottish Burgh Records Society, 1909).

McCrae, G. 'Renfrewshire's Historic Monuments – a Heritage under Threat', *Renfrewshire Local History Forum Journal* Volume 2 (1990).

Metcalfe, W.M. *A History of the County of Renfrew from the Earliest Times* (Paisley: Gardner, 1905).

Mort, F. *Renfrewshire* (Cambridge: Cambridge University Press, 1912).

Walker, F.A. *The South Clyde Estuary: An Illustrated Architectural Guide to Inverclyde and Renfrew* (Edinburgh: Scottish Academic Press/Royal Incorporation of Architects in Scotland, 1986).

Welsh, T.C. *Eastwood District: History and Heritage* (Eastwood: Eastwood District Libraries, 1989).

Wilson, J. *General View of the Agriculture of Renfrewshire* (Paisley: Stephen Young, 1812).

BOOKS ABOUT PARTICULAR AREAS

Anderson, E.G.R. *The Parish of Lochwinnoch* (Lochwinnoch: The Author, 1987).

Anon. *Guide to Paisley and Surrounding Districts* (Paisley: J. and R. Parlane, 1896).

Black, C. S. *The Story of Paisley* (Paisley: J. and J. Cook, 1948).

Brown, R. *History of Paisley,* 2 vols (Paisley: J. and J. Cook, 1886).

Blair, D.W. *Long Slope, Small Hill: The Story of Giffnock* (Glasgow: Vista, 1972).

Burgess, M. *Discover Erskine, Bishopton and Langbank* (Renfrew: Renfrew District Council, 1994).

Burgess, M. *Discover Kilbarchan, Bridge of Weir and Houston* (Renfrew: Renfrew District Council, 1995).

Burgess, M. *Discover Linwood* (Renfrew: Renfrew District Council, 1993).

Burgess, M. *Discover Lochwinnoch and Howwood* (Renfrew: Renfrew District Council, 1994).

Burgess, M. *Discover Renfrew and Inchinnan* (Renfrew: Renfrew District Council, 1993).

Clark, S. *Paisley: A History* (Edinburgh: Mainstream, 1988).

Crawfurd, A. 'The Cairn of Lochwinnoch' (unpublished MS held in Paisley Public Library).

Deighton, J.S. *Eaglesham, An Earl's Creation* (London: Johnson, 1974).

Dennison, E.P., Stronach, S. and Coleman, R. *Historic Barrhead: Archaeology and Development,* The Scottish Burgh Survey (Edinburgh: Historic Scotland, 2008).

Dunn, J.A. *History of Renfrew* (Renfrew: Renfrew Town Council, 1971).

Eastwood District Libraries. *A Planned Village: History of Eaglesham* (Eastwood: Eastwood District Libraries, 1988).

Eastwood District Libraries. *Calico, Cotton and Character: A History of Busby* (Eastwood: Eastwood District Libraries, 1988).

Eastwood District Libraries. *Crum's Land: A History of Thornliebank* (Eastwood: Eastwood District Libraries,).

Eastwood District Libraries. *Fairest Parish: A History of Mearns* (Eastwood: Eastwood District Libraries, 1988).

Eastwood District Libraries. *Sandstone to Suburbia: A History of Giffnock* (Eastwood: Eastwood District Libraries, 1988).

Hamilton, T.W. *How Greenock Grew* (Greenock: James McKelvie, 1947).

Houstoniana: an Historical, Antiquarian, Topographical and General Record (Houston: Campbell, 1864).

Johnstone Community Council. *Old Johnstone in Pictures* (Johnstone Community Council, 1982).

Lyle, W.H. *History of Bridge of Weir* (1975).

McCarthy, M. *A Social Geography of Paisley* (Paisley: Paisley Public Library, 1969).

McClelland, R. *The Church and Parish of Inchinnan: A brief History* (Paisley: Alexander Gardner, 1905).

Murray, J. *Kilmacolm, A Parish History* (Paisley: Gardner, 1907).

Murray, R. *Annals of Barrhead* (Barrhead: Barrhead Community Council, 1994).

Parker, D.P. 'A History of Elderslie' (Elderslie Community Council, 1999).

Pride, D. 1910 *History of the Parish of Neilston* (Paisley: Gardner, 1910).

Roe, D. *Kilmacolm: A History – Secrets of a Renfrewshire Village* (Edinburgh, 2007).

Ross, Revd W. *Busby and its Neighbourhood* (Glasgow, 1883).

Scott, Revd A.B. *Old Days and Ways in Newton Mearns* (Glasgow, 1939).

Simpson, A.T. and Stevenson, S. *Historic Renfrew; the archaeological implications of development*, Scottish Burgh Survey (Glasgow: Dept of Archaeology, University of Glasgow, 1981).

Simpson, A.T and Stevenson, S. *Historic Paisley; the archaeological implications of development*, Scottish Burgh Survey (Glasgow: Dept of Archaeology, University of Glasgow, 1982).

Smith, R.M. *The History of Greenock* (Greenock: Orr, Pollock and Co., 1921).

Wilson, A. *Eaglesham Bicentenary Year, 1769 – 1969* (Paisley: Renfrew County Council, 1969).

Winters, J. *Linwood* (Stroud: Tempus, 1999).

PREHISTORIC RENFREWSHIRE (CHAPTERS 1–4)

Alexander, D. 'Aerial photograph sites in Renfrewshire', *Renfrewshire Local History Forum Journal*, Vol. 4 (1992): 17–24.

Alexander, D. (ed.) *Prehistoric Renfrewshire: Papers in Honour of Frank Newall* (Paisley: Renfrewshire Local History Forum, Archaeology Section, 1996).

Alexander, D. 'Sites and artefacts: the prehistory of Renfrewshire' in D. Alexander (ed.), *Prehistoric Renfrewshire* (1996), pp. 5–22.

Alexander, D. 'Previous archaeological work' in D. Alexander (ed.), *Prehistoric Renfrewshire* (1996), pp. 1–4.

Alexander, D. 'Prehistoric Archaeology of Renfrewshire: the evidence' in S. James and G McCrae (eds) *Renfrewshire Studies* (Paisley: University of Paisley, 1997), pp. 13–29.

Alexander, D. and Henry, B. 'Picketlaw hut circle, Moyne Moor – an interim report' in D. Alexander (ed.), *Prehistoric Renfrewshire* (1996), pp. 29–32.

Boyd, W.E. 'Stratigraphy and Chronology of late Quaternary Raised Coastal Deposits in Renfrewshire and Ayrshire'. Unpublished PhD thesis, Glasgow University, 1982.

Bruce, J. 1908 'Report on investigations upon the Langbank pile dwelling', *Trans. Glasgow Archaeology Society*, New Series, 5 (1908): 43–53.

Hale, A.G.C. 'Marine crannogs: previous work and recent surveys', *Proceedings of the Society of Antiquaries of Scotland*, 130 (2000): 537–58.

Livens, R. 1996 'Knockmade homestead, Lochwinnoch' in D. Alexander (ed.), *Prehistoric Renfrewshire* (1996), pp. 33–42.

Love, R. 1875 'Notices of the several openings of a Cairn on Cuffhill . . .', *Proceedings of the Society of Antiquaries of Scotland*, 11 (1874–6): 272–97.

Morrison, A. 'A Bronze Age burial site near South Mound, Houston, Renfrewshire', *Glasgow Archaeological Journal* 6 (1979): 20–46.

Morrison, A. 'The Mesolithic period in South West Scotland: a Review of the Evidence', *Glasgow Archaeological Journal* 9 (1982): 1–14.

Newall, F. *Excavations at Walls Hill, Renfrewshire* (Paisley: Paisley Museums and Art Galleries, 1960).

Newall, F. 'Early Open Settlement in Renfrewshire', *Proceedings of the Society of Antiquaries of Scotland* 95 (1961–2): 159–70.

Newall, F. *Excavation of prehistoric and medieval homesteads at Knapps, Renfrewshire* (Paisley: Paisley Museums and Art Galleries, 1965).

Newall, F. 'Late Neolithic Settlement in Gryfesdale, Renfrewshire', *The Western Naturalist* 1 (1972): 42–58.

Newall, F. 'The destruction of a Bronze Age cairn on East Green Farm, Kilmacolm', *The Western Naturalist* 2 (1973): 97–106.

Newall, F. 'Renfrewshire in Prehistory: The Stone Ages', *The Western Naturalist* 3 (1974): 3–14.

Newall, F. 'Renfrewshire in Prehistory: The Bronze Ages', *The Western Naturalist* 5 (1976): 81–105.

Newall, F. 'Renfrewshire in Prehistory: The Iron Ages', *The Western Naturalist* 7 (1978): 3–20.

Nisbet, H. 1996 'Craigmarloch hill fort, Kilmacolm', in D. Alexander (ed.), *Prehistoric Renfrewshire* (1996), pp. 42–58.

Ramsay, S. 1996 'Human impact on the vegetation around Walls Hill', in D. Alexander (ed.), *Prehistoric Renfrewshire* (1996), pp. 59–64.

Scott, J.G. 'A. hoard of bronze weapons from Gavel Moss farm near Lochwinnoch, Renfrewshire', *Proceedings of the Society of Antiquaries of Scotland* 85 (1950–1): 134–88.

Scott J.G. 'The ditched enclosure at Shiels, Govan, Glasgow', in D. Alexander (ed.), *Prehistoric Renfrewshire* (1996), pp. 65–70.

Smith, J A. 'Note of the remains of the Irish Elk found in Scotland', *Proceedings of the Society of Antiquaries of Scotland* 9 (1870–2): 345–50.

Stables, D. 1996 'South Mound cairn, Houston', in D. Alexander (ed.), *Prehistoric Renfrewshire* (1996), pp. 23–28.

Toolis, R 'Bronze Age pastoral practices in the Clyde Valley: excavations at West Acres, Newton Mearns', *Proceedings of the Society of Antiquaries of Scotland* 135 (2005): 471–504.

ROMAN RENFREWSHIRE (CHAPTER 5)

Keppie, L. *Scotland's Roman Remains* (Edinburgh: John Donald, 1986).

Keppie, L. and Newall, F. 'Excavations at the Roman fort of Barochan Hill, Renfrewshire, 1972 and 1984–6', *Glasgow Archaeological Journal* 20 (1996–7): 41–76.

Murray, D. 'Note on a bronze handled pot of Roman manufacture, and two bronze falling handles found at Barochan, Renfrewshire', *Transactions of Glasgow Archaeological Society*, New, 1(4) (1890): 498–514.

Newall, F. 'Excavations at Outerwards', *Glasgow Archaeological Journal* 4 (1976): 111–23.

Newall, F. 'Romans in Strathclyde; first century AD occupation', *Western Naturalist* 4 (1975): 79–93.

Newall, F. 'The Roman Fort on Whitemoss Farm, Bishopton, Renfrewshire. Part 1: The Excavations of 1950–1954 and 1957', *The Scottish Naturalist* 109 (1997): 55–96.

Newall, F. 'The Roman Fort on Whitemoss Farm, Bishopton, Renfrewshire. Part 2: Whitemoss and the Antonine Wall: The Place of Whitemoss in Roman Scotland', *The Scottish Naturalist* 110 (1998): 13–43.

Tacitus. *Agricola* (Harmondsworth: Penguin, 1970).

EARLY HISTORIC RENFREWSHIRE

Alcock, L. and E.A. 'Reconnaissance excavations on Early Historic fortifications and other royal sites in Scotland, 1974–84: 4, Excavations at Alt Clut, Clyde Rock, Strathclyde, 1974–75', *Proceedings of the Society of Antiquaries of Scotland* 120 (1990): 95–149.

Allen, J.R. and Anderson, J. *The Early Christian Monuments Scotland* (Edinburgh: Society of Antiquaries of Scotland, 1903).

Craig, D. 'The early medieval sculpture of the Glasgow area', in A. Ritchie (ed.), *Govan and its Early Medieval Sculpture* (Stroud: Alan Sutton Publishing Ltd, 1994).

Driscoll, S. *Alba: the Gaelic Kingdom of Scotland ad 800–1124*, The Making of Scotland Series (Edinburgh: Birlinn, 2002).

Graham-Campbell, J. and Batey, C.E. *Vikings in Scotland: an Archaeological Survey* (Edinburgh: Edinburgh University Press, 1998).

Hughson, I. 'The sculptured stones of Govan and Renfrewshire', *Renfrewshire Local History Forum Journal* 6 (1994): 22–8.

Johnson, M., Rees, A. and Ralston I 'Excavation of an Early Historic palisaded enclosure at Titwood, Mearnskirk, East Renfrewshire', *Scottish Archaeological Journal* 25(2) (2003): 129–45.

Lacaille, A.D. 'The Capelrig Cross, Mearns, Renfrewshire; St Blane's Chapel, Lochearnhead, Perthshire; and a sculptured slab at Kilmaronock, Dumbartonshire', *Proceedings of the Society of Antiquaries of Scotland* 61 (1926–7): 122–42.

Macquarrie, A. *Crosses and upright monuments in Strathclyde: typology, dating and purpose* (Glasgow: Friends of Govan Old, 2006).

Steel, A. *Place-Names and Social Organisation in Clydesdale: Territorial Organisation in Pre-Feudal Strathclyde* (Unpublished MS, no date).

Stuart, J. *The Sculptured Stones of Scotland* (Aberdeen, 1856).

MEDIEVAL RENFREWSHIRE

Alexander, D. 'Duchal Castle: an initial survey', *Renfrewshire Local History Forum Journal* 4 (1993): 17–24.

Alexander, D. 'Feudal Renfrewshire and the Stewards: History and Archaeology', *Glasgow Archaeology Society Bulletin*, No. 40 (Spring 1998): 4–9.

Alexander, D. 'Excavation of a medieval moated site in Elderslie, Renfrewshire', *Scottish Archaeological Journal* 22(2) (2000): 155–77.

Alexander, D. and Steel, A. *Wallace, Renfrewshire and the Wars of Independence* (Edinburgh, 1997).

Clark, S. 'Queen Blearie, The vicissitudes of a legend', *Renfrewshire Local History Forum Journal* 9 (1998): 3–6.

Denholm, P.C. 'Excavations at Levan Castle, Gourock, 1966 and 1970–72', *Glasgow Archaeological Journal* 16 (1993): 55–80.

Howell, A.R. *Paisley Abbey: Its History, Architecture and Art* (Paisley: Gardner, 1929).

Lewis, J. 'Excavations at Newark Castle, Port Glasgow: 1984 and 1997', *Proceedings of the Society of Antiquaries of Scotland* 128 (1998): 905–921.

Lewis, J. 'Excavations at Crookston Castle, Glasgow 1973–75', *Scottish Archaeological Journal* 25(1) (2003): 27–56.

Malden, E. *Unpublished Descriptive List of Renfrewshire Castles, Tower-houses and Manor Places* (c.1970? Held in Paisley Museum).

Malden, John (ed.) *The Monastery and Abbey of Paisley.* (Paisley: Renfrewshire Local History Forum, 2000).

MacGibbon, D. and Ross, T. *The Castellated and Domestic Architecture of Scotland from the Twelfth to the Eighteenth Century*, Vols 1–5 (Edinburgh, 1887–92).

MacGibbon, D. and Ross, T *The Ecclesiastical Architecture of Scotland from the Earliest Christian Times to the Seventeenth Century*, Vols 1–3 (Edinburgh, 1896–7).

Mason, G.W. *The Castles of Glasgow and the Clyde* (Musselburgh: Goblinshead, 2000).

Poll Tax Roll 1695, Paisley Central Library, Reference Dept.

Steel, A. *Timothy Pont's Renfrewshire* (Paisley: University of Paisley, 2003).

Steel, A. *In the Name of the Lion: Wallace, Renfrewshire and the Wars of Independence* (Paisley: Renfrewshire Local History Forum, 2007).

Talbot, E.J. 'Early Scottish castles of earth and timber: recent fieldwork and excavation', *Scottish Archaeological Forum* 6 (1974): 48–57.

Topen, D. *The Castle and Lands of Stanely, Paisley: Renfrewshire*, Renfrewshire Local History Forum Occasional Paper No. 7 (2003).

Tranter, N. *The Fortified House in Scotland. Volume 3. South West Scotland* (Edinburgh: James Thin, 1986), pp. 149–65.

SIXTEENTH- TO TWENTIETH-CENTURY RENFREWSHIRE (CHAPTERS 9–13)

Alexander, D. 2002 'Dam Busters: the breaching of Greenock Reservoirs No 1 and 2', *Renfrewshire Local History Forum Journal* 11 (2001–2): 21–7.

Alexander, D., Addyman, T. and Roberts, J. 'Life's Rich Tapestry: Excavating the Kilbarchan Weavers', *History Scotland* 4(6) (Nov/Dec 2004): 48–53.

Butt, J. *The Industrial Archaeology of Scotland* (Newton Abbot: David and Charles, 1967), pp. 297–301.

Clark, S. 'The Shaws Water Falls in Greenock', *Renfrewshire Local History Forum Journal* 14 (2007–8): 26–31.

Clark, S. *Industrial Archaeology of Paisley* (Paisley: Renfrewshire Local History Forum, 1998).

Gow, B. *The Swirl of the Pipes: a History of Water and Sewage in Strathclyde* (Glasgow: Strathclyde Regional Council, 1996).

Hills, R.L. *James Watt Vol.1:His Time in Scotland 1736–1774* (Ashbourne: Landmark Publishing, 2002).

Hinxman, L.W., Anderson, E.M. and Carruthers, R.G. 'The Economic Geology of the Central Coalfield of Scotland. Area 1 Paisley: Barrhead, Renfrew . . .' *Memorials of the Geological Society of Scotland.* (Edinburgh: HMSO, 1920).

Hughson, I. and McCrae, G. 'Cowden Hall' *Renfrewshire Local History Forum Journal* 3 (1992): 28–31.

Hughson, M. *John Robertson, Engineer; Designer of the Comet's Engine* (Barrhead: Barrhead and Neilston Historical Association, 1989).

Hughson, M. 'Neilston Corn Mills' *Renfrewshire Local History Forum Journal* 6 (1994): 14–19.

Kelso, W.W. *Sanitation in Paisley: A Record of Progress, 1488–1920* (Paisley: Gardner, 1922).

Kelso, W. *The James Watt Story* (Greenock: The Author, 1997).

McCrae, G. 'Tannahill's Landscapes', in *Renfrewshire Studies II* (University of Paisley, 1998).

McIntosh, N.A. 'Changing Population Distribution in the Cart Basin in the Eighteenth and early Nineteenth Centuries' *Transactions of the Institute of British Geographers* No. 22 (1956): 139–57.

Milligan, T. 'The West of Scotland and the Slave System', in *Renfrewshire Studies II* (University of Paisley, 1998).

Nisbet, S. 'The Growth of Port Glasgow in the eighteenth Century', *Renfrewshire Local History Forum Journal* 3 (1992): 24–7.

Nisbet, S. 'A Note on the Midtown Limekiln near Howwood', *Renfrewshire Local History Forum Journal* 9 (1998): 30–1.

Nisbet, S. 'An Eighteenth Century innovation: Meikle Corseford lime quarries and mines', *Renfrewshire local History forum Journal* 10 (1999): 1–4.

Nisbet, S. 'The Four Paper Mills of Cathcart', *Scottish Local History Journal* 49 (2000): 29–33.

Nisbet, S. 'A Loch in Sheep's Grazing? Early Drainage of Castle Semple Loch', *Renfrewshire Local History Forum Journal* 12 (2004): 26–32.

Nisbet, S. 'The Archaeology of the Lime Industry in Renfrewshire', *Renfrewshire Local History Forum Journal* 13 (2005): 41.

Nisbet S. 'The Rise of the Cotton Factory in eighteenth Century Renfrewshire', BAR Report No. 464 (Archaeopress 2008).

Nisbet, S. 'A Sufficient Stock of Negroes', *Renfrewshire Local History Forum Journal* 14 (2008): 32.

Nisbet, S. *Castle Semple Rediscovered* (Paisley: Renfrewshire Local History Forum, 2009).

Nisbet, S. and Welsh T.C. *Robert Allason and Greenbank* (Eastwood Libraries, 1991).

Ramsay, P.A. *Views in Renfrewshire* (1839).

Robertson, C.J.A. *The Origins of the Scottish Railway System, 1722–1844* (Edinburgh: John Donald, 1983).

Rock, C.H. *The Weaver's Cottage, Kilbarchan* (Edinburgh: The National Trust for Scotland, 1962).

Shaw, J. *Water Power in Scotland, 1550–1870* (Edinburgh: John Donald, 1984), pp. 331–6.

Skillen, B. 'The Copper Mines of Renfrewshire', *Renfrewshire Local History Forum Journal* 8 (1997): 23–9.

Stephenson Locomotive Society. *The Glasgow and South Western Railway* (London: The Society, Undated).

Taylor, C. *The Levern Delineated* (Glasgow: W.R. McPhun, 1831).

Welsh, T.C. 'Horse and Water Power on Eaglesham Farms', *Eastwoodian Magazine* 2 (Eastwood District Council, 1991).

Index

Entries in bold, following the page numbers, denote Figure numbers. Colour plates are listed also in bold as **Pl. 3** etc.

Abbotsinch 202, 257
Aberdeen Breviary 137
Act of Union 151, 161, 171, 180, 182, 186
Adam of Kent 97
Addyman, Tom and Associates 176, 178, 266
Adelphi House 175
aerial photography 28, 42, 61–64, 66, 76–77, 105
Africans 183
Agricola 60, 71–73, 76
agriculture
  abolition of runrig 196
  buildings 111
  change 151, 171
  cycle 68
  destruction of sites1 59
  General View of County of Renfrew 190, 215, 221
  improvement 172
  increased productivity 180, 197, 240
  land clearance 26
  plots 148
  pre-improvement 161, 163
  pressure 47
  produce 140
  use of lime 198, 230
agricultural improvements
  abolition of runrig 196
  agent of change 148
  destruction of archaeological sites 6, 102, 196
  discontent with 196
  enclosure 173
  funding 184
  lack of early sites 147, 190
  mapping 263

new farms 7, 192, 196
prior to industrial change 197, 204
revolution 190, 261
Statistical Accounts 209
Aikenhead family 128
Ainslie, John surveyor 25, 102, 124, 148, 193, 209, 230
Aitken, Andrew 25
Alan, Steward of Scotland 106
Alba, Kings of 87
Albert dock 243
Aleynd Glasfrith 103
Alexander I, King of Scots 95
Alexander III, King of Scots 129
Alexander III, King of Scots coins 112
Allason, Robert 172, 176, 184–85, 249
Alt (Old) Patrick Water 215
alum 200, 232
America, trade 167, 201, 208, 219
American War of Independence 208, 219
Anchor Mills 241–2, **97**
Anderson, John 224
Andersonian Institute, Glasgow 227
Angles of Northumbria 81–83
Anglian 83
Anglo-Saxon 82
Anglo-Norman 98, 263
animal bone
  cattle 65
  Castle Levan kitchen midden 127
  comb 65
  Mote Hill, Ranfurly 101
  teeth 62
  use of 19
animals

carvings of 88–90
  pens 111
  wild 16
anti-aircraft battery 256–58, **102**, **Pl. 15**
Antonine Wall 75, 77
AOC Archaeology Ltd 43, 50, 51, 63–64 194
Aquila Airways 256
Arden limeworks 232
Ardgowan 125, 130
Ardgowan mill 140
Ardgowan, John of, 157
Ardrossan canal 217–18, 228, 248
Argyll Stone (St Conval's Chair) 153, **66**
Argyll, Duke of 169
Argyllshire 47, 81, 205
Arkleston 97
Arkwright, Richard 209
armour 119
Arran 19, 26, 33
Arrol-Johnston car factory 259
arrowheads 19, 22, 26, 33
artefacts
  early historic 86
  medieval 110, 122, 139, 261
  prehistoric 1, 6, 9, 11, 28–29, 32, 35–38,
    41–43, 48, 53–54, 58, 65–68
  post-medieval 157
  Roman 72
Arthgal, King of Strathclyde 84
Arthurlie cross 89–90, **43, Pl. 6**
Art Nouveau 255
Artnocks farm 195
Atlantic 181–2
Auchenbothie castle and farm 132,158–61,191
Auchenfoyle Farm 26
Auchentiber 162
Auchinleck church 109
Auldhouse Burn 91
Auldbar 91
axes
  carving on Barochan Cross 89
  copper/bronze axes 36–7, 48, **15**
  stone axes 10, 22–23, 26–27, 35, 38, 203, **5, 10**
  stone battleaxes 38–9
Ayr 166, 236
Ayr railway 237
Ayrshire 2, 7, 25–26, 38, 72, 77, 89, 93, 97–98,
  111, 123, 125, 141, 169, 217, 237, 246–47

Baldwin of Biggar 98
Balgray dam 238–9
Ballageich Hill 39
Balliol, John 113
Baltic trade 219, 233
Barbours of Kilbarchan 185, 203
Barcapel farm 9, 91

Barclay, Robert of Capelrig 173
Bargarran 151, 169
Bargrennan cairns 24
Barmufflock dam 214
Barngreen 202
Barns Farm, Whitecraigs 256
Barns, John 167
Barochan 20, 39
  Cross 88–90, **42, 43**
  Cross base 61, **30**
  Flemings of 145
  Roman patera 72, **36**
Barochan Hill, Roman fort 71–73, 76–77, 265,
  37, 38
Barr castle 7, 1 25–6, 158
Barr Loch 192
Barr Meadows 192
Barrhead
  alum works 232
  railway 248
  station 27
  Gap 17, 242
  Grampian Way 204
  industry and housing 216
  St Matthew's church 255
Barrhouse farm 13, 190, 193, 194, **78**
Barscube, Stewarts of 131
Barshaw Park
battles 5, 84, 95, 97, 106, 113–14, 120, 122, 124,
  134, 139, 140, 152, 248
  of Inchinnan (Knock) 97
  of Langside 122–23, 134, 140
  of Muirdykes 152–53, 169
Bayeux Tapestry 98
beads 26, 41, 68, **19, Pl. 1**
Beauchamp House 201
Beith roads 200
Bell, Henry 232
Bell Street hoard 112, **Pl. 9**
Ben Lawers 19, 30
Bennan Loch 37
Benston Pit 229
Bishops of Glasgow 135, 149
Bishopton Ordnance Factory 236–37, 252, 256
Bishopton railway cutting 236
Bishopton station 237
Black Cart Water 22, 128, 192, 200–01, 214
Black Cart, bridges 220
Black Dyke mine 197
Black, W.O. 9
Blackbyres station 248
Blacketty water 107
Blackhall 144, 154, 157
Blackhall ironstone 231
Blackston house 173
Blaeu map 6, 132

Blantyre Estate, Erskine 236
bleach-fields 13, 185, 187, 189–90, 204, 215,
    239, 249
bleaching 150, 175, 180, 189, 207, 211
Bluebell woods, Johnstone 229
Bluebell Woods, Langside, cup-and-ring
    marked boulder 31, **12**
Board of Trustees for linen manufacture
    187,189
Bogston station 252
bone see animal bone and see human remains
Bonnyton Moor homestead 49, **22**
Boulton and Watt 224
Bow and Maclachlan engineers 244
Bowling 38
bracelets 48, 54, 58, 64, 68
Bradley, Prof. Richard 30
Braehead 13
Braehead enclosure 63, 67–68, **32**
Braehead shopping centre 106
Braidbar quarries 245
bricks 106, 127, 211, 228, 242–43, 257–58
    kilns 231
    works 231, 245, 249
Bridge of Weir 41, 201, 213
    Castle Terrace 246
    cotton mills 214
    development of 216, 247
    railway 246
    Ranfurly Hotel 246
Brigantines 78
Brimstone Bridge lint mill 188
Britons 81–82
British Museum 113
Broadlie Mill 211–12, **83**
bronze
    cannon 133–34, **59**
    key 101
    prehistoric artefacts 35–38, 41, 53–54, 65, 68
    Roman patera and handles 72–73, **36**
Brock Burn 238
brooch 65
Broom bleachfield 190
Broom estate 252
Broomlands 201
Brown, David, Mill of Syde 162
Brown's brick works, Ferguslie 231, 245
Brownside farm 190, 222
Bruce, Marjorie 97, 113–14
Bryden, Andrew, John and Janet 202
Buchannan church 109
burghs 95, 120, 134–36, 140, 148, 163–66, 168
burial 32, 35, 68, 176–77, 179, 181, 261
    cairn 22, 32, **14**
    chamber 25
    cist 30, 39

deposits 45
goods 32
ground 86–87, 93, 143, 145
monument 41
mound 98
plot 182
site 1, 24, 27–53
tomb **65**
vault 143
burnt mounds 14, 42–43, 261
Busby place name 85
    cotton mills 211, 226, **82, 85, Pl. 13**
    development 247
    glen waulk mill 163, 188
    Home Guard 258
    industry and housing 216
    printfield 247
    railway 247, 251
Bute 72, 97, 226
Byres Hill, Barshaw Park 6, 105

Caird's shipyard 256
Cairn of Lochwinnoch 161, 185, 197
cairns
    Neolithic chambered cairns 7, 8, 24–26, 265
    Bronze Age cairns 12, 22, 26–27, 29, 32, 36,
        39–41, 44–45, 98, 101
Calder Glen copper mines 245
Calder U. F. (Burgher) Church 175
Calder Valley and Barytes mines 16, 246
Calderbank bleachfield 187
Calderbank lint mills 188
Calderglen Mill 228
Calderhall estate 216
Calderhaugh cotton mill 213, 228
Caldwell Tower and Hall 129, 154, 158,
    229–30, **92**
Caledones 81
Caledonian Railway Company 246–7
Campbell, Archibald, Earl of Argyll 153
Camphill, Queen's Park, enclosure 103, 105,
    265
Camphill Reservoir 252
Canada trade 219, 233
canals 149, 150, 165, 192, 216–18, 224–25, 234,
    236–37, 24–28, **87**
    see also Glasgow to Johnstone canal
    see also Johnstone canal
    see also Ardrossan canal
Candren Burn 218
Capelrig Cross 9, 91, **6, 43**
Capelrig house 172–3
Cardonald 36
Cardross house 113
Caribbean trade and plantations 149, 167,
    181–82, 263

Carling Craigs 32
Carlisle family 185
Carriagehill housing 249
Cart basin 159, 180, 197, 209
  aqueduct 218
  bridge 161
  lade 138
  navigation 217, 244
  river 234
  valley, mines 197
Cartsburn shipyard 243
Cartsdyke barony 164
Cartsdyke station 252
Cartside cotton mill 211
castles 1, 8, 12–13, 93, 97, 102, 105–09, 111,
  114–33, 140, 144, 158, 261
Castle Hill (East Barnaigh) fort 58, 76, 101, **26**
Castle Semple (Castleton) 122–23, 127, 129,
  132, 134, 183–85, 192
  Collegiate Church 142, **62**, **Pl. 10**
  estate 262
  house 172–73, 184, **75**
  loch 7, 133–34, 142
Castlehead 103, 231
Castlehill House and Gardens 106
Castle Levan see Levan Castle
Castlewalls farm 222
Cat Craig homestead and hut circles 48, **22**
Cathcart bridge 201
  castle 12, 121, 201, **55**
  church 109
  family 121–22
cattle 51, 101
cave 67
CFA Archaeology Ltd 85, **40**, **52**, **90**
Ceredig (or Coroticus) king 82
Chapel farm 143, 145
Chapell House, West Arthurlie 144, 173
chapels 82–3, 103, 109–10, 122, 136, 142–46,
  216, 221
Chapelton, Castle Semple 263, **103**
Chapelton Farm, Port Glasgow 145
Charles II, King of Great Britain 166
Chopin, Frederick 130
Chrisswell Chapel 115, 145–46
Christison, David 7
churches
  Early 82, 84, 86, 90
  Medieval 109–110, 118, 123, 136, 139–40,
    142–44, **53**
  Post-reformation 127–28, 143, 151, 166–67
    171, 175–76, 181, 201, 203, 216, 221, 254–5
churchyards 13, 82, 90, 168, 176, 181
cists 6, 25, 30, 32–33, 35, 39, 41, 68, 266
Clark, thread manufacturers 241
Clark, Patrick 228

Clark, Sylvia 13, 113, 150, 228
Clarkston 251
Claudius 71
Clippens Shale Oil Company 245
Cloak Burn 228
Cloch Lighthouse 220
Cloch Point anti-aircraft battery 257
Clochoderick stone 16, 94
Cluniac monks 97, 109
Clyde river and deepening 149, 164, 182, 220,
  225, 233
Coatbridge 249
Coats, thread manufacturers 218, 241, 243
Cochran, John Earl of Argyll 152–53
Cochrane family 161
Cochrane, Alex of Dundonald 158
Cochrane, Wm of Ferguslie 204
coins 1, 78, 83, 86, 95, 112–13, 118, **Pl. 9**
Coldstream Mill, Beith 192
Comet, the 232–3, **94**
Commore Dam 189, 213
Compton's mule 209
Connal or Conval, St 82, 137, 144
Constantine, St 84
Constantine I, King of Scots 84
Coplie Burn homestead 204, **22**
copper 36, 38, 100, 118, 205, 245–46
copperas 198, 200, 231
Cornalees bridge 200
Coronation Park, Port Glasgow 232
Corse, Robert 175
Corslie Hill 61, 72, 88–89, 105, **30**
cotton see mills
Couper, James and Robert 249
Covenanters 129, 151, 154, 168
Covenanter's Stones 39
Coves Reservoir 253
Cowden Glen animal bones 17, **8**
Cowden Hall 154, 157–58, 202, 243
Cowglen 97
Cowglen coal mines 229, **91**
Craigends castle 132
Craigends limeworks 198
Craigenfeoch water works 252
Craigmarloch fort 9, 11, 12, 39, 52–54, 66–8,
  93, **26**, **Pl. 2**
Craigie see Duncarnock
Craigminnan 168
Craigston Wood cup-and-ring marks 31, **13**
crannogs 8, 64–66, 72, 265
Crawford, Andrew 161
Crawford, James of Kilwynet 136
Crawfordsdyke and harbour 167, 180, 182
Crawfurd, Andrew 185, 197
Crawfurd, George 5, 228
Crawhin dam 253

Croc, Robert 97, 103
Crofthead 17
Crofthead cottages 243
Crofthead cotton mill and bleachfield 188–89, 237, 242, **Pl. 14**
Cromwell, Oliver 168
Crook Hill 91
Crookston Castle 2, 12, 265
  ringwork 97, 103–04, 105, **49**
  tower 117, 120, **54**
  cropmarks 64, 105
  crosses
  cross-base 11, 61, 91, 153
  cross-shaft 87–8, 90–3, 261, 265
  cross-slab 86, 88,90
  market crosses 136, 163–65, 191, **69**
  medieval cross-marked gravestones 143
Crosslee cotton mill and lade 213, **85**
Crosslee, industry and housing 216, 259
Crosslees cairn 39–40
Crum family 255
Crum Memorial Library 254
Cuff Hill 7, 24–25, **8**
cultivation 98, 173, 193
Cunningham family of Craigends 115, 123, 134, 143, 183, 198
Cunningham, barony of 119
cup-marks 5–6, 29–32, **12, 13**

Daff Reservoir 253
Dalriada 81
dams
  mill dams 56, 69, 142, 162, 187, 189, 192–93, 209, 211, 212–16, 221, **81, 96, 100, Pl. 3**
  reservoir dams 225–27, 238–39, 243, 252–53, **90, 100**
Damnonii 60, 72
Danielstoun, Hugh de 100
Danzielstone family 126
Dargavel House 158, 256
Darien Scheme 167, 180
Darluith mining 245
Darnley limeworks 232
David I, King of Scots 95–96, 134–35
David II, King of Scots 113
David's Tower, Edinburgh Castle 114, 124
Deaconsbank Golf Course 31
Deil's Wood (Castlehill Plantation) 101, **47**
Denniston (Milton bridge) motte 7, 99–100, 265, **47, Pl. 7**
  artefacts from 100, **48**
Derwent water 209
designed landscapes 173, 175
Douglas, Archibald, Lord of Galloway 124
Douglas, Francis 202
Douglas, James 142

Dovecothall cotton mill 209
Dowries Farm Hill 40
Dripps waulk mill 163
Drumcross anti-aircraft battery 257
Drumcross farm enclosure 64
Drumgrain mill 140
Duchal Castle 93, 98, 107, 120, 143, **50, 51**
Duchal house 172–73
Duchal moor and railway 204, 237, 249
Dumb Proctor, Lochwinnoch, cross shaft 91, **43, 45**
Dumbarton Rock 79, 83–84, 86, 120
Dumbuck 8, 64, 76, 165, 182
Duncan, King of Scots 95
Duncarnock (the Craigie) hill fort 9, 14, 16, 56–59, 67–68, 93, **27, 28, Pl. 3**
Dunconnel Hill 58, 67–68
Dundonald, Earl of 128, 154
Dunrod Hills 226
Duntocher fort 76
Dunwan Dam 212
Dunwan fort 55, 93, **27**
Dykebar station 248
dykes 173, 191

Eaglesham, barytes mines 246
  by-pass 85
  cairns 39
  church and churchyard 144, 154, 175
  cotton mills 211–12, 252
  Kirkton Burn, 225
  Montgomerie Street 204
  moor 73
  motte 101–02, **Pl.12**
  parish 220–2
  Polnoon Street 204
  village development 180, 191, 204, 216, 259, **Pl.12**
  water supply 253
Earl of Argyll 152
Earl of Arran 122
Earl of Carrick 114
Earl of Eglinton 122, 123, 144, 191, 204, 217
Earl of Lennox 118, 120
Earl of Mar/Mar, Earl of 204
earthwork castles see mottes and ring-works
East Fulton mining 245
East Green 10, 12, 44
East Kilbride railway 245, 7
East Revoch cairn and burnt mound 40, 43
East Yonderton anti-aircraft battery 257, **102, Pl. 15**
Easter Cochrane (Johnstone) castle 129
Eastwood church 109
Eastwood High School 173
Edward I, King of England 105

Edward I, II and III coins 112
effigies 143, 145, **63**, **64**
Elderslie 13, 111, 231
  distillery 215
  industry and housing 216
  moated enclosure 111–12, **52**
  mill 162
  station 237
  water supply 252
  see also Wallace's House
Elliston castle 115, 128–29
Elliston Mill 187
emigration 196
Empire Exhibition 173
English Sewing Company 243
English trade 181
Erskine Bridge 259, **33**
  church 109
  crannog 66,72
  development 131, 259
  estate 262, **Pl. 16**
  quarry 234
Espedair Burn 225, 238
estates 3, 93–4, 111, 125–26, 129, 132, 134,
  183–84, 172–73, 175, 185, 188–9, 204, 216,
  232, 251, 259
European trade 181

Fairhurst, Horace 105
Fairlie castle 125
farms 1, 6, 13, 111, 140–1, 159, 162, 190–92,
  195–96, 204, 217, 221, 251, 256, 262
farmsteads 7, 13, 52, 141, 159, 194, 266, **78**
Feachem, Richard 9
Fereneze Bleachfield 189
Fereneze Braes 73
Ferguslie 218
  brickworks 231
  mills 241
  mineral railways 245
Ferguson's shipyard 243
fieldbanks 46
field system 46, 160
field walking 10, 21, 261
Finlayston and castle 22, 115, 154
First World War 248–49, 256
Fitz Alan, Walter 96
Flavian 73
Fleemingston 263, **103**
Fleming and Fergusson engineers 244
Flemings of Barochan 105, 145
Flenders Farm, Mearns 196
flints 1, 19, 20–2, 26–7, 33, 41, 43, 261, **10**
Floak burnt mound 43
Floakside 13, 194, **78**
Flodden, battle of 143

Floors Farm, Eaglesham 258
food 17, 19, 23, 27, 84, 97, 155, 191, 197
Forehouse house 173
forest 2, 16–17, 26, 107–8, 141
Fort Matilda station 252
forts/hill forts 1, 6–7, 9–10, 14, 52–61, 67–69,
  79, 84, 93, 105, 141
  Roman forts 10, 27, 71–78
  vitrified fort 54, 265, **Pl. 2**
Foxbar House 249
French Wars 223
Fullarton, engineers 244

Gantocks 220
Garnieland mill 162
Garnkirk railway 235
Garvel graving dock 243
Garvel Park house 172, 175, 182
Garvock hill 39
Gavel Moss hoard 36–37, **15**
Gemmell, James of Garvel 175
geology 150
Georgetown 21
Georgetown Ordnance factory 256
Giffnock 112
  development 247, 251
  quarries 232, 245, 247
  station 245
Glanderston Dam 56, **Pl. 3**
Glasgow 207, 220, 232, 234
  and Renfrew Joint Railway 236, 248
  and South Western Railway 246
  Archaeology Society 104
  Barrhead and Neilston Direct Railway 237
  gliding club 256
  Guild of Hammermen 224
  Paisley and Greenock Railway 236, 246
  Paisley, Kilmarnock and Ayr railway 236, 246
  region 149
  shipping 225
  to Johnstone Canal 237, **87**
  Town Council 200, 225
glass 89, 122, 137, 195, 203
Glassford 103
Glen Burn 238
Glen Hall, Neilston 254
Glenburn Dam 252
Glencairn family 122–23
Glenfield station 248
Glenhuntly Burn 253
Gleniffer Braes 15, 73, 108, 222, 258
Glentyan house 172,175
Glentyan mill 162, 192
Gododdin 81
Golborne, John 220, 225, 182
Gorbals Gravitation Water Company 238

Gotter burn west 46
Gourock barony 164
  golf course 32
  pier and station 247–48, 252
  rope work 182
  water works 253
  Battery Park 256
Govan stones 85–87
Granny Kempock stone 29
grave goods 32, 35, 39, 41
gravestones 86, 143, 176
graveyards 243–45, 176–77, 179, 266, **Pl. 11**
Green Water 45, 107
Greenbank house 13, 172, 185, 249, **71**
Greenbank lint mill 188–9, **76**
Greenlaw junction 235, 247–48
Greenlaw House 175
Greenock 202, 204, 209, 212, 215, 223, 226,
  232
  and Ayrshire Railway Company 236, 246
  burgh and barony 164,166, 249
  Brisbane Street 250
  Custom House and Lane 166, 220, 243
  docks and harbour 166, 219, 224, 232, 237,
    243, 249
  East Harbour 243
  Gaelic church 216
  flying-boat terminal 256
  gas works 239
  James Watt Dock 243
  Lynedoch St 215
  Lynedoch Street 225
  planned town 191, 238
  Princess Pier and station 243, 247, 252
  reservoirs and water supply 225–27, 238, 252,
    90
  road(s) 200
  rope work 182
  Roxburgh Street 215
  Sheriff Court 254
  shipping and shipbuilding 220, 225, 232, 243
  timber trade 233
  turnpike 149
  tenements 216
  town hall 254
  Victoria Harbour 243
  West Blackhall Street 215, 238
  West End 215
  West End 249
  West Harbour 232, 243
Grimketil 97
Gryffe Castle 99, 101, **47**
Gryffe Children's Home 101
  dam 253
  reservoir 11, 26–27, 32
  river 22, 211

  valley 213
  Water 100
guns
  anti-aircraft guns 257–58, **102**, **Pl. 15**
  guns/canons 120, 133, 134
  gun loops 125, 129–30, 133–4, 154–5, 158, **59**

Haakon, King of Norway 97
Hadrian 74
Hairlaw Craigs 5
Halidon Hill, battle 113
Hall of Caldwell 173
Hamilton family 123, 134
Hamilton of Wishaw 166
Hamilton, Claud 122, 140, 154
Hamilton, John, Abbot of Paisley Abbey 122,
  139
Hamilton's shipyard 243
Hamiltons of Ferguslie 126
Harelaw Dam 213, 238, 252–53
  stone axes 26, 39, **10**
Hawkhead station 122, 248
Hawkhead, Ross of 143
hearths 7, 43–44, 50, 141, **20**
Hector, William 7
Helensburgh 232
Henry I, King of England 95
Hersington 263, **103**
Hess, Rudolph 258
Hessilhead 25
High Castlehill, Kilmacolm 55, **26**
High Mathernock anti-aircraft battery 258
Highlands, migration 202
Historic Scotland 3, 13, 103, 118, 154
Hillhouse 120
hill forts see forts
hoards 35, 37, 48, 53, 85–86, 112–3, **15, Pl. 9**
Hodgart and Barclay engineers 244
Holehouse 243
Holmwood House 13, 249, **99**
Holyrood chapel 122
Honourable Society of Improvers 190
housing estates 90, 102, 129, 132, 252, 259, 262
Houston church 109,143
  Alexander & Co. 183
  barony of 164
  family 198
  George 215, 225
  industry and housing 216
  Market Cross 164, **69**
  North Mound 41
  of Johnston 129
  Sir John 216
  Sir Patrick 143
  South Mound 6, 12, 41, 27–28
  village 216, 259

Howwood limeworks 229
Howwood water works 252
Hugh de Danielstoun 100
Hugh de Morville 96
Hugh of Pettinain 98
Hughson, Irene 12
human remains 179
  bones 6, 24, 176–7, 179
  skeletons 41, 86
  skulls 6, 24, 176, 203
Humbie farm and place name 85–86
hunting 17, 19–21, 23, 25–7, 107–08, 168, 261
Hunter, Jim 131
Hunter, Robin and Susan 13
Hunterian Museum 49, 76, 113, 224
Hurlet 200, 218, 228, 237, 245
Hurlet limekiln 231, **93**
Hurlet mines 150, 180, 197–98
Hurlet waggonway 225, 232, 234, **93**
Hurlet–Barrhead road 232, 234
hut circles 1, 13, 19, 33, 43–51, 53, 58, 60, 69,
  262, 266
  see also Picketlaw

Inchinnan
  bridge 200, 217, 220, 244, **98**
  carved stones 21, 82, 89–90, 153, **43, 44**
  palace 118
  village 259
India Tyre factory 256
Industrial Archaeology of Paisley 150
industrial revolution 171, 190, 204, 207, 215,
  217, 223–24, 227, 261
Ingleston 97
Inkerman mines and railway 150, 197, 245
Inkerman pits and brickworks 245, 249
Inverkip (Ardgowan) castle 125
Inverkip 98, 200, 226
  barony 164
  castle (Ardgowan) 130
  church 109
  marina 130
  parish 169, 220
  railway 247
Ireland 238
Irish trade 149, 181
iron 67–8, 84, 148–9, 198, 200, 220, 226,
  229–31, 237, 243, 245, 249

Jacobite rebellion 151, 204
Jamaica 183
James II and VII, King of Great Britain 152–53
James IV, King of Scots 107, 122–23, 139, 135
jetton 100, **48**
Johnstone canal 149, 217, 234
  Bluebell woods 198

bridge 215
castle (Easter Cochrane) 129, 132
High Church 175
Houston square 215
industry and housing 216
Laigh cotton mill 211
Ludovic square 215
mills 213, **84**
mining 245
Old Mill 175, 209, 211, **85**
planned town 191
station 237
water supply 252

Kaim copper mines 197, 245–46
Kaimhill limekiln 231, **93**
  mines 197
Kelly dam and cut 253
Kelso, Wm. 202
Kelvingrove Museum 9, 36
Kempock Point 29
Kenmuir Hill, folly 173
Kenneth II, King of Scots 84
Kentigern (Mungo), saint 82, 86
Kerr family 185
Kerr, Dr 238
Kerr, Peter 228
Kidd, William, Capt., 169
Kilbarchan 200, 203
  barony 164
  bleachfields 190
  Chapel (St Catherine's) 144
  church and graveyard 13, 109, 143, 176–79,
    203, **72, 73**
  development 187, 247, 259
  steeple 169, 202
  station 248
  Weaver's Cottage 13, 203
  West Parish Church 176
Kilellan church and manse 109–10, 141, 154,
  158
Kilmacolm and railway 246–47
Kilmacolm barony 164
  church 109–10, 143
  housing 249
  Hydropathic 247
  parish 220
  railway 237
Kilpatrick church 109
Kilwinning Abbey 123
Kilwinning cross 89
King's Inch 106
Kingarth church 109
Kingdom of Strathclyde 81–4, 88, 93, 95
King Ywain 95
Kirkton enclosure 64

Kirktonfield Dam 214
Knapps 10, 47, 68, **21**, **22**
Knapps farm 141
Knock Farm, Renfrew 39
Knock Hill 6, 97, 102
Knock or Kemp Knowe 102
Knockbartnock Farm 26
Knockmade 7, 10, 12, 40, 48, 67–69, **4**, **22**
Knocknairshill dam 253
Kyle and Carrick 115

Lacaille, A.D. 9
Lady Burn 46
Ladymuir Farm 168
Laggan Hill 44, 141, 159
Laigh Corsford limeworks 229
Lamont's shipyard 243
Lanarkshire iron works 149
landscapes
  medieval 16, 107, 120, 134, 140, 147
  modern 7, 148, 173, 192, 196, 238, 253
  prehistoric 29–30, 46, 51, 55, 62
  Renfrewshire 2, 15–6, 147, 197, 256
Lang Dyke 183
Langbank 219, 233, 236–37
  comb 66, **34**
  crannogs 64–65, 72
  raised beach 20
Langside, Battle of 123, 134, 140
Langstilly, Lochwinnoch 37
Largs church 109
Largs, battle of 97, 106
Larkfield reservoir 253
Law castle 125
Law Hill 101
Lawfield, Kilmacolm 39
Laxlie Hill cist 68
Leeward Islands, trade 182–83
Legerwood church 109
Levan castle 12, 125, 127
Levern cotton mills 213
Levern Delineated 218
Levern valley 211, 232
Levern water 36, 232, 243
lime 159, 180, 189, 198, 214, 230, 232
lime burner 25
lime kilns 13, 197–9, 230–31, **92**, **93**
limestone 13, 15, 25, 183, 197, 199, 228, 230, 245
limeworking 159, 180, 189, 198, 214, 230, 232
Linwood 21
  bridge 201
  car plant 259
  cotton mill 214, **85**
  industry and housing 216
  mining 245

moss 20, 37
  Napier Street 238
  road 231
Lithgow, John de 139
Lithgow's Kingston shipyard 243
Lithgow's shipyard 243
Littleton reservoir 238
Livens, Robin 49
Loch Fad, Bute 227
Loch Leven castle 122
Loch Libo Gap 247
Loch Lomond re-advance 20
Loch Thom 22, 32, 39
Lochar rivers 22
Lochend Hill 29, 39
Locher bridge 201
Lochgilphead church 109
Lochnaw Castle 124
Lochwinnoch 204, 228
  church 109
  cross shaft see Dumb Proctor
  dam & lade 212
  development 191, 216, 259
  old cotton mill 212
  parish 161, 221
  parish church 175
  station 237, 248
Locke, Joseph 236
Lockhart, Robert, Covenanter 154, 168
London 201
Long Dam, Greenock 226
Long Loch 39, 159, 190
Longhaugh Lodge enclosure 42, 64
Lonie, W.F. 9
Lord of the Isles 97
Love, Robert 25
Lugton Junction 248
Lugtonridge, Ayrshire, bronze shields 38, **16**
Lurg Moor fortlet 33, 46, 71, 77, **38**, **Pl. 5**
Lyle family 107, 143, 173
Lyle, Sir Robert 120
Lyles Hill hut circle 45

MacBeth, King of Scots 95
MacDowell family 173, 198
McLennan, W.D., architect 250, 255
Maetae, tribe 78–79, 81
Malcolm II, Kings of Scots 95
Malcolm III, Kings of Scots 95
Malcolm IV, King of Scots 96–97
Malden, John 13, 137, 266
Mansionhouse Road, Paisley 172
maps
  Ainslie's 25, 102, 148, 193, 195, 209–10, 212, 215, 222, 230
  Blaeu's 6, 132

distribution maps 64, 99
estate maps 232, 262–63
general use of 3, 5, 84, 87, 108, 110–11, 146, 250
geological maps 20, 150, 228
Ordnance Survey 2, 6–7, 105, 148, 194, 239, 245, 262
Pont's 132, 159, 162, 165
Ptolemy's 59, 72
Roy's 193
Taylor's 218
Wilson's 215
mapmaker 223
Mar Hall, Erskine, enclosure 63–7, **32**, **33**
Margaret's Mill (Maul's Mill), Kilmacolm, 192–95, **77**
Market Cross, Houston 164–65
Marshall Moor 55, 58,
Mary, Queen of Scots 122–23, 134
Maxwell families
of Dargavel 158
of Newark 126, 155, 166
of Pollok 118
of Stanely 123
Lord 128
Maxwellton, Paisley 187
Mearns 98
castle 125, 127–8
parish church 109, 143
Meikle Cloak, rotary querns 67, **35**
Meikle Corseford, Spateston, limeworks 198, **79**
Melrose Abbey 96, 139
Merchiston limeworks 23, **93**
Mere, Lutkyn, Danish pirate 120
Metcalfe W. M., historian 151, 167
Mid Linthills, Lochwinnoch 162, 190
Middleton, Newton Mearns, homestead and hoard 37, 48, 49, **22**
Midton limeworks 230–231, **93**
Mile End Mill, Paisley 241–2
Mill of Gryffe grain mill 192
mill dams 187, 192, 213, 214–15, 221
mill lades 187, 193, 211, 213–15
mill tunnel 210–11, **82**
Millbank Mill, Lochwinnoch 192
Millholm paper mill, Cathcart 250–1, **99**
Milliken House, Kilbarchan 175
Milliken, James 183
Milliken Mill 213
mills 2, 7, 215–16, 220, **76**, **77**, **81–85**, **89**, **Pl. 13–14**
cotton mills 13, 148, 185, 188–9, 191, 197, 204, 207–15, 221, 225, 227–28
crushing mills 246
flax mills 187, 226

grain/corn/flour mills 137–38, 140, 162–3, 192–93, 214, 222, 226
lint mills 185, 187–8, 209–10
paper mills 250, **99**
plash mills 187
textile mills 188, 192, 198, 210, 225
thread mills 228, 241–22, **97**
threshing mills 222
wash mills 189
waulk mills 163, 188
woollen mills 226
millstones
quarry at Deaconsbank 32
in situ at Millbank Mill 192
see also querns
millwright 209, 232–33
Milton Bridge, motte *see* Denniston
minerals 148, 150, 183, 197–98, 204, 231, 234, 237, 245–46, 249
mines and mining 3, 197, 198, 229–30, 234, 237, 245
barites 237, 246, 249
clay 230–31
coal 198, 200, 218, 225, **91**
copper 245–6
ironstone 200, 230–1, 245
lime 200, 230–31
Mittown bleachfield, Lochwinnoch 187
Moat Hill, or The Mote, Eaglesham, 102
moated site 111, 266
Mons Graupius, battle of 73
Mons Meg, cannon 117, 120
Monteath, Rev. John 7
Montgomery family, 98, 102, 119, 123
Morow, John, master mason 139
Morton family 127
Morrison, Dr Alex 12, 41
Mote Hill, Ranfurly see Ranfurly, motte
mottes 7, 93, 96, 98–103, 105–08, 111, 124, 128, 141, 231, 265, **47**, **48**, **Pl. 7**
moulds 36, 38, 54, 68
Moyne Moor neolithic sites 28–29
Muirdykes, battle of, 152
Muirshiel barytes mine 237, 246, 249
Muirshiel Country Park 48
Mure of Caldwell 129
Murray Chapel, Kilmacolm, 110, 143
Murray, Rev James 7–8, 246, 265
museums
British Museum 113, 205
Hunterian Museum 49, 67, 76, 113, 224
Kelvingrove Art galleries and Museum 9, 11, 31, 36, 91
National Museum of Scotland 65, 113, 134
Paisley Museum 9, 10–11, 13, 27, 52, 91, 113, 131, 254

Science Museum 232
Summerlee Museum 249
Myres Hill 39

National Museum of Scotland 65–66, 113, 134
National Trust for Scotland 118, 172, 202, 250
Neilston
  'dispersed village' 245
  parish church 109, 143, 176, 266
  station 247
  stone artefacts 10, **5**
  stone axes 26
Neilston and Barrhead Direct Line 247
Nethercraigs limeworks 230–31
Netherhouses limeworks 230
New Mill, (Calderhaugh) Lochwinnoch 210, 213
New (Orry) Mill, Eaglesham 211
Newall, Frank 10–12, 32, 44, 48, 60
Newark
  castle 130, 132, 144, 154–5, 157, 266, **67**, **68**
  parish church 175–76, 182
Newfield cotton mill 213
Newton limeworks 231
Newton Mearns 252
Newton Woods cross 91–92, **45**
Nisbet, Stuart 13, 197, 204, 262
Norse 81, 84–6, 97, **41**
North Kirktonmoor cairn 39
North Mound, Houston 41
North Wood, Pollok Park, enclosure 62, 104, **31**
Northbar House, Inchinnan 173

oak 16, 52, 105, 118
Old Bar Castle 130–1, 265, **57**, **58**
Old Kilbarchan Church *see* Kilbarchan church
Old Mains, Inchinnan 192
Old Mill, Eaglesham 212
Old Mill, Johnstone 209, 213–14
Old mill, Lochwinnoch 212
Oldbar, Paisley, rig-and-furrow 160, 191
Orchard quarry, Giffnock 245
Ordnance Survey *see* maps
Ouse Hill cairn 40
Overlee weems 7
Overton Reservoir, Greenock 226

Paisley
  burgh 135–36, 140
  industrial development 228
  stocking factory 185
  street cleaning 202
  Waterworks Company 238
Paisley, Abbey of **Pl. 8**
  building projects 139

drain 137–39, 266
  foundation 109
  ground plan 110, 138, **61**
  sedilia **60**
  St. Mirin Chapel 136–7
  wall 135, 137–8
Paisley and Renfrew Railway Company 235
Paisley Co-op tenement, Lady Lane, Paisley 255
Paisley Museum and Art Gallery 27, 113, 254
palisades 13, 47, 51–52, 54, 60, 63–64, 86, 103, 261, 266
Paper Mill, Cathcart cinerary urns 39
patera 72–73, **36**
Paton's Mill, Johnstone 210
peat 15, 17, 20–21, 26, 38, 43, 46–47, 52, 69, 227
Peel of Castle Semple 7, 132–33, **59**
Peel meadows 192
Pennytersal motte 99–100, **47**
Picketlaw hut circle 43, 44, 51, 266, **20**
pits
  coal 197–99, 214, 229, 230–32, 245
  gun 257
  prehistoric 27–9, 41, 43, 45, 60, 86
place-name evidence 84–86, 92–94, 143, 159, 192, 263
plantations
  conifer 6,12,45
  sugar 183, 263
  trees 25, 101
pollen 26, 62, 69, 72, 142
Pollokshaws 36
Poll Tax Roll 132, 147, 158–61, 166, 190, 193–94, 203, 222
Polnoon Castle 99, 102, 122–23, **47**
Pollok House 118
Pollok Park
  castle 105
  possible motte 105
  ringwork 103
population
  decline 190, 196, 220–21, 252
  distribution of 148, 159
  Greenock 166
  health of 179
  housing of 204
  increase 181, 190–91, 202, 204, 215, 226, 238, 240, 246–47, 252
  Paisley 164, 202
  prehistoric 52–53
  Roman Catholic Irish 216
  support for Covenants 168
  support for Hanoverians 205
Port Glasgow
  hoard 86–87, **41**
  economic development 157, 167, 181–83, 219

shipbuilding 232, 243
 timber ponds 219, **88**
pottery
 early historic 84
 medieval 51, 101, 103–05, 111, 118, 122, 127,
  137,
 139, 141, 176, 179, 195, **48**
 modern/industrial
 prehistoric 23, 27–29, 32, 35, 39, 43, 45,
  47–48, 51–52, 54, 58, 60, 64, 66–67, 72
 post-medieval 122, 176–77, 181
 Roman 76–7, 101
Pride, Dr David 8, **5**
Pudzeoch Burn, Renfrew 217
Pulpit Rock, Greenock 168

Quarrelton coalmines, Johnstone 150,
 199–200, 218, 225, 228–29, 245
Quarriers Homes 254
quarries and quarrying 3, 7, 13, 43, 230, 234,
 245
 lime 198–99, **79**
 millstone 32
 stone 31, 45, 183, 187, 232, 245, 247, 251
 querns 50, 66–67, 69, 104, **35**
 hand mills at Overlee 7

radiocarbon dating 11, 28, 44, 48, 51–52, 54,
 62, 64, 66, 86,111, 203, 262
railways 31,150, 165, 188, 191, 234–37, 240–41,
 243, 245–48, 251–52, **88**
 construction 7, 17, 148–49, 218, 248
 gravity183, 234
 horse drawn 234–35
 mineral 246
 narrow gauge 237
 sporting 237
 see also Caledonian Railway Company
 see also East Kilbride railway
 see also Garnkirk railway
 see also Glasgow and Renfrew Joint Railway
 see also Glasgow and South Western Railway
 see also Glasgow, Barrhead and Neilston
  Direct Railway
 see also Glasgow, Paisley and Greenock
  Railway
 see also Glasgow, Paisley, Kilmarnock and Ayr
  Railway
 see also Greenock and Ayrshire Railway
 see also Paisley and Renfrew Railway
Ralston 97
Ranfurly
 castle 128
 motte, Castle Hill, 99, 101, **47**
Ranfurly Hotel 246
Rashielee 131

Renfrew
 airport 256
 burgh 135, 140, 164
 castles 106–07, 114, 115, 266
 parish church 143
 Town Hall 254
Renfrewshire
 history of archaeology in, 5–14
 geology of 15
 as part of the 'Glasgow region' 149
Renfrewshire Local History Forum 12, 261
Revoch Cut, Eaglesham 212
Richieston enclosure, Erskine 64
rigs 159–60, 173, 191
ring-work 98, 103–106, 117, 128, 265
roads
 construction 7, 12, 25, 85–86, 120, 232
 excavated 179
 expansion of 148, 165, 204
 Roman 73, 75, 77–8
 turnpike 180, 200–01
Roadside, Mearns 185, 188
Robert Bruce, King of Scots 97, 110, 112–13
Robert II, Kings of Scots 114, 146
Robert III, King of Scots 114, 135, 139, 146
Robertson, John, engineer 233–34
Robinson, George, surveyor 226
Roman forts see forts
rope-works164, 182
roundhouses 13, 51, 63–64, 266
Ross family 106, 122, 143
Ross, Charles, surveyor 215, 262
Ross, Sir John of Hawkhead, 144, **63**
Ross Hall, enclosure 5, 105
Ross Mill, Eaglesham, meal mill 162
Rouken meal mill 162, 193
Rouken Glen Park mill dams
Rowbank Burn 210
Rowbank Reservoir 252
Royal Commission (RCAHMS) 3, 9, 131–4,
 42–43, 57, 262
runrig 161, 196

St Bryde's, chapel and well 145
St Conval (St. Congal) 82, 137
 chapel and well 144–45
St Kentigern 82, 86
St Mirren 82, 83,
 chapel and altar screen 136–37
 chapel 136
St Mungo 82
St Nicholas chapel 145
St Roque's chapel 145
Samian ware 76, **Pl. 4**
Saucel Mill 162
scheduled monuments 31, 90, 134, 227

sculptured stones 90–92
Scots American Company of Farmers 196
Scottish Aviation Company, Barrhead 256
Scott's Shipyard, Port Glasgow 232
Scroggy Bank, Gourock 33
Second World War 102, 150, 244, 253, 256, 258
Seedhill 82 162
Semple family 120–23, 127, 129, 133–4, 140,
    142–43, 145
Sempill, Sir Robert, First Lord Semple, 142,
    62, Pl. 10
Shaw, George, Abbot of Paisley 135, 138–9
Shaws Water Company 226–7, 238, 253
Shiels enclosure, Govan, 28, 62, 265, 31
shipbuilding 148–49, 219, 232–3, 241, 243–44
shipyards 2, 182, 215, 219, 256
Sibbald, William, surveyor 215
sieges 117
    Castle Semple and peel 123, 134
    Crookston 120
    Duchal 107, 117, 120
    Dumbarton 83–85
Simon and Lobnitz 244
Skiff Wood limeworks 230
slate 137, 139, 176, 202
slaves 183–84, 263
Sma' Shot Cottages 204
Sneddon quay, Paisley 163, 167
South Branchal fort 6
South Kirktonmoor farm mill 222
South Mound, Houston, cairn and cemetery 6,
    22, 27, 40–42, 68, 265–66, 17
    skeletal remains 41, 18
    jet beads 41, 19, Pl. 1
South Castlewalls, Lochwinnoch 222
Spateston limeworks 180, 198, 200
spears 36–37, 86–87, 92
standing stones 29
Stanely
    cross 89, 91, 126, 43, 56
    castle 125–27, 56
    reservoir 238
Stanger, Master David 143
Steed Stone cross 91
Stewart families
    of Ardgowan 130
    of Barscube 131
stone circles 28–9
Stonecraigs quarry, Paisley 232
Strathgryffe 97, 99, 108
suburbs and suburban 2, 237, 248–50, 252, 259
sugar 164, 182–84, 219, 226, 238, 263
swords 37–38, 84, 124, 134, 143, 154
    Sempill sword 134
    carvings of 143, 176
Syde, Mill of, Neilston 161

Tannahill's Cottage, Paisley 201
Tannahill's Hole 218
tax 100, 114, 132
    see also Poll Tax Roll
Telford, Thomas, engineer 217
Temple, Kenmure Hill 173
Tervas, Thomas, Abbot of Paisley 135, 139
textile industry 148–51, 161, 163, 181, 185–86,
    198, 201–02, 208, 228
    see also mills
Thom, Robert , surveyor, 226–27, 238
Thornliebank 213, 254–35
    printworks 255, 101
Threepwood 190
timber ponds 219, 89
Titwood, Mearns
    neolithic find at, 28
    palisaded enclosure 13, 85, 40
tobacco 173–4, 182, 184, 208, 71
tower-houses 105–06, 111, 114, 117, 124–132,
    145, 157–62, 171
trackways 28, 162, 243, 258
    see also railways
Turnershiel, Lochwinnoch 190, 195

Uplawmoor 248
Upper Busby mill 210
Upper Pollok 97–8
unenclosed settlements 12, 43, 51, 53
unenclosed land 159
urban
    archaeology 262
    growth 196
    industry 212, 225, 228
    middle class 250
    settlements 134, 148
urns 6, 39, 45

vegetation 16–17, 46–47, 62, 142
vitrification 54, 265, Pl. 2

Walkinshaw brick works 231, 245, 249
Wallace's House, Elderslie 111
Walls Hill 59–60, 66, 68–69, 72, 141, 265, 29
war see First World War and Second World War
warfare 54
Warlock Gates, Lochwinnoch
    chapel and well 145
    lodges 173
Wars of Independence 97, 103, 105, 110, 112,
    130, 142
Waterside, Neilston 184
Watt, James, engineer 223–25, 234
Waulkmill Glen limeworks 232
Weaver's Cottage, Kilbarchan 67, 162, 202–4,
    266, 80

weavers 160–61, 179, 187, 201, 203–04, 209, 216
weaving 161, 179, 185–87, 189, 196, 202, 207,
    211, 228, 266
Wellpark, Greenock, aqueduct 225
Wemyss Bay 247–48
West Acres, Mearns 13, 50–51, **23**, **24**
West Arthurlie mill 210
Wheatlands, Kilbarchan 39
Whinhill Reservoir 253
whisky 205, 215
White House, Milliken Park 175
Whitecraigs quarry, Giffnock 245
Whitefauld limeworks 230
Whiteforeland Point flying boat terminal 256

Whitelees bombing decoy control point 258
Whitemoss
  neolithic finds 27–28, **11**
  Roman fort 75–77, **38**, **Pl. 4**
Whittliemuir 69, 142
William the Lion, King of Scots 96, 134
Wilson, John, writer 190, 218–9, 221–22
Windy Hill, Lochwinnoch
  hut circle 45
wine 155, 163
witches 29, 151–52, 168–69

yew 26, 111
Yonderton grain mill 192